Wartime is costly. Whilst the human cost is a burden which remains part of our every waking thoughts for many years after the end of the conflict, the physical cost, at least in some cases, is easier to deal with.

Some, if not most of the physical cost of war, is spent in the constant supply of materials including armaments and machines to the troops – wherever they happen to be fighting. Of course the Services have always needed supplies of uniforms, equipment and machines. However, the rate of expansion of the Services and the rate of consumption of armaments increases dramatically in wartime. Pre-war traditional manufacturers simply could not cope with the sudden increase in orders.

The only solution was to fabricate what was needed, in the Second World War at least, in additional factories. 'Shadow Factories' was the term used to describe the use of third party factories and equipment used to manufacture components or complete units which were then passed on to the Services. These units could be anything from tanks, parts of aircraft to small pumps or rifles. The list was almost endless.

Clearly it would be impossible to walk into the nearest engineering shop and expect them to manufacture heavy components. The railway yards were used to dealing with heavy blocks of metals and so they were approached to help with heavier vehicles such as tanks. Similarly the motor manufacturers were asked to help out with producing trucks and Jeeps, for example.

Of course this need necessitated formal contracts, and as far as possible discretion so that the German bombers could not locate and destroy vital sources of supplies. In some cases, such was the level of secrecy that components for aircraft for example, were fabricated in a number of Shadow Factories and assembled in a different location. In that way the exact engineering drawings could be more easily controlled and a stray bomb would only destroy part of the plans and planes.

Where relevant, examples are provided from across the United Kingdom and cover an extensive range of machines and vehicles. Some details will also be provided concerning armament shells, some of which were made in one site and filled in other facilities. The government departments were certainly kept busy keeping track of it all!

David Rogers is a scientist by training, obtaining a doctorate in Chemistry before working for a Fellow of the Royal Society for his post-doctorate.

He went on to spend many years in British industry working for a multi-national company in both research and manufacturing departments inventing, developing or helping to manufacture a range of products.

He is a Fellow of the Royal Society of Chemistry, The Royal Photographic Society and of the British Institute of Professional Photography. He was a Visiting Professor in Business Psychology for three years and is now a Visiting Lecturer. He decided to transition to a career involving writing, consultancy and some teaching in 2004.

Since that time, David has written or edited 12 published books, mainly in the field of science/technology or wartime history.

Married with two children, David has spent some of his spare time as a School Governor.

Shadow Factories

Britain's Production Facilities during the Second World War

David Rogers

 Helion & Company Limited

Helion & Company Limited
26 Willow Road
Solihull
West Midlands
B91 1UE
England
Tel. 0121 705 3393
Fax 0121 711 4075
Email: info@helion.co.uk
Website: www.helion.co.uk
Twitter: @helionbooks
Visit our blog http://blog.helion.co.uk/

Published by Helion & Company 2016
Designed and typeset by Mach 3 Solutions Ltd, Bussage, Gloucestershire
Cover designed by Euan Carter, Leicester (www.euancarter.com)
Printed by Lightning Source Limited, Milton Keynes, Buckinghamshire

ISBN 978-1-910294-46-8

British Library Cataloguing-in-Publication Data.
A catalogue record for this book is available from the British Library.

For details of other military history titles published by Helion & Company Limited contact
the above address, or visit our website: http://www.helion.co.uk.

We always welcome receiving book proposals from prospective authors.

**Dedicated to my brother Ian
and my sister in law Janet**

Contents

List of Illustrations

Preface

Most interested readers of war history are used to reading of the exploits of pilots, the sound sights and even in some cases the smells of aeroplanes. There may be no thought to where were these manufactured, in what quantities, how were they moved from the source of manufacture to point of use, where were they stored in the meantime? In some cases, wings were made in one location and other parts elsewhere. These various parts were then assembled in a third location. The need to avoid concentrating all vital manufacturing plants in one location in case of bombing helped both to drive this dispersion strategy and to harness labour and accommodation where it was available. Tracing the manufacture and distribution of these various components of aircraft production makes for interesting reading, especially so given that some factories were set up just prior to and during the Second World War for this specific purpose.

Under the internal project name of the Shadow Scheme, and developed for the Air Ministry by Sir Kingsley Wood (with Sir Herbert Austin, later Lord Austin as its first head), British shadow factories were developed as a means of boosting additional manufacturing capacity principally, although not exclusively, for the British aircraft industry.

It is tempting to assume that the shadow factories were able to manufacture all types of aircraft in sufficient numbers to supply all of our needs during the Second World War. Nothing could be farther from the truth. Whilst this scheme led to a dramatic increase in aircraft production, the government still needed to import completed aeroplanes from abroad, notably Canada and the United States (under the lend–lease scheme), as well as much needed aero engines and spare parts. For this reason, Chapter 2 sets the scene and mentions some of the activities of the lend–lease scheme.

Importing materials of great variety also required a different mindset in government as a ministry was needed largely to undertake the necessary paperwork for the materials supply under the lend–lease agreement with the United States. This also needs to be mentioned in context with the wider aircraft supply chain. I have chosen to start with the British government departments concerned and then mention the contribution of the lend–lease scheme to the aircraft supply chain before mentioning shadow factories in detail. This seems to be a logical progression even though historically the shadow scheme started in 1936 and therefore well before the set-up of some of the government ministries or indeed the lend–lease scheme.

Finally, whilst there were some other factories set up in a similar way to that of the aircraft shadow factory scheme and, although vital to the war effort, they are not covered here in detail. In many ways, aircraft production serves a fine example of the activities of the other services, government departments and industrialists. Information of these activities, sometimes referred to as Agency Factories, can be found in The National Archives.

Acknowledgements

I first became aware of the Second World War aircraft whilst staring at my bedroom ceiling; let me explain. In those days, I shared a bedroom with my older brother, who had an interest in building model aircraft, principally from the Second World War. He attached lengths of string from them and persuaded my parents to let him pin the other end of the string to our bedroom ceiling. The last thing visible before lights out and the first thing in the morning I saw were these model aircraft. Few of them survived our youth as they made great targets!

My brother and I have had several conversations of these model airplanes as I started research for this book. We know for certain that there was a Lancaster bomber, a Spitfire, a Hurricane and a Boulton Paul Defiant. There were some others but we think they were the First World War aircraft. Our bedroom ceiling was crowded but interesting. The four model aircraft types mentioned above were popular models because the aircraft they depicted were all involved in the Second World War. Perhaps not surprisingly, these four aircraft are all mentioned later.

Over the years as I became more interested in war history I started to try and understand where the Second World War aircraft were made. For any others like me who also have this fascination, most if not all of the answers, appear below. So thank you brother Ian for your passive introduction to this topic.

I also owe a debt of thanks to my late father who compiled many documents, books and spoken material relating to the two World Wars. I have drawn on some of these during this study.

My patient wife, Carolyn, has also once again read a draft of the typescript looking for anomalies in my English, as indeed has Bill, a member of the RAF during the Second World War and who knows where to place apostrophes amongst other things. I continue to be amazed at the exploits of Fellows of the Royal Society who were active in the Second World War in many different guises. The shadow factories were no exception. My thanks to the library staff at the Royal Society who once again pointed me in the right direction in their archives.

My final thanks are to my late father-in-law who was a pilot during the Second World War. Rarely did he mention anything of his wartime activities, with two notable exceptions. He spent many hours discussing his exploits with his eldest grandson, Kev, and even let him see his log book, training records, etc., and to look at his pilot's wings (Figure 1).

Figure 1 Pilot's wings.

The other notable exception was when I took him, my mother-in-law and my young family to the RAF Museum at Hendon. Quite unexpectedly he looked at some of the aircraft and started to mention their performance either on take-off or whilst in flight. I was stunned that he recalled his war memories at that time but grateful for the insider knowledge he provided. His reticence in discussing his war was mainly due to the large number of friends he lost, the memories were too painful to discuss. He spent the latter stages in North Africa during which he tried to get posted closer to 'the action' by flying any aircraft that landed where he was stationed, hence his personal knowledge of performance.

Perhaps the following poem, a copy of which was always on display in his dining room, summed up his feelings whilst at the controls. It was written by John Gillespie Magee (1922–41).

High Flight

Oh, I have slipped the surly bonds of earth
And danced the skies on laughter-silvered wings;
Sunward I've climbed and joined the tumbling mirth
Of sun-split clouds – and done a hundred things
You have not dreamed of: wheeled and soared and swung
High in the sun-lit silence. Hovering there
I've chased the shouting wind along, and flung
My eager craft through footless halls of air;
Up, up the long, delirious, burning blue
I've topped the wind-swept heights with easy grace,
Where never lark nor even eagle flew:
And while, with silent lifting mind I've trod
The high untrespassed sanctity of space,
Put out my hand, and touched the face of God.

Introduction

The Origins of Shadow Factories

"Shadow Factories" was a term coined in the mid-1930s to describe a concept used in the manufacture of aircraft during the preparations for war. An account written at that time describes the scheme.

Note on the Air Ministry Shadow Factories

1. The origin of the Shadow Plan

The 'Shadow Scheme' was introduced with two purposes in view; firstly to assist in producing, with the speed which the programme demanded, the large numbers of aeroplanes and aero-engines needed for the expansion of the Royal Air Force, and secondly to develop a reserve of manufacturing capacity for use in war.

The production of the vast quantities of aeroplanes and engines which would be needed in war is naturally beyond the capacity of the peace-time aeroplane industry, and the plans drawn up against an emergency provided for supplementing the capacity of the aeroplane industry by turning over part of the motor-car industry to producing aeroplanes and aero-engines. Several large motor car firms were earmarked for this purpose. The rapid expansion of the Royal Air Force likewise involved producing a number of aeroplanes more quickly than they could be turned out by the ordinary aeroplane industry and the Air Ministry therefore invited certain of the selected motor car firms to manufacture the balance of aeroplanes and aero-engines which were beyond the capacity of the aeroplane industry; the greater part of this balance consisted of reserves.

To avoid interfering with the ordinary commercial work of the motor car firms, the scheme provided that new factories, the 'shadow' factories, should be built and equipped, at Government expense, close to the works of each of the motor car firms, who would act as managers of the shadow factories, but continue the production of motor cars in their own factories. When their present task is finished the shadow factories, which remain the property of the Government, will continue in readiness to start work again immediately a war breaks out. The presence of the shadow factories, and the experience which the parent motor car firms have gained during their period of management, will enable the whole organisation, both the shadow and the main factory, to start production of aeroplanes in war with the greatest possible speed.

2. The two airframe shadow factories

It was decided to establish two shadow factories for producing airframes, (i.e. the aeroplane structure without its engine). Lord Austin as Chairman of the Austin Motor Company, agreed to manage one of them and he at once prepared plans for its erection at the main works of his firm at Longbridge, Birmingham. That factory has been completed and is expected to start production in May. The airplane manufactured will be the Battle bomber, designed by the Fairey Aviation Company. Messrs Rootes Securities (controlled by the brothers W E and R C Rootes) undertook the management of the other airframe factory and immediately prepared plans for its establishment at White Waltham, near Maidenhead, but at a later date it was decided instead to locate the factory at Speke, near Liverpool. This change retarded progress and the factory is not expected to be ready until November to start production of Blenheim bomber aircraft designed by the Bristol Aeroplane Company.

3. The aero-engine shadow factories

The additional aero-engines immediately required were all of the Mercury VIII (840 bhp, 9 cylinder, radial, air-cooled) type, designed by the Bristol Aeroplane Company. The motor car firms which agreed in 1936 to undertake their production are:

- The Austin Motor Company Limited (Birmingham) – Chairman Lord Austin.
- Humber Limited (Coventry) – controlled by the brothers Rootes.
- Daimler Limited (Coventry) – Managing Director Mr G Burton.
- Standard Motor Company Limited (Coventry) – Managing Director Captain J P Black.
- The Rover Company Limited (Birmingham) – Managing Director S B Wilks.

A Government shadow factory has been established at or close to the main works of each of these firms. At a later stage the Bristol Aeroplane Company agreed to join this group and to manage a shadow factory (established at their Bristol works) to undertake work originally assigned to the Wolseley Motor Company which withdrew from the scheme.

A committee of Heads of these firms, under the chairmanship of Lord Austin, decided, with the approval of the Air Ministry that, in view of the limited time available it would be best for each firm to make in its shadow factory a particular group of components, which would then be passed to two of the factories for assembly into completed engines and be subjected to the usual tests. Assembly and testing is undertaken by the Austin Company and the Bristol Aeroplane Company.

The first full set of components was completed in the new factories in October 1937 (a notable achievement) and the engine constructed from them has since been fully tested with satisfactory results. The output of further sets of components is now steadily increasing and the scheme shows every promise of being entirely successful.

4. General

These shadow factories cover a total area of nearly 50 acres and they are giving employment at present to some 9,000 operatives, a number which will increase to about 16,000 when the factories reach full production later in the year.

The energy and enthusiasm displayed by the management of the motor car firms and the willing co-operation and advice of the two professional aeroplane and engine firms – the Bristol Aeroplane Company and the Fairey Aviation Company – whose products are being manufactured in the shadow factories, are, in the opinion of the Air Council, deserving of the highest commendation and are largely responsible for the successful development of this very substantial increase in productive capacity in such a remarkably short space of time.[1]

More details of the history of the early shadow factories can be found in Appendix I. The involvement, or rather lack of involvement, of Lord Nuffield in these early discussions is interesting. A booklet produced by Jaguar cars and handed out free to visitors of their Castle Bromwich factory tells more of the story. Incidentally, it was on this site that most of the Spitfires were manufactured (see later chapters).

Apparently, Lord Nuffield had disagreed with the then Air Minister, Lord Swinton, over something quite different and allowed personal animosity to gain the upper hand. This did not help matters, as it was vital that Nuffield be brought into the equation. Months slipped by and the scheme was revised several times.

On 16th May 1938, Swinton resigned and was replaced by Sir Kingsley Wood, who wasted no time and arranged a meeting with Nuffield for 19th May [more of which later]. At the meeting he urged Nuffield to join the scheme as they needed his industrial might and Wood offered him the opportunity to build a large factory to produce the Spitfire. After much discussion Nuffield agreed to join the scheme – for which he accepted no salary – and built a new factory …

Lord Beaverbrook, Minister of Aircraft Production, contacted Lord Nuffield in May 1940 to ask why Castle Bromwich had not produced even one complete Spitfire of the 1,000 ordered. There was no love lost between the two men and Nuffield offered to hand over control; Beaverbrook accepted and quickly appointed Vickers-Armstrong to take over from Morris Motors.[2]

Aircraft of the United Kingdom Flown in the Second World War

If, like me, you too were aware of some of the aircraft used in the Second World War but do not have an encyclopedic knowledge of the subject, it might be worth glancing through this section which is an attempt to list the major types of aircraft used at some point in the war – not necessarily at the beginning. The references from The National Archives have categorized these aircraft into the following types:

a.   Heavy bombers.
b.   Medium bombers.
c.   Light bombers and fighters.
d.   General reconnaissance.
e.   Transports and ASR.
f.   Naval.
g.   Trainers.

No attempt has been made to do this here; the table of bombers (Figure 0.1) is taken from *The World Encyclopedia of Bombers* and is in alphabetical order for ease of reference. Where known, the date of first flight and engine(s) used when the airplane was introduced is included. This is sometimes useful as shadow factories for engines and airplanes are also presented in the later text.

Figure 0.2 is taken from *Fighter Command 1939–45* and is also in alphabetical order. Finally, Figure 0.3 is compiled from *The Enclyclopedia of Military Aircraft* and documents those aircraft in this reference that do not appear in either of the other two tables.

The rationale for documenting as many of the operational aircraft as possible is both to demonstrate the competing needs of some of the engines and to show the number of types of aircraft needed to be manufactured. Of course, not all of the aircraft listed below were manufactured in shadow factories; however, the shadow factory scheme did bring vital production capacity at a time of greatest need to many of these aircraft.

Bombers

Designer	Type	First Flight	Engine Type
Armstrong Whitworth	Whitley Mark V	17 Mar. 1936	Rolls-Royce Merlin X
Avro	Anson Mark I	24 Mar. 1935	Armstrong Siddeley Cheetah IX
Avro	Manchester Mark I	25 July 1939	Rolls-Royce Vulture
Avro	Lancaster MRK I	9 Jan. 1941	Rolls-Royce Merlin XX
Bristol	Blenheim Mark I	25 June 1936	Bristol Mercury XV
Bristol	Beaufighter TF Mark X	17 July 1939	Bristol Hercules XVII
Bristol	Beaufort I	15 Oct. 1938	Bristol Taurus VI
Bristol	Brigand BI	4 Dec. 1944	Bristol Centaurus 57
De Havilland	Mosquito BIV	25 Nov. 1940	Rolls-Royce Merlin 21
Fairey	Battle Mark 1	10 Mar. 1936	Rolls-Royce Merlin
Fairey	Barracuda Mark II	7 Dec. 1940	Rolls-Royce Merlin 32
Handley Page	Halifax Mark III	25 Oct. 1939	Bristol Hercules VI or XVI
Handley Page	Hampden Mark II	21 June 1936	Bristol Pegasus XVII
Hawker	Typhoon IB	27 May 1941	Napier Sabre IIA
Short	Sterling Mark III	14 May 1939	Bristol Hercules XVI
Short	Sunderland Mark V	16 Oct. 1937	Pratt and Whitney R-1830 Twin Wasp
Vickers	Wellesley	19 June 1935	Bristol Pegasus XX
Vickers	Wellington IC	15 June 1936	Bristol Pegasus XVIII

Figure 0.1 Bombers in flight during the Second World War.[3]

Main Fighter Command Aircraft

Type and Mark	Engine	No. of Crew
Beaufighter IF	Hercules III	2
Beaufighter IIF	Merlin XX	2
Beaufighter IVF	Hercules IV	2
Blenheim IF	Mercury VIII	2/3
Blenheim IVF	Mercury XV	2/3
Defiant I	Merlin III	2
Defiant II	Merlin XX	2
Gladiator I/II	Mercury IX/VIIIA	1
Havoc I/II	Wasp S3C4-G	2/3
Hurricane I	Merlin II/III	1
Hurricane II	Merlin XX	1
Mosquito FB.VI	Merlin 21	2
Mosquito NF.II	Merlin 22	2
Mosquito NF.XIX	Merlin 25	2
Mosquito NF.XXX	Merlin 113/114	2
Mustang I/II	Allison V-1710-39	1
Mustang III/IV	Merlin V-1650-7	1
Spitfire I	Merlin II/III	1
Spitfire II	Merlin XII	1
Spitfire IX	Merlin 63	I
Spitfire V	Merlin 45/50	1
Spitfire XIV	Griffon 65	1
Spitfire XVI	Merlin 266	1
Tempest V	Sabre IIB	1
Tomahawk I/II	Allison V-1710-33	1
Typhoon I	Sabre IIB	1
Whirlwind I	Peregrine I	1

Figure 0.2 Main Fighter Command Aircraft types.[4]

Designer	Type	Engine	Purpose
Airspeed	Oxford	Armstrong Siddeley Cheetah IX	Trainer
Armstrong Whitworth	Albermarle	Bristol Hercules XI	Transport and glider
Avro	Lincoln	Rolls-Royce Merlin 85	Heavy bomber[a]
Avro	York	Rolls-Royce Merlin XX	Transport
Blackburn	Skua	Bristol Perseus XII	Naval dive-bomber
Spitfire Mk 1	Defiant	Rolls-Royce Merlin III	Fighter
Fairey	Albacore	Bristol Taurus XII	Naval torpedo-bomber
Fairey	Firefly	Rolls-Royce Griffon IIB	Naval fighter
Fairey	Fulmar	Rolls-Royce Merlin VIII	Naval fighter
Fairey	Seafox	Napier Rapier	Reconnaissance biplane
Gloster	Gladiator	Bristol Mercury VIIIA	Fighter biplane
Westland	Lysander	Bristol Mercury XII	Army co-operation
Westland	Welkin	Rolls-Royce Merlin 61	High altitude interceptor
Westland	Whirlwind	Rolls-Royce Peregrine	Long-range fighter-bomber

Note:
a The maiden flight was on 9 June 1944. Deliveries began in the Spring of 1945 – too late to see active service in the Second World War.

Figure 0.3 Other aircraft flown in the Second World War.[5]

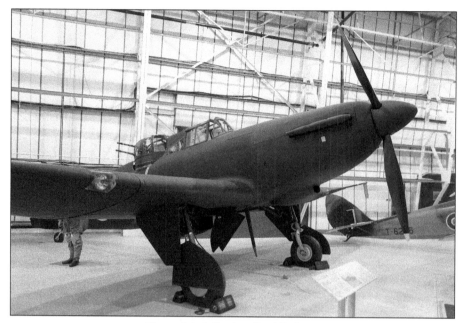

Figure 0.4 A Boulton Paul Defiant.

The Defiant I and II are listed in Figure 0.2 as being part of fighter command. Whilst this is the case, there was a (sometimes) fatal flaw with the design in that there were no forward-facing armaments, with all of the firepower concentrated in the rear turret. This problem led to its withdrawal from daylight operations for night work, which was deemed safer. Whilst the Defiant was slightly more successful in night operations, there was a lack of radar early in the war. By the time that radar-equipped Defiants were reaching squadrons, they were being replaced by more effective Beaufighters and Mosquitos. Figure 0.4 shows a Boulton Paul Defiant I (N1671). Although the Hawker Hart (Figure 0.5) is not listed above, it was a crucial airplane, at least in the early part of the war. The information board at RAF Hendon mentions the following:

> Many of the early Second World War Royal Air Force bomber pilots learned to fly on the Hart Trainer and with a production run of over 500 this is hardly surprising. The latter half of the 1930s was a time of great expansion in RAF front-line units and equal growth took place in training facilities.
>
> The Hart light bomber laid the foundation for a whole family of types that equipped the RAF in the 1930s ... Differing little from the day bomber, except for the deletion of rear cockpit armament and the installation of dual controls, the new aircraft allowed trainee pilots to experience the characteristics of Hawker biplanes they were likely to meet in service.

Figure 0.5 A Hawker Hart (K4972) used to train bomber pilots.

As monoplane fighters and bombers entered service the importance of the Hart Trainer in the UK training establishments declined.[6]

Of course, the Hurricane and Spitfire aircraft are two of the most iconic ever to be flown in the Second World War, at least for those of us who are not pilots. Whilst most Spitfires were a well-conceived mix of engine and airframe, there was at least one exception, the Mk 5b (Figure 0.6).

During 1940 the Spitfire Mk I and Mk II barely maintained superiority over the Messerschmitt Bf109E so the Air Staff turned their attention to the question of a replacement. Their preferred successor was the Mk III, fitted with a Merlin XX engine and incorporating a new wing design.

Realising it would take time to tool up for a new production aircraft and because of the problems with the Merlin XX, the Air Ministry asked Rolls-Royce, as an interim measure, to install the Merlin 45 engine in the Spitfire Mk I airframe. Between 1941 and 1943 over 6,500 of this Mk V were produced. The Spitfire Mk III never did go into production but some of the new design features intended for it were incorporated into the Mk V.[7]

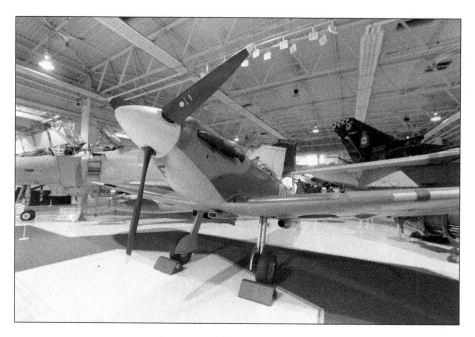

Figure 0.6 The Spitfire Mk 5b.

Key Members of the Motor Industry in the Mid-late 1930s

Several members of the motor industry were key to the supply of parts, sub-assemblies and indeed completed aircraft during the immediate pre-war period and throughout the Second World War. Listed below are some biographical sketches of these individuals and are listed here as they played a part in several ventures, including shadow factories. An understanding of their roles and responsibilities will help in later chapters.

Lord Austin

The following entry for Herbert Austin and is taken from the Encyclopaedia Britannica.

> Founder and first chairman of the Austin Motor Company, whose Austin Seven model greatly influenced British and European light-car design. An engineer and engineering manager in Australia (1883–90), he became manager and later director of the Wolseley Sheep-Shearing Company in England. In 1895 he designed the first Wolseley car—a three wheeler—and in 1900 drove the

first Wolseley four-wheeled car, also of his design. He began production of his own cars at the Longbridge Works, Birmingham, in 1906. Knighted in 1917, he was a Conservative member of the House of Commons from 1919 to 1924 and was created a baron in 1936.[8]

Sadly Lord Austin died aged 75 on 23 May 1941.

Lord Nuffield

Uniquely amongst the motor manufacturers, William Richard Morris, otherwise known as Lord Nuffield, was a Fellow of the Royal Society. The following is an extract of Lord Nuffield's Royal Society biographical memoir.

At this time Nuffield was also energetically considering how he could contribute to the rearmament program. Some of his businesses were already working for the War Office, but following a dispute with the Air Ministry he was unable to make satisfactory arrangements for Wolseley aero-engines under the shadow factory scheme, and the works were closed. Nuffield, therefore, concentrated his energies on War Office work, and undertook to produce fast light tanks at Morris Commercial and later under a new company Nuffield Mechanisations and Aero Ltd The first prototype was completed by the end of 1937, and by 1938 production vehicles were available. Nuffield Mechanisations also began making Bofors guns which were produced in rapidly increasing quantities from 1939.

Despite his early difficulties with the Air Ministry, Nuffield soon returned to his interests in aircraft. In 1938 he played a leading part in an aircraft project based on the prototype Napier Sabre engine, and intended to attack the air-speed record. The project ran into difficulties, especially because the design required modification when the Germans raised the record to 469 mph in April 1939. Because of the war only one prototype was constructed and, although this flew successfully in its maiden flight, it was subsequently so badly damaged on landing that it was decided to abandon the project. In 1938 Nuffield was also invited to construct and operate a factory for the large scale production of Spitfire aircraft, and a vast project with some 52 acres of buildings was planned for a site near Castle Bromwich. The new factory was complete by June 1940, but Nuffield had encountered considerable difficulties in working with the Supermarine organisation who were responsible for designing the aircraft. Eventually Lord Beaverbrook decided that in the national interest another management company should run the factory. ...

When war came, the branches of Morris Motors that were already concerned with the rearmament program changed over to full-time war work quite quickly. The change could not, however, take place so rapidly in the main assembly shops, and when private car production stopped at Cowley there was initially considerable unemployment. Although the construction of light vehicles required by the

Forces and Civil Defence soon began, the Cowley works had to transfer its main effort to different fields and began to play a major part in the repair of aircraft. ...

In addition to these activities, the Cowley works became heavily involved in other aircraft contracts and produced Tiger Moths for training, Beaufighter and Lancaster power units, and components for Horsa gliders. Large contracts were also obtained from the Admiralty and the Ministry of Supply for a wide range of armament jobs. There were similar changes to war production in other Nuffield works. The Radiator Branch, besides making a wide range of small components, became a major centre for the design and production for aircraft-engine coolers and had to erect an entirely new works at Llanelly to meet its orders. Morris Industrial Exports and the MG factory became fully engaged in work on tanks and aircraft, and SU Carburettors, despite damage by air raids, became a leading supplier of aircraft carburettors. The Riley Company constructed aircraft components, Morris Commercial a wide range of army vehicles, and the Wolseley Company produced some 22,000 Bren-gun carriers. Nuffield Mechanisations continued as a centre of tank design and production, as well as making guns and other equipment. ...

Morris was awarded the following for these and other activities: OBE 1917; Bt 1929; Baron 1934; Viscount 1938; GBE 1941; CH 1958.[9]

Lord Rootes

William Edward Rootes threw some of his considerable energy and expertise into many national committees including the following:
- Member of the Board of Trade Advisory Council 1931–34.
- Board of Trade Departmental Committee on Gift Coupon Trading Stamps 1933.
- Member of the Delegation to British Week in Finland 1933.
- Member of the Committee of Education and Training of Students from Overseas (1933–34).
- Member of the UK Trade Mission to Poland 1934.
- Member of the Joint Aircraft Engine Committee (Shadow Industry) 1936–40.
- Chairman of the Joint Aircraft Engine Committee (Shadow Industry) 1940–41.
- Chairman of the Ministry of Transport Motor Vehicle Maintenance Advisory Committee 1941.
- Member of the Supply Council, Ministry of Supply 1941–42.
- President of the Society of Motor Manufacturers and Traders 1939–42.
- Member of the Engineering Advisory Council, Board of Trade 1947–62.
- Member of the UK Trade Mission to Canada 1958.
- Chancellor Designate University of Warwick (from 1964).

He was created KBE (1942), GBE (1955), 1st Baron (1959), and died on 12 December 1964.[10]

1

Key Ministries in the National War Cabinet

A government has the same fiscal and social responsibilities in wartime as in times of peace; there are, however, obvious additional needs and responsibilities during conflicts. For example supplying the services and indeed the home front with the essential components of living is made much more difficult when shipping is affected, air raids a daily occurrence and workforces disrupted or have had their work redirected to other things Additionally, some commodities taken for granted prior to 1939 were simply unavailable during the Second World War. Of course, there is also the need to manufacture or import the machinery of war. Whilst the work of the whole National War Cabinet and the underlying ministries was important, of concern here were the three key ministries, namely the Ministries of Aircraft Production, of Supply and of Production. These three ministries were at the vanguard of the supply chain for wartime supplies of arms and ammunition to the services, and indeed the home front.

Ministry of Supply

The Ministry of Supply (MoS) was created by an Act of Parliament in 1939 to *establish a Ministry of Supply and for the purposes connected therewith.*

Clearly an Act of Parliament brought to the statute books in 1939, needed to be considered and the Act written well before the outbreak of war.

> The reason which finally led to the establishment of a Ministry of Supply in time of peace was the decision to double the Territorial Army. In an announcement in the House of Commons on 29th March 1939, the Prime Minister, after announcing that the Territorial Army would be brought up to war establishment and then doubled, stated that this important decision would involve a number of consequential decisions in order to provide inter alia for the necessary increase in equipment and reserves and for the war potential necessary to maintain the increased forces.

On 19th April 1939 the Cabinet considered the proposals of the Minister for Co-ordination of Defence and the Chancellor of the Duchy of Lancaster for a Ministry of Army Supply, and authorised plans for a Ministry of Supply to be worked out in detail and a draft bill to be prepared.

On the 20th April 1939, the Prime Minister announced in the House of Commons that His Majesty's Government had decided that a bill should be introduced as soon as possible to set up a Ministry of Supply under a Minister who would be a member of the Cabinet.

Thus, in spite of agitation in favour of a complete Ministry of Supply to deal with the supply of all three Services, the Government decided to limit the functions of the Ministry of Supply for the time being to the supply of Army needs only, on the grounds that the existing supply services for the Navy and Air Force were fully adequate for their purpose.[1]

As time went on, it became clear that this decision introduced a limitation to the swift delivery of supplies wherever they were needed. Consequently, plans were revised. This led to the formation of two further ministries, which are mentioned later.

Part 1 of the Act establishing the Ministry of Supply sets the scene, some of the key parts of which are as follows:

1.1. It shall be lawful for His Majesty to appoint a Minister of Supply (hereafter in this Act referred to as 'the Minister') who shall hold office during His Majesty's pleasure and shall have such functions as are or may be conferred on him by or under this Act.

1.2. The Minister may appoint a Parliamentary Secretary to the Ministry of Supply.

2.1. Subject to the provisions of this subsection, the Minister shall have power:

   a. To buy and otherwise acquire, manufacture or otherwise produce, store and transport any articles required for the public service, and to exchange, sell or otherwise dispose of any articles bought or otherwise acquired or manufactured or otherwise produced by him.

   b. To buy or otherwise acquire any articles for the purposes of exchanging them for articles required for the public service.

   c. To do all such things (including the erection of buildings and other execution of works) as appear to the Minister necessary or expedient for the exercise of the foregoing powers.[2]

The first individual appointed as Minister of Supply was Rt. Hon. Leslie Burgin MP. From then onwards, the ministry grew as it took on more responsibility such that the organisation chart for the period between September 1939 and May 1940 contained the following directors who oversaw their respective departments, or groups of departments in the case of the director-generals:[3]

- Directors of engineers and signals equipment.
- Director of finance.
- Director-General of explosives and chemical supply.
- Director-General of equipment and stores.
- Director-General of finance.
- Director-General of munitions production.
- Director-General stores.
- Director-General of tanks and transport.
- Director of instrument production.
- Director of mechanisation.
- Director of movements and components.
- Director of ordnance factories.
- Director of progress and inspection.
- Director of storage.
- Director of scientific research.
- Director of transportation equipment.

The director-generals and the minister met weekly as they were all members of the Supply Council where the work of the departments and other special business was discussed.

The Minister of Supply was also concerned with three of the permanent executive committees of the Anglo-French Co-ordinating Committee, namely:

1. Munitions and Raw Materials.
2. Textiles and Hides.
3. Timber.

The minister was also concerned with the British Supply Board in Canada and the United States, sometimes known as the Greenly Mission. This committee effected British Government purchases of certain kinds of goods in Canada and the United States. The Board operated in Canada through the Canadian War Supply Board and in the USA through the British Purchasing Commission under Mr A B Purvis.

By 28 May 1940, the headquarters staff of the new ministry consisted of 4,400 people distributed over many branches. As the war progressed and with roles and responsibilities becoming clearer, the duties of the Ministry of Supply were split into two functions, supply and production.

Supply functions:

1. <u>For the Army</u>. Supply of munitions of war is the responsibility of the Ministry alone. The supply of clothing and equipment for the army is also

the responsibility of the Ministry, subject to the power of the War Office to make local purchases of comparatively small quantities in these two spheres.

2. Admiralty and Air Ministry. The Ministry of Supply exercises concurrently with the Admiralty and the Air Ministry the powers and duties relating to supply of such classes of munitions and other stores as may be agreed from time to time between Ministers. This function is derived from arrangements existing before the formation of the Ministry of Supply. It covers articles such as small arms, small arms ammunition and explosives.

3. 'Common User' articles. The Ministry of Supply furnishes 'common user' articles, i.e. articles used by more than one department, the three Service Departments, the Home Office under the Civil Defence Act and the Office of Works being the Departments mainly involved.

4. Control of Royal Ordnance Factories. The Ministry has assumed responsibility for the control and administration of the Royal Ordnance Factories which were previously administered by the War Office. These constitute a principal source of the supply of munitions.

5. Design, Inspection, Research and Experimental work. As a corollary of its supply functions in respect of munitions, the Ministry has assumed responsibility for design, inspection, research and experimental work relating to munitions of war required by the army (including optical and scientific stores) and has taken over control of the former War Office establishments engaged on experimental and development work ...

Production functions:

There are five departments which are concerned with production, each under a Director-General:

1. Department of Munitions Production – Production of guns, machine guns, small arms, shells, cartridge cases, fuses, instruments, optical glass, machine tools etc.

2. Department of Explosions and Chemical Supplies – Production of explosives and related chemical materials.

3. Department of Tanks and Transport – Production of tanks, mechanised vehicles, transportation equipment, etc.

4. Department of Equipment Stores – Production of clothing, equipment, general stores etc.

5. The Royal Ordnance Factories – The Director-General of Ordnance Factories is responsible for the production of the Royal Ordnance Factories as well as for their control and administration. His production programme is derived from other production departments.

The first four production departments are sub-divided into a number of directo-rates, which are responsible for surveying and planning the productive capacity of the country as regards the particular articles under their control. Investigations are made into the productive capacity of existing firms through the Area Officers of the Ministry, who are located in the Regional Areas of the country, and records are kept against future production requirements. Offers of capacity from firms are similarly investigated and recorded.[4]

Once formed and the minister appointed, there was a need to establish some of the infrastructure, including a budget!

22 November 1939

Dear Compton,
I enclose an official letter asking for delegated financial powers for the Ministry of Supply in respect of losses etc.,works services and urgent cases in which capital assistance is required in connection with defence expenditure. This is on the lines indicated in Gilbert's letter to Dobbie-Bateman of 3rd November.

We should be glad to have a very early reply as regards losses, etc. and works services as we are waiting to issue instructions.

You will remember I spoke about this a week or so ago. Accordingly, if there is likely to be any delay in approving the capital assistance proposal (paragraph 6 of the letter), we should be glad if it could be dealt with separately.

Yours sincerely,
Burgin[5]

Burgin's words were to prove prophetic as there were indeed losses in transit, although the majority were later in the war. For example, the losses in transit of ilmenite, a raw material, amounted to over £16 million. This was in addition to the losses in ships.[6]

The issue of timely supplies of materials and munitions was a recurring factor in many discussions. By way of an example, the War Cabinet Chiefs of Staff Committee considered a memo written by the Ministry of Supply pointing out the threat to supplies from invasion and bombing.

The danger to war factories through invasion is slight compared to that from bombing. We, therefore, consider that there are no areas from which all govern-ment work should be removed on account of the invasion danger. As a general principle, however, those areas from which vital war production should be excluded on account of invasion are the same as those shown in the attached map. Existing production should remain, but no new war production should be initiated in these areas (the areas marked on the map consisted of all areas within 20 miles of the coast of Great Britain).

The area thus indicated includes a large number of important towns which have grown up round the main ports, in which a high proportion of the industry of the country is normally situated. It also includes the whole of the industrial areas of West Cumberland, Northumberland and Durham, as well as industrially important parts of Lancashire and Scotland.

The area boards have continually drawn attention to congestion on the one hand and to under employment on the other, and the Northern Area Board on 15th January passed the following resolution:

That in our opinion County Durham should again be considered as a suitable place to which business should be transferred because of the available labour supply, and that the present line of demarcation as to vulnerability should be reviewed.[7]

Not only was the issue of potential loss of manufacturing taken seriously but there was also the matter of ensuring that storage of materials owned by the Ministry of Supply and stored in warehouses was scattered round the British Isles. Where possible this was done in unpopulated areas. An audit undertaken in August 1942 showed the following (Figure 1.1):[8]

Area	Covered Storage (Sq. Ft.)
Scotland	1,900,879
Birmingham	1,322,134
Wales	903,396
Bristol	666,741
London	1,157,498
Yorkshire	1,210,135
North Midlands	790,114
Reading	276,543
North West Midlands	2,613,440
Northern[9]	935,833
Lancashire	7,167,246
Northern Ireland	102,030
Special Depots	1,331,541
Total	20,377,530

Figure 1.1 Ministry of Supply covered storage depots.

As we shall see later, locating new shadow factories was subjected to the same concerns, which ensured that some of the newer shadow factories were in parts of the country not previously used for aircraft manufacture. For example, there was a shadow factory in Yeadon, adjacent to which an airfield was built, now the Leeds Bradford Airport.

The distribution of manufacture and supply brought with it some other issues, one of which was the amount of accommodation needed for the workers. Over time, hostels were built in some locations. In notes prepared for the minister's speech on the estimates (27 April 1943), the opening remarks reflected on the hostel project.

> At the beginning of April there were approximately 11,000 residents in the 20 specially constructed hostels attached to Royal Ordnance Factories, and some 400 in smaller industrial hostels, mainly large houses specially adapted for the purpose. In a number of cases the former include residents not employed in the ROFs and the Ministry of Supply has been glad to help other Departments, particularly the Ministry of Agriculture, in this way. Accommodation for approximately 1,000 senior staff of the ROFs is also provided in 13 cases in premises acquired or adapted for the purpose.[10]

In most if not all cases, the land used for these wartime hostels has been used for other purposes and their exact location lost. In their book *Civilians in Silsden*,[11] J. Rogers and D. Rogers managed not only to determine the location, which was known as the National Service Hostel (more locally as the Howden Hall Hostel) in Silsden, but also to determine the groups of workers this hostel housed. The residents included (from page 126):

a. Female navy personnel.
b. Royal Ordnance Factory workers, many from Ireland.
c. Girls from the Newcastle and Hartlepool areas.
d. Land Army personnel (thought to number approximately 100).
e. Others not specified.

This hostel was used after the war to house refugees of different nationalities. A plaque was erected by the Association of Ukrainians, some members of which lodged there, Figure 1.2.

Owning lodgings created some minor headaches for some of the senior staff in the Ministry of Supply. In some cases, activities such as dance programmes required entertainment licences,[12] and if available for consumption, alcohol licences.

Whilst creating and maintaining a file on theatre, cinematograph, dancing and music licences may not seem like core business for senior members of the MoS, creating and maintaining a record of important decisions was a more mainstream activity. The list from the Raw Materials Department is interesting. This hand-written document covers many commodities from paper, timber, metals to silk, industrial diamonds and most things in between.[13]

The Ministry of Supply evolved its infrastructure as needs arose. For example, the Supply Council chairman was Sir William Rootes in April 1942, the car manufacturer intimately connected with the shadow factories. It must have seemed a daunting

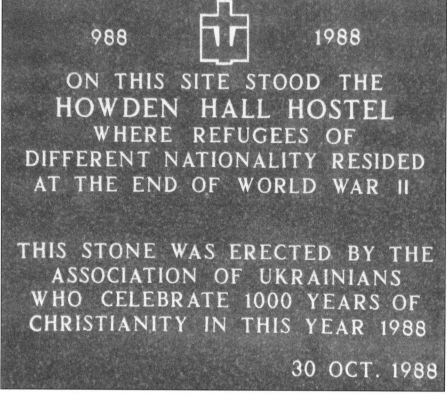

Figure 1.2 The site of a Second World War hostel, later used to house refugees.
(Author's photograph)

task to ramp up production of much needed commodities at the same time as maintaining relationships with other countries needing materials, parts and machines.

With these and other duties, it is not surprising that the Ministry of Supply simply could not cope with maintaining the supply chain or armaments and other common commodities to the RAF and expanding its remit to include the production of aircraft. The Ministry of Aircraft Production, more commonly known as MAP, was therefore created specifically to provide the necessary infrastructure for the many other needs of the RAF.

Ministry of Aircraft Production

The Ministry of Aircraft Production (MAP) was constituted by Order of Council on 17 May 1940, with the London headquarters housed in the offices of Imperial Chemical Industries Milbank.[14] Written in June 1940, the following brief describes the functions of the new Ministry.

11th June 1940

Functions of the Department

1. With reference to paragraph 6 of office memorandum No 1, it has been decided that the Ministry of Aircraft Production will be responsible for:
    a. Production of aircraft, armament and all equipment hitherto dealt with by the department of the Director-General of Production, Air Ministry.
    b. Control of the arrangements for repair of aircraft and equipment in industry, technical control of the Royal Air Force Repair Depots in this country and Salvage Units, and responsibility for production of aircraft up to the stage at which they are fully equipped for issue to operational units.
    c. Research and development as hitherto dealt with by AMDP (for purposes of technical administration the Experimental Establishments will come under the Ministry of Aircraft Production in the same way and to the same extent as they have hitherto come under AMDP).

Arising out of (b) above, the following arrangements have been made:

Civil Repair Organisation

2. The Ministry of Aircraft Production has taken over from the Air Ministry complete control of the Civil Repair Organisation.

Royal Air Force Repair Depots

3. The technical control of the repair work in the Royal Air Force Depots at home has been transferred to the Ministry of Aircraft Production subject to the Air Ministry retaining the right to impose a priority call on certain personnel for special work unconnected with repairs and for repair work outside the depots on aircraft in operation squadrons.
4. Responsibility for administration of the depots as service units remains with the Royal Air Force and the Air Ministry.

Salvage Organisation

5. Technical control of the RAF Salvage Units, both at home and overseas, will be exercised by the Ministry of Aircraft Production. Technical directions will normally be conveyed by the Ministry of Aircraft Production through No 43 Group, Royal Air Force, in respect of salvage units at home, and through the Maintenance Officer-in-Chief in France in respect of salvage

units in France. Copies of such instructions will simultaneously be sent to the Air Ministry.

6. Salvage units, both home and overseas, will remain under the Air Ministry (through the AOC Maintenance Command) for purposes of administration.[15]

The first minister of aircraft production was Lord Beaverbrook (1940–41), who was subsequently appointed Minister of Supply 1941–42, British lend–lease administrator in the United States 1942 and Lord Privy Seal 1943–54.[16] He was succeeded by the following:

1. Baron John Moore-Brabazon (1941–42).
2. Baron John Llewellin (1942 –42).
3. Sir Stafford Cripps (1942 –45).
4. Ernest Brown MP (1945 –45).

The Minister of Aircraft Production chaired a committee known as the Aircraft Supply Council, the members of which, at least in 1943, were as follows:[17]

- The Rt. Hon. J T C Moore Moore-Brabazon MP.
- F Montague MO, parliamentary secretary.
- Sir Charles Craven, controller-general.
- Sir Archibald Rowlands, permanent secretary.
- Air Marshall F J Linnell, controller of research and development.
- W C Devereux, controller of North American aircraft supplies.
- Sir Henry Tizard FRS.

W C Devereux was a key part of the council for at that time lend–lease from the United States was in full flow (see Chapter 2). This was just one of the many collaborations with the North American continent concerning aircraft manufacture.

It might seem unusual for one member of the council to be the president of Magdalen College, i.e. Sir Henry Tizard FRS. A First World War member of the Royal Flying Corps, Sir Henry was chairman of the Aeronautical Research Committee and a member of the Council of the Ministry of Aircraft Production in addition to his work on the Aircraft Supply Council.[18]

Whilst the distributed manufacturing policy mentioned above provided a measure of protection against blanket bombing, it required closer liaison with regional organisations, particularly on matters affecting aircraft production. The Ministry of Aircraft Production regional organisation, therefore, became a significant undertaking:

The functions of the regional representation are:

a. To represent the Ministry on the Regional Boards.
b. To co-operate with the local officers of other government departments in all matters of common interest in order to avoid overlapping and waste of effort and to contribute as far as possible to the rapid and local settlement of difficulties of allocation of industrial capacity, priority etc., within the general priority directions issued from Headquarters.
c. To be responsible for the efficient performance of certain important executive functions which have been decentralised to the regions in connection with:
  i.   Industrial capacity.
  ii. Labour.
  iii. ARP and fire prevention.
  iv. Location of factory space.
  v.   The repair of air raid damage.
d. To maintain contact with the Regional Commissioner and his staff and in the event of interruptions of communications between the Regions and Headquarters (e.g. in invasion conditions) to assume responsibility, subject to the general control of the Regional Commissioner, for MAP matters in the region and to ensure in consultation with the local officers of the production directorates the maintenance of MAP output.
e. Generally to be the local 'eyes and ears' of the Department in the regions.

The attached chart, which is based on the Midland Region, shows in its lower half the layout of a typical regional office (and is reproduced below as Figure 1.3).

Arguably, 1943 saw some unexpected changes within the Ministry of Aircraft Production:

1. The transfer of the Directorate-General of Aircraft Production Factories to the Ministry of Works.
2. The organisation of staffs dealing with jet engines and aircraft.

Both of these are interesting for different reasons.

The following arrangements were made during the transfer mentioned above as point 1.

The Directorate-General of Aircraft Production Factories will be transferred to the Ministry of Works on the 1st March 1943, and the following arrangements will then apply:

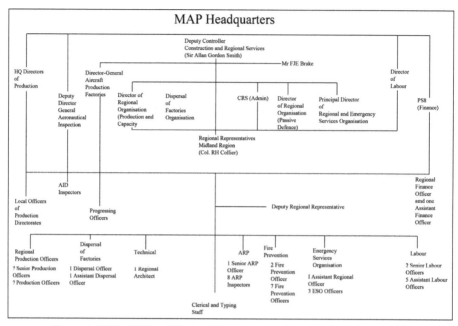

Figure 1.3 The Midland Region Map regional office. (Author's diagram[19])

1. The MAP will retain responsibility for final decisions on the nature and extent of schemes whether involving buildings and works services only or plant and equipment only or both buildings plant and equipment, including approval, in the light of advice received from the Ministry of Works, or estimates of cost and of major variations.

2. The MAP will continue normally to employ managing firms as agents and in such cases will look to the Ministry of Works for advice on such matters as:

    a. The reasonableness of the estimates of cost of building work, services, plant of equipment submitted to the MAP by managing firms.

    b. The suitability of sites from the building aspect.

    c. The layout and design of buildings and works in terms of constructional design and economy in the use of labour and materials.

    d. The selection of architects and of contractors to be invited to tender, paying due regard to the wishes of the managing firm by whom the commissions or contracts will be placed.

    e. The terms and conditions of the contracts for works and services to be entered into by managing firms.

    f. The relative merits of tenders received.

    g. The progress of the work both of buildings and services and of the construction and installation of plant and equipment.[20]

The potential introduction of the jet engine, designed by Sir Frank Whittle FRS, led to the formation of a new department.

> I have worked out the main features of a new organisation, under Dr Roxbee-Cox as Director of Unconventional Projects (DUP), to attain the following objects over the next two years:
>
> i.   To accelerate development and supply of unconventional aircraft and power units which are now in hand.
> ii. To press forward new development and research for more advanced aircraft and engine projects and to plan to produce these at the earliest dates possible.
> iii. To lay the foundations of new development and research for longer term projects.
>
> Under the DUP it is proposed to set up sections to deal with:
> a. Engine Development.
> b. Airframe Development.
> c. Airframe and Engine Research.
> d. Engine Manufacture.
> e. Airframe Manufacture.
> f. Contracts.
> g. Future projects.[21]

The move of MAP to shift from conventional aircraft to jet engine-based aircraft is best illustrated with the following:

> Memorandum of the Drive to Jet Propulsion
>
> 1. Objectives.
>   i.   To get as many gas turbine aeroplanes based on engines at present under development into operation as quickly as possible.
>   ii. To produce gas turbine aeroplanes of higher performance as quickly as possible, urgently investigating the adaptation of current types of aircraft.
>   iii. To produce vehicles capable of supersonic speeds.
>
> 2. The following steps are considered to be necessary.
>   a. To put aerodynamic and thermodynamics, airframes and engines, research, development, and pilot production under one man responsible to CRD.
>   b. To give this man top priority in obtaining suitable staff, labour, machine tools and capacity.
>   c. To keep the directing staff small, compact and expert.

d.   To include in the staff Wing Commander Whittle and a first class fuel chemist.
e.   To engage in intensive research and development on aero-thermodynamic ducts, boundary layer control, low drag and compressibility at Power Jets Ltd, RAE and NPL.
f.   Quickly to get defined ample airframe capacity for work on (i) and (ii).
g.   To get allotted capacity for high speed construction of experimental aircraft, flying models and devices, and for the adaptation of existing aircraft, in connection with (iii).
h.   To extend the experimental facilities generally on the engine side, notably at Power Jets which should be under the direct technical direction of the controller mentioned in (a).
i.   Immediately to build aero-thermodynamic ducts on to the E28 or the F9/40 or anything else suitable for experiments aimed to reach supersonic speeds.
j.   To concentrate flight research and development at a single aerodrome under Wing Commander Wilson, at present in the USA.
k.   To take risks in the hope of big dividends.[22]

Ministry of Production

The Ministry of War Production was created to fill a gap between the Ministry of Supply, the Ministry of Aircraft Production, the Admiralty and the Ministry of Labour and National Service. The draft white paper concerning the duties of the Minister of War Production as he was initially known (the word 'war' was removed shortly after the ministry's creation) outlined the following:

General

1.   The Minister of War Production is the War Cabinet Minister charged with responsibility for general production policy, under the instructions of the Minister of Defence and the War Cabinet. He will carry out the general co-ordinating duties at present performed by the Production Executive, other than in field of man-power and labour. These duties include the allocation of available resources of raw materials and productive capacity, and the settlement of priorities of production where necessary.

Allocation and common services

2.   All common services in the field of production will continue to be administered by the Departments at present responsible for them, subject to general direction by the Minister of War Production.

3. These common services include the controls administered by the Ministry of Supply and the Ministry of Aircraft Production. The Minister of War Production will have direct access to the Controllers.
4. The allocation of industrial capacity, machine tools, and all raw materials, will be under the direct authority of the Minister of War Production. These allocations will cover the requirements of all Departments of State, including the requirements of the general public sponsored by Government Departments.
5. All Regional Organisation and Capacity Clearing Centres will be included in one group under the direction of the Minister of War Production.

Labour Questions

1. Under the general authority of the War Cabinet, the functions of the Production Executive in regard to man-power and labour will in future be carried out by the Minister of Labour and National Service. These functions include the allocation of man-power resources to the armed forces, to the Production Departments and to the civil industries, as well as general labour questions in the field of production.
2. As part of his function of dealing with demands for the allocating man-power, the Minister of Labour and National Service has the duty of bringing to notice any direction in which he thinks that greater economy in the use of man-power could be affected.[23]

The outline also mentioned duties in relation to naval production and merchant shipbuilding, in relation to the Board of Trade, in relation to building programmes, representation in the House of Commons, the Combined Assignments Boards and the responsibilities of department ministers.

As was often the case, Churchill offered some advice:

I feel that the Ministry of Production would benefit by having a civil servant of high position and ability as its Secretary. The Ministry has to deal with so many of the established Departments that there might be great advantages in having an Officer of long experience and understanding of inter-departmental workings and relations in this position.

I suggest that Sir Arthur Street should be considered for this appointment. In this case Sir Henry Self, who is well qualified by experience of aircraft production matters, might be appointed Secretary of the Ministry of Aircraft Production, thus releasing Sir Archibald Rowlands, who was at one time Deputy Under Secretary of State in the Air Ministry, to succeed Sir Arthur Street as Secretary of that Department.

I trust that the Ministers concerned will be prepared to give these proposals favourable consideration and will discuss the matter with the Deputy Prime Minister.

W S C

1.8.42[24]

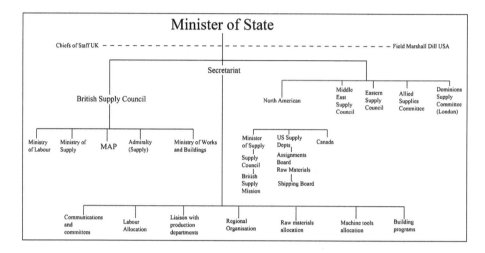

Figure 1.4 Organisation chart for the newly formed Ministry of Production. (Author's diagram)

Figure 1.4 shows the organisation chart for the resulting ministry, the permanent secretary for which was Sir Henry Self.

Further advice from Churchill followed:

Directive by the Prime Minister on the duties of the Minister of Production

1. I made a statement on the 12th March last in the House of Commons (Hansard Columns 1205–7) about the powers of the Minister of Production. That statement still stands, but it appears advantageous that the powers should be further defined in certain particulars.
2. The general duties of the Minister of Production in relation to the Ministers in charge of the Supply Departments are as follows:
    i.   The Minister of Production is responsible for production policy and for those specific matters which lie at the root of production policy, namely:
        a. The Settlement of Priorities.
        b. The Allocation of Capacity.
        c. The Program of Raw Materials (including the import program, the development of home and Empire resources, and the conservation of materials).

    ii. In these matters the Supply Ministers (while, of course, retaining their constitutional right of appeal to the War Cabinet in matters of special importance) will accept the directions of the Minister of Production.

3. In the field of raw materials, the questions for which the Minister of Production is responsible interlock with those for which the Minister of Supply is responsible. The necessary arrangements are to be made between the staffs of the Minister of Production and of the Ministry of Supply to define the channels through which the Minister of Production will obtain the information which he requires for the proper discharge of his duties, and through which he will issue directions in regard to raw materials.

W S C[25]

The creation of this ministry was of importance to shadow factories as all of the imported aero engines and complete airplanes were ordered and the paperwork processed through this organisation. Indeed, some shadow factories concerned with the assembly of aircraft as distinct from the manufacture of airframes or aero engines would have ground to a halt had not this part of the process been transparent to the shadow factory managers. To further clarify the process, the following two paragraphs elaborate on the organisational structure from the North American part of the shadow factory raw materials supply chain.

1. The Minister of Production is the War Cabinet Minister responsible among other things for the program of raw materials: he is therefore responsible for planning the development of home resources, arranging the import program and settling the allocation and release of stocks. The Ministry of Supply, as Agent for the Ministry of Production, carries out the raw materials program under his general supervision and direction according to the broad lines of policy laid down by him.

2. Broadly speaking, the Raw Materials Department with its controls is responsible for developing in detail and carrying out the policy laid down in broad lines by the Minister of Production. Its organisation is based upon two principles which the problems to be dealt with have suggested. In the first place issues of policy related to a specific commodity or group of commodities are dealt with so far as possible together and by the same person. In the second place those issues which involve common action for all or a number of commodities are, where possible, dealt with together, especially when the issues involve negotiations with other Departments and it is of importance that the Raw Materials Departments speaks with one voice. The distinction between general and particular issues is necessarily a relative one and must not obscure the fact that both types emerge in the work of the department at the same level.[26]

2

Overseas Capacity and Infrastructure

Modern industries are aware of the concept of just-in-time manufacturing. That is to say that a manufacturer produces whatever products have firm orders in the required timescale for their sale to the end customer. This and other concepts have their modern 'branding' in what is called lean thinking or lean manufacturing which started in the Toyota Motor Company in Japan, created by one of their senior workers, Taiichi Ohno.

Whilst the concept was unchanged from the early days of manufacturing until restated by Ohno, that is just-in-time management, the practical implications in wartime are fundamentally more complex. Raw materials supplies, from home and abroad, were compromised by many factors. The ability to create a stable workforce was almost impossible and the air raids and shortages led to many human difficulties. These and other factors honed the wartime interpretation of just-in-time materials supply.

Industrial Capacity Committee

For these and many other reasons, the War Cabinet needed to understand the contribution that industry could make to the over-arching goal of keeping Britain supplied with its many and varied needs. Accordingly, the War Cabinet established the Industrial Capacity Committee.

Production Council

The utilisation of industrial capacity for war production

The Industrial Capacity Committee (ICC) was 'charged with the duty of considering general questions relating to the utilisation of industries as a whole, in consultation with such industries'. At a meeting of the Production Council on the 26th June 1940, when the ICC was set up, the Minister of Supply pointed out that *the production of munitions is now so highly specialised that anything in the way of general utility is not wanted but that the plant could be organised when it is clear what work it is required to do.* We have studied the offers of capacity that have been flowing in from almost every branch of industry and we have entered into consultations with a considerable number of Trade Associations. While these studies were proceeding, the Area Boards were strengthened and developed, and these more vigorous organisations were immediately directed to the task of enlisting as much of the spare capacity as possible by an extension of sub-contracting. It has been clear from the outset, however, that nothing can be done by the Area Boards which would substitute for a national policy in relation to the various industries, and that the problem is not one of discovering capacity but is, as the Minister of Supply so rightly stated, one of organising specific needs. It is, in a word, a production problem. And the significance of this simple observation is that it can be solved only by those who have full information of the detailed needs and day to day difficulties of production departments, and who have the requisite technical staff with a knowledge and experience of produc-tion engineering. That is to say, however helpful the ICC may be in regular-ising the flow of capacity offers and in organising the co-operation of advisory industrial bodies, the problem can be solved only by the production departments themselves.

We have found it convenient to consider the various branches of industry in three broad categories:

a. Those in which there is capacity to produce in excess of the requirements of the production departments plus civilian demand, limited as it will continue to be by war conditions, and whose plant and machinery cannot be used in the branches of munitions production where there is a shortage of capacity.
b. Those in which there is (or ought to be) an immediate shortage of capacity or in which a shortage may be expected to occur as the war production program develops.
c. Those in which there is a surplus of capacity for their normal types of product but which can to varying extents be adapted to relieve the overload in the industries under (b) above.[1]

Of course, production capacity issues are the purview of specialists, able to under-stand materials flow through a factory and the implications of lead times. Fortunately, the Production Council were able to make use of the memorandum written to the Rt. Hon. Arthur Greenwood PC (the chairman of the Production Council) by the War Emergency Committee of the Institution of Production Engineers.[2]

In some of its opening remarks, this memorandum offers three specific suggestions which *should be adopted for the further improvement of designs with the object of facilitating production*, all worthy and no doubt welcome suggestions.

Additionally, some key posts were staffed by various individuals with experience of industrial production.

8th July 1940

Organisation of the Industrial Capacity Committee and its relation with the
Area Boards

In order to carry out effectively the tasks assigned to it, the Industrial Capacity Committee proposes to appoint an Assistant Secretary and the appropriate staff to perform secretarial duties. Treasury authority has been obtained for the appointments to be carried on the Ministry of Supply vote.

It proposes to appoint Sir James Lithgow as an industrial expert, to act as Deputy Chairman of the Committee. The First Sea Lord of the Admiralty had agreed. The Admiralty has appointed Engineer Rear-Admiral W R Parnell CB as its representative in Sir James Lithgow's place.

It is also proposed that while each individual Area Officer should remain responsible to his own department, the Area Boards in their corporate capacity should in future be responsible directly to the Industrial Capacity Committee, and that the Area Board's Secretaries should be under the direction of the Committee.

I submit these proposals for approval of Council.

Harold McMillan MP
Chairman
Industrial Capacity Committee[3]

Incidentally the functions of the Regional Boards were defined in broad general terms as follows:

i.   To ensure the rapid, effectual and continuous co-ordination of the efforts of all government officials in the region in connection with the production of essential stores.

ii.   To provide for the speedy exchange of information between ministries and service departments and the regional advisory committees.

iii. To settle by agreement, in so far as is possible, all local difficulties likely to delay output.

iv.   To transmit to headquarters proposals for the exploitation of additional capacity found in the region.

v.   To advise headquarters on the adjustment of difficulties over priority contracts.

It will be seen that this is a very wide definition authorising the Boards to interest themselves in every difficulty that may arise likely to impede the maximum production in their regions. It should be understood that this general instruction is issued not to certain members of the boards who have no other official duties to perform, but to all members.[4]

At the same time as he was appointing key individuals with industrial experience to relevant posts, Harold McMillan was surveying key individuals in government and the forces to understand the distribution of orders to industry. This reply was from the First Lord of the Admiralty.

12th August 1940

My Dear McMillan,

Thank you for your letter of July 31st on the question of absorbing into war work those factories which were formerly engaged in civil trade. I fully sympathise with your position, and I can assure you that the Admiralty is at all times anxious to spread these orders as widely as possible, and I have asked my Department to use their best endeavours to supply the information which the Industrial Capacity Committee wishes to obtain on the lines set out in the enclosure to your letter.

A V Alexander
First Lord of the Admiralty[5]

Industrial capacity has a direct relevance to shadow factories because of the need for the newly created concerns to receive supplies of rivets, springs, small motors and indeed a whole myriad of parts which were not made in shadow factories. The priority of manufacturing was defined in one of the Defence Regulations:

Priority of Production

In exercise of the powers conferred on him by Regulation 55 of the Defence (General) Regulations, 1939, the Minister of Supply hereby directs as follows:

a. You shall give first priority to any work on which you are or may be required to be engaged of or in connection with producing articles of any of the following descriptions:
   i. Fighter, bomber or trainer aircraft.
   ii. Instruments or equipment for such aircraft.
   iii. Anti-aircraft equipment (especially Bofors guns and instruments and ammunition therefor).
   iv. Small arms and small arm ammunition.
   v. Bombs.
   vi. Components parts of any of the above mentioned articles.

b. Subject to (a) above you shall give priority to any work on which you are or may be required to be engaged of or in connection with producing articles of any of the following descriptions:
   i. Anti-tank weapons.
   ii. Field artillery.

    iii. Tanks.
    iv. Machine guns.
    v. Ammunition (including mines).
    vi. Component parts of any of the above-mentioned articles.[6]

Just so there was no doubt about priorities, Churchill provided his input:

War Cabinet Priorities

The very highest priority in personnel and material should be assigned to what may be called the radio sphere. This demands scientists, wireless experts and many classes of highly-skilled labour and high grade material. On the progress made, much of the winning of the war and our future strategy especially Naval, depends. We must impart a far greater accuracy to the AA guns, and to a far better protection to our warships and harbours. Not only research and experiments, but production must be pushed hopefully forward from many directions and after repeated disappointments we shall achieve success.

The 1A priority must remain with Aircraft Production, for the purpose of executing approved target programs. It must be an obligation upon them to contrive by every conceivable means not to let this priority be abused and needlessly hamper other vital departments. For this purpose they should specify their requirements in labour and material beforehand quarter by quarter, if practicable month by month, and make all surplus available for others immediately. The priority is not to be exercised in the sense that aircraft production is completely to monopolise the supplies of any limited commodity. Where the condition prevails that the approved MAP demands absorb the total supply, a special allocation must be made, even at prejudice to aircraft production, to provide the minimum essential needs of the other departments and branches. This allocation, if not agreed, will be decided at Cabinet level.

Special aid and occasional temporary priorities must be given to the laggard elements. Among these stand out the following:

a.   Rifles.
b.   Small arms ammunition, above all the special types.

Intense efforts must be made to bring the new factories into production. The fact that scarcely any improvement is now expected until the end of the year, i.e. 16 months after the outbreak of war, is a grave reflection on those concerned. Twelve should suffice for a cartridge factory. We have been mercifully spared from the worst consequences of this failure through the armies not being in action as was anticipated.

Trench mortar ammunition and AT gun ammunition are also in a shocking plight and must be helped.

All these laggards must be the subject of weekly reports to the Production Council and to me.

The Navy must exercise its existing priorities in respect of small craft and anti-U-Boat building. This applies also to merchant shipbuilding, and to craft for landing operations. Delay must be accepted upon all larger vessels that cannot be finished in 1941. Plans must be made to go forward with all processes and parts which do not clash with prior needs. The utmost possible steel and armour-plate must be ordered in America.

W S C
10 Downing Street
15th October 1940[7]

Such was the pressure to deliver results that McMillan wrote a report of the first 10 weeks of the Industrial Capacity Committee to the chairman of the Production Council (the minister without portfolio). The report was detailed, some 92 pages long. Whilst it would serve no purpose to reproduce it here, the introduction might add value and appears as Appendix II.

The radio sphere mentioned above by Churchill underlined the need for production of as many valves and bulbs as possible. On at least one occasion, the Ministry of Supply became directly involved as the following communication reveals:

Mr Owen reviewed briefly the events leading up to the present position in which the Board of Trade had arranged for two Westlake bulb blowing machines to be erected in a UGB factory at St Helen's. As the firms concerned had asked for certain financial assistance in carrying this scheme through and as this assistance could, as a matter of departmental convenience, be provided more easily by the Ministry of Supply than by the Board of Trade, it has been decided that this project would be sponsored by the Ministry of Supply. The Board of Trade, however, would retain responsibility for bulbs in general.[8]

Priorities of this complexity (each of the main items is composed of many individual components) required further organisation. The scientific and optical instruments industry needed inclusion into the planning. Accordingly, a sub-committee of that name was created under the auspices of the Industrial Capacity Committee. In their report dated 26 June 1944, their committee commented:

In war-time instruments of precision are essential and include gun directors and predictors, range finders, gyroscopic equipment, telescopes and binoculars, specialised radio apparatus and tank and aircraft instruments of many types.

Industrial instruments include testing equipment of all kinds, optical measuring mechanisms, optical alignment instruments, pressure, temperature and flow meters, time measuring equipment, spectrophotometers, and instruments controlling many mechanical engineering processes.[9]

Sir Frank Smith FRS chaired this committee which also included Viscount Falmouth, Sir Charles Darwin FRS, Sir Peter Bennett, Mr Hugh Roberts, Mr C S Wright, Mr A W Angus, Mr P A Cooke and Mr G Roberts.

Perhaps with a sense of concern, there was the need to create a sub-committee of the Industrial Capacity Committee called the Sub-Committee on Removal of Factories. This sub-committee had following remit:

1.   The sub-committee was appointed under minute 5 of the meeting of the Committee on 14th October to investigate and report on the principles to be followed in view of the need for the removal of factories damaged in air raids.
2.   A number of factories engaged in war production, export trade and other essential processes are being removed, with the knowledge and assistance of the department concerned, for the following reasons:
      i.   Because the factory has been seriously damaged by enemy action.
      ii.   Because the factory is situated in a coastal area, and other factors indicate its removal before it is put out of action.
      iii. Because dispersal is advised. This practice has been largely adopted by the Ministry of Aircraft Production for air frame and aero-engine works, and the example may be followed by some firms working for the Ministry of Supply. The Board of Trade have also some dispersal schemes for storage.[10]

Later in the report:

The bombing of London has greatly increased the number of removals, both of damaged war production factories and of non-essential factories. Some at least of the latter are removing as a precaution and because of labour difficulties. The movement has already created a number of problems. If it were only a passing phase, the difficulties might be left to sort themselves. But if air raid damage continues, and war production is to develop as intended, the task of re-housing damaged factories and providing labour, housing, transport, etc. will become increasingly serious.[11]

Sir Frank Edward Smith FRS was involved in numerous activities during the war. An entry in his *Royal Society Biographical Memoir* documents the following:

The Minister of Supply very early on in the war appointed him Director of Instrument Production, a key executive post which he held until 1942. To this was later added the Chairmanship of the Ball and Roller Bearings Panel. Both of these posts were unpaid.

The Ministry of Supply also set up a Scientific Advisory Council in 1941, together with a series of specialist committees. Sir Frank accepted the Council Chairmanship and held the post until March 1947. This Council enabled the Minister to claim that he had readily available the best advice in the country, a claim which was fairly widely accepted. One of the members of the Council wrote of Smith *I was impressed by the width of his experience, by his practical grasp of the problems discussed, by his ability to bring out the best from the members of the Committee and by the co-operation that he succeeded in generating between them.*

Sir Frank took on equally important responsibilities for the Minister of Aircraft Production. In June 1940 Lord Beaverbrook, on Robert Watson-Watt's (the inventor of radar) recommendation, appointed him as Controller of matters relating to the production of RDF and VHF and all other radio equipment ... to have full authority to issue the necessary directions to all departments of the Ministry, subject only to my responsibilities. In a less flamboyant manner this post was described as Controller of Telecommunications (later Communications Equipment). Sir Robert Renwick took over that responsibility in 1942.

Finally, Sir Frank's collection of posts apparently included the Chairmanship of the Technical Defence Committee, MI5, 1940–1946.[12]

Sir Charles Darwin FRS was director of the National Physical Laboratory (NPL) and in that capacity he had oversight of many of the experiments involving aircraft that were sent to the NPL. More of the work of Sir Charles, culled from the Royal Society Archives and the National Archives, is available in *Men Amidst the Madness*.[13]

Of course, labour concerns continued throughout the war, in many cases women appeared on the factory floor of some industries for the first time.

Figure 2.1 shows official figures compiled at the time.

Date	Males	Females	Total	% of females to total
June 1939	1,668,000	282,000	1,950,000	14.5
June 1940	1,863,800	364,100	2,227,900	16.3
June 1941	2,055,200	602,000	2,657,200	22.7
Sept. 1941	2,092,300	678,100	2,770,400	24.5
Dec. 1941	2,131,300	834,900	2,966,200	28.1

Figure 2.1 Employment in the engineering and allied industries.[14]

Later in the war, the Industrial Capacity Committee was merged with the Location of Industry Committee.[15]

Non-munitions

If Britain had a continuous supply of raw material, and unlimited industrial capacity, and indeed no allies needing our help, the Industrial Capacity Committee would have solved most of the wartime supply issues. However, none of those statements were anywhere near the truth. Later in this chapter, a brief section concerning the import of goods and materials, mainly from North America, describes the help we provided to our allies through the Commonwealth Supply Council. The idea behind the creation of this body and its sub-committees was that it should act as a co-ordination body similar to the Joint War Planning Staff in London and the Combined Raw Materials Board in Washington. The Council comprised of the following committees:

i.   **The Machine Tools Committee** – Sir Percy Mills (Chairman)
     Was aptly named co-ordinating the manufacture and distribution of machine tools. It was not thought necessary to include representatives of United Kingdom departments other than the Colonial Office, India Office and Machine Tool Control.

ii. **The Munitions Committee** – Sir Walter Layton (Chairman)
     The intention was that the first task for this committee was to consider army munition requirements in Australia.

iii. **The Non-Munitions Committee** – Sir Nigel Campbell (Chairman)
     This committee covered production within the whole Empire. It was not the intention to channel all requests through London for all non-munitions, only those important critical items which looked as if they were likely to be in short supply were considered. For those critical items, London was the obvious location to co-ordinate requests, as the necessary economic information was available there on the needs and production in all of the United Kingdom.

In a separate document, the following Washington policy decision was proposed:

Inasmuch as it is the policy of the US Government to make separate allocations for military and civilian purposes and have therefore set up their administrative machinery accordingly, it follows that the military and civilian requirements of the British Empire on the USA must be considered separately. The extent to which the British Empire requirements for all purposes can be presented in a single unified program is limited because OLLA [the Office of Lend Lease Administration – more of which later] and the US War Department programs cover different periods and are reviewed at different times. In the field of non-munitions supplies, however, the principle of a single program for all requirements of non-munitions goods irrespective of their military or non-military end use, is accepted by the BSC (British Supply Council) and all British Missions in Washington as one which, in agreement with the US Government we should strive to establish.[16]

However, a meeting held in Sir W Palmer's room on 12 August 1942 suggested a level of co-ordination on behalf of British and Commonwealth and Dominions, especially at the outset of the committee.

The object will be to establish:

i.   By what machinery in this country programs of the non-munitions requirement of the UK, Dominions and Colonies (where these will involve calls on US capacity) can be collated, scrutinised, and communicated to Washington (with an indication of the extent to which such programs can be conveniently met from UK capacity).

ii. What organisation will be needed as a counterpart, in Washington in order to discuss and to defend the programs vis-a-vis the appropriate US organisations and to secure that as far as possible our needs are allowed in the planning of US industrial concentration.[17]

ii. **The Raw Materials Committee** – Lord Portal (Chairman)
     This committee replaced the Empire Clearing House which was set up by the Ministry of Production after the establishment of the Central Raw Materials Board in Washington, for the purposes of co-ordinating the Empire's demands on the USA, and of representing them to Washington.[18]

Of course, the prime consideration here is that of shadow factories and the needs for items and raw materials in the construction undertaken in those facilities. The following letter discusses representation.

30th November 1942

Sir,

I am directed by the Minister of Aircraft Production to refer to Mr Chegwidden's letter of the 10th November 1942 regarding the four committees set up by the Commonwealth Supply Council at its meeting on 28th October 1942 and to state that the question of this Department's representation on these bodies has been considered.

In accordance with the suggestion made in the letter under reply, it is agreed that it will suffice if an officer of this Department is nominated to receive all agenda papers, minutes of meetings and memoranda of the four committees, reserving to the Department the right of attendance or representation at meetings of these bodies when desired.

I am directed to inform you that I have been nominated for the purpose of receiving these papers. It will be convenient if they can be addressed to me at room 110, IC House.

Should it appear at any time to the Minister that the continuous representation of this Department on one of the four committees has become necessary, a further communication will be addressed to you nominating a representative on that committee.

I am Sir,
Your obedient servant,
W D Wilkinson[19]

Unfortunately, these committees could not in themselves solve the many and varied supply issues. The Minister of Production issued the following memorandum on 31 July 1942.

It has become necessary for me to make special arrangements for dealing with my responsibilities in connection with production from industries other than those that are generally regarded as the munitions industries. I am concerned in three ways:

1.   War production can no longer be distinguished from civil production. What have hitherto been regarded as civil industries have for the most part been cut so far that contraction would be likely to have harmful effects on the war effort of the country. These industries therefore require as assured an allocation of materials, capacity and labour as do those industries producing military requirements. Furthermore in many cases the Services and the civil population require the same article so that the requirements of one cannot be catered for without taking those of the other into consideration. The most obvious examples are the textile and clothing trades but there are and will be others. It is my responsibility to ensure that our productive resources are properly distributed and therefore to make appropriate provision for non-munition as well as munition industries.

2.   For some of our requirements we are or may be partly dependent on supplies from the United States. As the US authorities are cutting down on non-essential production it will be necessary for us to state our requirements in comprehensive form in advance and to demonstrate that they are essential. It will then be for the United States War Production Board and the Combined Production Board, which is directed to take into account of the essential needs of the civilian populations to determine how best to make provision for these requirements.

3.   To an increasing extent, the provision of the essential minimum requirements of the United Nations and of the neutrals will become a liability

falling on the planned productive resources of the United Kingdom and the United States. I am not concerned with export policy as such, or with economic warfare. But I am responsible for the allocation of resources for the production of goods for export.

I therefore propose to set up in my office a section to deal with non-munitions supplies. It will be the duty of this section:

a.   To keep itself informed of military and essential civil requirements from the non-munitions industries and of the arrangements for meeting these requirements.

b.   To initiate any inter-departmental action (other than that already in progress) that may be necessary.

c.   To serve as a focus for placing requests for American assistance in this field.

d.   To collect information needed for planning that part of the combined production program of the CPRB which will be devoted to non-munitions requirements.

In addition to reviewing UK requirements, it will be necessary to take special measures to obtain comprehensive information about the requirements of the other United Nations and of neutrals for the products of the non-munitions industries. I intend to propose to the Empire Clearing House that it should agree to the extension of its function to cover this aspect of the matter. It will be the duty of the Non-Munition Supplies Section of my Office to see that the necessary information is collated. In doing so, it will make use of the facilities of the Board of Trade or of any other Department specially equipped to deal with particular commodities.[20]

Later in the same year (31 December 1942), the Ministry of Production announced some appointments:

As a result of criticism from the Supply Departments, the Ministry of Production has abandoned his idea for the setting up of a Joint Industrial Staff and proposed to set up:

1.   A Progressing Section within his own department.
2.   A Chief Production Executive Committee of the Supply Departments.

The new Progressing Department would be required, by following the day to day progress, to assist centrally in seeing that the necessary resources were put at the disposal of the Supply Departments. The Chief Production Executive Committee would not meet regularly, but only from time to time as necessary.

The oral statement which the Minister of Production wishes to make is on the subject of the appointment of Sir Charles Craven as his Industrial Advisor and Sir Percy Mills as his Chief Adviser on Production Progress. It is proposed that Sir Charles Craven shall be Chairman of the Chief Executive Committee of the Supply Departments on which Sir Percy Mills will be the Minister of Production's representative. It is also proposed that Sir Charles Craven shall serve as the Chairman of the new Munitions Management and Labour Efficiency Committee (the new title of the 'Five Man Board'), on which Sir Percy Mills will again be the representative of the Minister of Production.[21]

The situation further changed later on in the war as one might expect. By August 1943, there was a joint committee of the Non-Munitions Committee and of the London Food Committee. Even at that stage in the war they were planning for 1945.

In order to plan for the 1945 production year, our requirements for that year must be submitted to Washington before the end of 1943. It will, therefore be necessary that all countries should consider their total crop programs and the necessary agricultural machinery therefore for 1945, and report the latter to the Secretariat of the Committee on, or before, 30th November 1943. In submitting their requirements, countries should state the total number of each item required and the source from which they would prefer to obtain them, in order that other machinery manufacturing countries such as the United Kingdom, Canada, Australia etc. can also draw up their programs. The requirements should be divided into two categories:

a. Those requirements to maintain agricultural production at the 1943/1944 level.
b. Those for any specified program of agricultural expansion.[22]

Of course, food and agricultural supplies have little in themselves to do with shadow factories. However, there were potential effects to the supply of parts used in the shadow factories. Labour, especially in some parts of the country, could be hard to find as was some of the components used in the manufacture of agricultural machinery and aircraft, or indeed other items needed by the services, such as iron, steel, springs, instruments, etc.

Lend–Lease and the Anglo-American Co-ordinating Committee (Supply)

The *Encyclopaedia Britannica* offers the following about lend–lease:

On 10th June 1940 when Italy entered the war on the German side and when the fall of France was imminent, US President Franklin D Roosevelt declared that the United States would *extend to the opponents of force the material resources of this nation*. After France fell he pursued this policy by aiding the British in their struggle against Germany. Roosevelt arranged for the transfer of surplus American war material to the British under various arrangements, including the exchange of 50 old American destroyers for certain British-held Atlantic bases, and he facilitated the placing of British orders for munitions in the United States. The British decided to rely on the United States unreservedly and without regard to their ability to pay. By December 1940 they had already placed orders for war materials that were far more than they could possibly muster the dollar exchange to finance.

Churchill suggested the concept of lend–lease to Roosevelt in December 1940, proposing that the United States provide war materials, foodstuffs and clothing to the democracies (and particularly Great Britain). Roosevelt assented, and a bill to achieve this purpose was passed by the Congress in early 1941. The Lend–Lease Act not only empowered the president to transfer defence materials, services and information to any foreign government whose defence he deemed vital to that of the United States, but also left to his discretion what he should ask in return. An enormous grant of power, it gave Roosevelt virtually a free hand to pursue his policy of material aid to the *opponents of force*.[23]

Less than two years later, the total lend–lease aid up to 31 December 1943 amounted to $20,000,000,000 of which $10.8 billion (44%) was on military items, $4.1 (21%) billion on industrial items, $2.5 billion (12%) was on food stuffs and $2.6 billion (13%) was on services rendered.[24] Of course, American soldiers based in Britain also needed help. In some cases, there was the need to provide land or buildings, apart from the need to provide some equipment from time to time.

2nd February 1943

Dear Norman,

The Treasury have recently had under consideration the question of maintaining records of reciprocal aid given to US Forces in this country and elsewhere. While they are anxious to avoid introducing the dollar and pound signs into our relations with the United States in connection with Lend–Lease, they feel that reciprocal aid is mounting up to such a size that we would do well to maintain as full a record as possible of physical deliveries made together with some account as far as may be practicable, of services rendered to US Forces.

The above named committee, one of the Bolero series, already maintains a record of demands for war-like stores placed on the Service Departments by the US Army in this country, and the Treasury have asked us to extend this record to include supplies made by other departments. They feel that since we are in any case doing some part of the work it would be sensible and advantageous to have it all in one single hand, where it may be properly digested and overlapping may be avoided. …

I should make it clear that what we are concerned with at the moment is physical statistics. The Treasury is still impressed by the strength of the arguments against using figures of value …[25]

Another letter on the same subject was written a short time later.

16th February 1943

To: The Rt. Hon. Oliver Lyttelton

My Dear Minister,

Thank you for your letter of the 3rd February about reciprocal aid. The figures which we are obtaining from the various Departments about reciprocal aid, which are now being co-ordinated by the Anglo-American Co-ordinating Committee, already include figures of value over a large part of the field, and I agree with you that it would on the whole be desirable that an attempt might now be made to obtain estimates of value over as wide a part of the field as possible. I feel, however that we must take great care in giving any overall estimate of the value of reciprocal aid for it is essential for us to continue to keep out the dollar sign and not to encourage any impression that we can give a total of reciprocal aid which can be deducted from a total of lend–lease, leaving a figure in dollars which will inevitably tend to be regarded as a pecuniary debt.

Yours ever
Kingsley Wood[26]

As with all contracts the details matter. The following letter discussed a wording of the forthcoming agreement.

3rd April 1943

To: The Rt. Hon. A V Alexander Admiralty

Dear Albert,

Thank you for your letter of the 19th March, agreeing to my proposals for the reconstitution of the Anglo-American Co-ordinating Committee (Supply). I note that your representative will be Mr. le Maitre.

As you may know there has been some discussion at the Principal Administrative Officer's Committee on the wording of sub-paragraph 6(d) of the note and this sub-paragraph has been amended to read as follows:

The Committee should provide the channel whereby problems connected with the provision of equipment and supplies for US Forces in the UK (including requirements put forward by SOS, ETO, USA for other theatres in emergency) may be resolved when difficulties arise which cannot be settled by direct discussion with the Departments concerned through existing machinery.

The new wording defines more closely the way in which it is intended the Committee should function and makes it clear that in the same way as the other Committees of Bolero (of which it remains an integral part) the Committee will exist for the co-ordination of executive action and will only be called together

wholly or in part (as in the past) to resolve individual cases of difficulty specifically referred to it.[27]

In some cases, reverse lend–lease spending amounted to large sums (Figure 2.2),
although there is no record of the total figure running into the billion dollar amount
as was the case for us under the lend–lease scheme proper.

Nature of Service	American Fighting Services		American Red Cross	
	Total to 30 June 1943	Quarter ended 30 Sept. 1943	Total to 30 June 1943	Quarter ended 30 Sept. 1943
Erection of new buildings	–	–	–	–
Major alterations to existing buildings	65,000	12,000	152,000	73,000
Rents (including compensation rentals for requisitioned buildings and assessed rentals for Crown buildings)	111,000	83,000	53,000	72,000
Repairs, occupational charges (cleaning, lighting, water, etc., furniture and other stores)	311,000	33,000	281,000	37,000

Figure 2.2 Pound amounts for reverse lend–lease.[28]

The formal agreement between the governments of the United Kingdom and the
United States of America on the principles applying mutual aid in the prosecution
of the war against aggression is dated 23 February 1942.[29] Appendix III records the
principles applying to reciprocal aid, the note below details the arrangements for
helping American procurement in the United Kingdom:

1. This note is intended to clarify the arrangements for handling supply and
    production problems arising out of the provision of American service
    requirements in the United Kingdom.
2. The Bolero Combined Committee (Chairman Sir Findlater Stewart) is
    intended to deal with general matters arising out of the Bolero movement.
    It will not normally concern itself with supply matters, for which a special
    sub-committee has been formed – see paragraph 4.
3. Where the American forces require tangible goods of any kind, the first
    approach should, in every case, be to the Service Department concerned, i.e.
    in the great majority of cases the War Office.
4. A Supply Sub-Committee of the Bolero Combined Committee has been
    set up. Sir Findlater Stewart is chairman of this sub-committee – in this

capacity he is responsible to myself. The sub-committee has an executive secretary and will have its own independent staff. It will be the duty of the executive secretary, in consultation with the sub-committee:

a. To maintain a complete record of all requests made by the American Forces. For this purpose, it is requested that copies of any request made to service departments as in paragraph 3 shall be sent to the executive secretary.

b. To keep himself informed of the disposal of all requests. The responsibility for acting upon them rests on the service departments, whose duty it will be to make all the necessary enquiries from, and place the necessary orders on, the production departments. The executive secretary will, however, keep in touch with the progress of requests and make it his business to give Americans all possible help; and to expedite decisions by all means in his power.

c. To see that all production questions involving more than one department or raising matters of general principle, are promptly referred for decision to the appropriate authorities. Where matters of general principle arise, these authorities will be the Joint War Production Staff and the London Combined Production Resources Board.

d. To see that all other questions, such as shipping and food matters, involving more than one department or raising matters of general principle are promptly referred to the appropriate authorities.

Signed O L
27th July 1942[30]

Incidentally, Bolero was the code word used to cover all arrangements for the reception of American forces into the United Kingdom. It was often used loosely to cover the requirements for operations (in connection with supplies) by the US forces after their arrival in the United Kingdom.[31]

As one might expect, VJ Day (15th August 1945) brought many changes including the need to wind down the lend–lease arrangement which had proved so successful. This telegram shortly after VJ Day spoke of this need.

30th August 1945

In order to avoid misunderstanding with regard to your post VJ Day require-ments I think it important that we should agree on a standard terminology covering the status of existing requisitions and lend–lease contracts especially cases where you either do not want any more of a particular material or only want a portion of the total amount not covered by requisitions or contracts. We list below the various points at which cut offs can be arranged and would suggest that branches be instructed to advise us at which of these points they wish cut offs to be made:

a.   Un-exported balances in this event we would notify Treasury procurement that no more of the material should be manufactured and also request them to repossess all material shipped from plants but not yet exported.
b.   Undelivered balances from plant. In which event we will export any mate-rial which has already left plant.
c.   Un-contracted balances. In which event we would arrange with Treasury procurement that existing contracts should be completed.
d.   Un-contracted requisitions. In Treasury procurement for purchase but no contracts yet placed.
e.   Unapproved requisitions. In FEA but for which funds have not yet been obligated.

As far as we can judge, goods already exported but not yet consumed would form part of the UK stocks as of VJ Day and terms of payment would be a matter of bargaining … with regard to goods coming under (b), (c), (d) and (e) we hope to have clearer understanding by tomorrow as to which of these categories would be considered as pipeline stocks and we will cable further.[32]

North American Built Aircraft

As mentioned earlier, the additional supplies of engines, airframes, etc. from the shadow factories was still insufficient to supplement the production of aircraft by the British aero industry. The North American programmes were, therefore, as much of a key component of the supply chain as were the shadow factories. For this reason, some of the issues relating to aero engines and aircraft will be mentioned here. For example:

25th July 1940

3,000 planes per month program

1.   Requirements (Figure 2.3).

Type	No. of engines per plane	No. of planes per month	No. of engines per month
a. Heavy bombers	4	250	1,000
b. Medium bombers	2	600	1,200
c. Patrol boats	2	250	500
d. Dive bombers	1	400	400
e. Pursuit	2	400	800
f. Pursuit	1	600	600
g. Trainers – advanced	2	300	600
h. Trainers – advanced	1	200	200
Totals		3,000	5,300
Spare parts (10%) in terms of complete units		300	530
Grand total		3,300	5,830

Figure 2.3 Requirements for the 3,000 planes per month plan.

2.   Facilities (Figure 2.4).

	Delivery units per month	No. of plants	Total floor area (million sq. ft.)	Total employees (thousands)	Cost of facilities in $1 m Buildings	Machine tools	Total
Airframes	3,300	15	33.2	332.0	116.0	226.0	382.0
Engines	5,830	6	15.0	75.0	52.5	240.0	292.5
Propellers	5,830	2	1.8	14.4	6.3	27.0	33.3
Misc.	–	23	18.6	130.6	58.5	113.8	172.3
Total		46	68.6	552.0	233.3	646.8	880.1

Figure 2.4 Facilities for the 3,000 planes per month plan.

3. Facilities cost (Figure 2.5).

Airframes	$382,000,000
Engines	$292,500,000
Propellers	$33,300,000
Miscellaneous parts	$172,300,000
Grand total	$880,100,000

Figure 2.5 Facilities cost for the 3,000 planes per month plan.

No mention of the individual manufacturers of airframes is made in this document. The engines were documented as being made by Wright Aero, Pratt and Whitney, Allison and Lycoming and the propellers by Hamilton-Standard and Curtiss-Wright. The above information provided by the Aeronautical Section of the National Defence Advisory Commission, however, is incomplete, at least as far as the whole supply position is concerned.[33]

The orders on the supply chain, however, are well documented, for example:

6th October 1940

Memorandum for the information of Lord Lothian on progress of air and munitions in North America on behalf of the UK Government

The AirProgram
1. UK and French orders prior to March 1940. Value approximately $400,000,000. Proceeding satisfactorily. Large part of deliveries already made.
2. UK and French orders under program of April 1940. Value $600,000,000. Deliveries October 1940–October 1941. Estimated yield 750 aircraft complete per month by middle 1941.
3. Prior to French collapse they had a program for production of engines to be installed in aircraft built in France. These have been taken over for:
    a. Additional aircraft orders placed since (2) above in the US, value $100,000,000.
    b. Delivery to UK for aircraft being built there.
        Some difficulty being experienced with regard to (b) – discussions now proceeding with US which, it is hoped, may ensure recognition prior need for delivery these engines to UK, US hesitant in view their own defence requirements.
4. Supplementary schemes of engine production, i.e., joint Packard contract with US and UK for 9,000 Rolls-Royce engines, 6,000 to be exported to

England starting May 1941, working up to 600 engines per month by end 1941.

5. All programs now in train in US on UK account represent at cost of, roughly, £1,750,000,000:

    a. Complete aircraft at rate of 250 per month at present, rising steadily to 750 per month by July 1941 and continuing at that rate to March 1942.

    b. Engines for export to England at rate of 400 per month to 1,000 per month by end 1941.

        Supply of engines at (b) is equivalent to about 600 combat planes. All the above arrangements, therefore, cover a total ultimate yield of approximately 1,350 aircraft per month.

6. In addition to the above, discussions now proceeding with US for additional joint program of 3,000 aircraft per month on UK account. Scheme will be introduced in two instalments, first stage being the creation of additional capacity for further 1,500 per month. Bottlenecks are:

    a. Aluminium and its fabrication into light alloys.

    b. Machine tools.

    c. Production of engines.

Financial aspects – possibilities of assumption of capital cost under RFC or other suitable loan procedure now being discussed with the US. Such assumption by US will probably entail acceptance of US types involving probable final assembly of British types in Canada where small program of Hurricanes and Hampdens already in production.[34]

Figure 2.6 details the British War requirements for 1941 and 1942 from North America.

	US deliveries against British contracts		Total US effort (contracted deliveries plus deficiencies)		Canadian production	
	1941	1942	1941	1942	1941	1943
Bombers and general reconnaissance	5,000	1,250	8,000	17,000	250	330
Pursuit	3,500	–	3,500	5,000	550	600
Flying boats	180	100	300	700	30	40
Miscellaneous	320	250	1,500	1,500	210	200
Total operational	9,000	1,600	13,300	24,200	1,040	1,170
Advanced trainers	600	300	6,200	6,300	800	1,480
Grand Total	9,600	1,900	19,500	30,500	1,840	2,650

Figure 2.6 British war requirements 1941 and 1942 from North America.[35]

The Canadian supply of aeroplanes to the UK was in most instances a matter of ordering the relevant aeroplane, taking delivery and paying for the goods (the transaction usually involved both spare parts and aeroplanes). Whilst this scheme worked well in the majority of cases, there were some issues needing resolution, for example (this is a copy of a transcript sent electronically):

14th October 1941

To: Bewley

You will presumably have seen BRINY 9122 and MAP 9963 relating to production of Lancasters in Canada. The Canadian offer, which Ministry of Aircraft Production have accepted, involved a financial point in which we shall welcome your views. It is as follows:

1. Canadian production of Lancasters will absorb capacity allocated by Ottawa for production of B26 bombers for our CAF. We must therefore undertake to supply B26 bombers for Canadian needs and we can do so only off lend– lease allocations. It is suggested in BRINY 9122 that dollar value of deliveries of B26's to Canada should be offset against the dollar value of Canadian production of Lancasters for us. Would there be any difficulty about obtaining the consent to transfer of B26s to Canada under Article 4? Precise dollar value of B26s would presumably be unknown and as adjustment between Canada and ourselves would only be approximate, would it not be better to omit all reference to dollar value and treat this as a purely barter deal? Would this be acceptable to United States and Canadian Authorities? Alternatively, if above proposal falls through, could B26s be treated as un-identifiable components under the Phillips–Clark memorandum?

2. Canadian capacity must be kept occupied in interval before Lancaster production can begin, and this can be arranged by production of 400 Hurricanes already authorised provisionally by DMS. These Hurricanes may be transferred to Russia and United States authorities have asked us to contribute half of necessary engines off our own contracts. This may involve a financial point, on which we may wish to consult you later. But since Moscow discussions may affect matter we are waiting for more details before deciding whether we need trouble you on this aspect of transaction.

Treasury[36]

The following is an unsigned reply to the above suggestion.

31st October 1941

Dear Mr Stettinius,

In view of the serious deficiency of heavy bombers which faces us we have been endeavouring to augment the supply in every possible way, and to this end negotiations are now in progress for manufacturing in Canada the latest type of British four-engine bomber known as the Lancaster.

The manufacture of an aircraft of this size on the scale envisaged makes it necessary that the plant and assembly facilities operated by the National Steel Car Corporation at Toronto should be brought within the scheme. These are at present scheduled for the production of 200 Martin B26 bombers required for the Royal Canadian Air Force, and preliminary work on the contract has already commenced. Plans for the expansion of the Royal Canadian Air Force make it essential that the B26 bomber should be furnished. Canada are not, therefore, in a position to cancel the contract for these airplanes unless they can be provided from some other source. This presents a serious difficulty on which I am venturing to seek your advice.

As the Lend–Lease Act is not applicable to Canada, the obvious solution that we should seek permission to transfer 200 Martin B26 bombers from the 500 which are included in the British program under Defence Air Contract no. 46, is not open to us. A possible course, and one which has the merit of simplicity, is that we might be authorised to exchange 200 of these B26 with Canada for an equivalent number of Lancasters on a barter basis. I do not know how far this would be practicable, but if some arrangement on these lines is acceptable, it would be a very great help to us.

I wonder if you would be good enough to consider this proposal and let me know your reactions. I am of course, entirely at your disposal if you would wish to discuss it with me at any time.

Yours[37]

Perhaps, the total number of individual items shipped from North America to the United Kingdom through lend–lease will never be known, because the paperwork is scattered in many folios and documents. Some of the aircraft and aero engines were used in this country and some were used by British forces overseas. By way of an example, Figures 2.7, 2.8 and 2.9 are of a Kittyhawk, a Lysander and a Merlin 23. Known as the Kittyhawk in the UK, this aircraft was renamed prior to shipment from the United States:

The Kittyhawk was the final development of the Curtiss Hawk line of monoplane fighters. During the Second World War it provided the Royal Air Force with valuable reinforcements in the Middle East at a time when British resources were overstretched.

Over 3,000 Kittyhawks were delivered to Commonwealth Air Forces. First introduced into service in January 1942 a conversion program began six months later to allow them to carry bombs. The RAF continued to operate Kittyhawks in Italy until the summer of 1945 when they were finally replaced with North American Mustangs. Known as the Warhawk in United States service, the British renamed the early P-40A, B and C models Tomahawks. In an effort to continue production the manufacturer fitted a more powerful Allison engine into a re-designed cowling and concentrated the gun armament in the wings; the resulting P-40D Warhawk was renamed Kittyhawk I by the British.[38]

Perhaps more than any other markings, the Kittyhawk was certainly distinctive (Figure 2.7)!

The Westland Lysander was designed to operate closely with the army and had a remarkable performance which allowed it to get into and out of extremely small fields. A radical change in army co-operation tactics meant that its lasting fame is not in this role but as a special duties aircraft ferrying Allied agents in and out of enemy occupied Europe.[39]

Figure 2.7 A Curtis Kittyhawk. (Author's photograph)

Figure 2.8 A Westland Lysander. (Author's photograph)

The total number of Lysander manufactured during the war was 1,593 of which 225 were built in Canada. This aircraft type is included here to demonstrate that Westland were unable to manufacture our total requirements, which was not surprising given all the other aircraft they were producing.

Finally, the Merlin 23, which is shown in Figure 2.9, was arguably one of the most important engines of the Second World War. The information board at the RAF explains:

> Early marks were fitted into Spitfires and Hurricanes which took place in the Battle of Britain in 1940.
>
> Continuous development allowed the Merlin engine to continue in production throughout the Second World War. The Merlin 23 was fitted with a two-stage supercharger and was used in many of the Mosquito variants.
>
> The Merlin engine series was also built under licence in the United States by Packard. Final production totalled over 168,000.[40]

Figure 2.9 A Merlin 23. Some of these were made by Packard in the United States.
(Author's photograph)

3

Set-up and Contracts

Early Discussions

With hindsight, it is easy to suggest that the creation of shadow factories was not going to be easy. Whilst at one point it was thought that motor manufacturers would simply be able to switch to producing aero engines and parts, reality soon set in. There were just so many differences in the two types of products that there was never going to be a simple solution. Additionally, the motor manufactures were used to dealing with higher profit margins than their counterparts in the aero industry. Unsurprisingly, the first few contracts and factories were, to put it mildly, less than productive – at least initially. The following are the notes from one of the early meetings.

Note of a meeting with representatives of automobile firms

Present: Secretary of State (Chair), Lord Weir, Sir Arthur Robinson, AMRD, AMSO, Secretary, Major Bulman, Sir Herbert Austin (Austin), Mr R C Rootes and Mr Heath (Rootes), Sir A Roger and Mr Burton (Daimler), Mr Herington (Standards), Mr Wilks (Rovers), Mr Bullock (Singers) and Mr Cannell (Wolseley). After thanking the representatives of the firms for attending the meeting, the Secretary of State said that, under the Government War Plan, the companies there represented had been allotted to the Air Ministry entirely (except for 25% of one firm) for the production of aircraft or aero-engines in time of war. The problem before him was two-fold. First, to arrange for the organisation of the firms for turn-over to war production in an emergency, and secondly, to obtain from them an output of aero-engines to meet those requirements of the Air Force Expansion Program up to March 1939, which were beyond the capacity of the professional aero-engine industry. In ordinary circumstances he would simply have to arrive at a paper scheme for the turn-over to war production, but the present emergency rendered it necessary for the Government to seek the assistance of the allotted firms as a 'shadow' to the professional industry in order to help in the production during the limited period which he had stated.

It must be clearly understood, first, that this shadow activity was not to inter-
fere with the existing commercial work of the firms, and secondly, that he was
not approaching them with a commercial proposition, or inviting them to enter
the professional aero-engine industry, as there would be no work for them after
the period was concluded unless political conditions were still so grave that the
present high rate of output had then to be maintained.[1]

Although history has shown that the shadow factory scheme, as outlined in the
introduction and Appendix I, did indeed work, there were some who thought the
whole scheme impractical.

To: AMSO

27th April 1936

Shadow Engines

I have read your file on this subject and also, as you know, discussed it in a general
way with Lord Weir and also Mr Clegg. I would like to put forward the following
scheme for your consideration.

Bristol Type Engines

Total estimated requirements	6,900
Capacity of Bristol as at presently constituted	2,900
Balance to be made	4,000

I consider that the risk entailed in placing the whole of these 4,000 engines
with shadow firms is not justified in view of the fact that we know that, humanly
speaking, we could get them for certain by expanding Bristols. On the other
hand, I am aware of all the arguments against this course of action being taken.
These arguments are not, in my opinion, weighty enough to justify our placing
about 57% of our total requirements with untried sources; I have studied the
scheme put forward by the seven companies, with the greatest care, but consider
it to be too cumbersome to be efficient in practice, too extravagant in managerial
fees and too restricted in the number of firms it will create capable of assembling
and testing complete engines.
    As an alternative I would suggest:

a.   That a shadow factory be established at Bristols for the manufacture of a
      further 2,000 engines. We should then be assured of approximately 71% of
      our total requirements of engines.

b.   That educational orders for 650 engines each be placed with shadow factories in association with:

i.   Austin Motor Company.

ii.   Rootes Securities Ltd.

iii. Wolseley Motors Ltd.

c.   That each of these shadows should be required themselves to make at least crankcases, cylinders and probably a few other important items, and to assemble, test, strip and rebuild complete engines.

d.   That these shadows should be free to sub-contract for other parts, but such sub-contracts must be placed with the management company whenever practicable.

The advantages of such a scheme appear to be:

i.   71% of our total requirements are assured.

ii.   In the event of war, four separate and distinct units would be trained to make complete engines and the management company of each would already be trained to make many of the parts required.

iii. Management fees would be payable to 4 firms instead of 7.

iv.   The only serious objection I can see to this scheme is that the major jigs and tools and test gear would exist in four complete sets. This is, of course, a very expensive matter, but do not the advantages accruing in the event of war outweigh this consideration?

H A P Disney
Director of Production[2]

There were almost more 'solutions' to this problem than there were people who knew the scheme even existed! Incidentally, Sir Herbert Austin was raised to the peerage (the introduction has further details) during the pre-war years, becoming Lord Austin, and in some of these letters appears as Sir Herbert and in others as Lord Austin.

Manufacture of airframes and engines under the Shadow Scheme

Note of a meeting with Sir Herbert Austin and members of the Air Ministry 30 April 1936.

Present: The Secretary of State, Lord Wier, the Air Member for Supply and Organisation, the Secretary, the Director of Contracts and Sir Herbert Austin. The meeting had been called to discuss the draft scheme which Sir Herbert Austin had submitted on 21st April 1936 on behalf of the seven engine firms, following the conference with representatives of the firms on 7th April 1936.

The Secretary of State, referring to paragraph 2 of the scheme, said that, as AMSO had already explained to Sir Herbert Austin, he was not altogether satisfied that division of the engine into seven sections, with each of the firms making only one section, was the most suitable arrangement. It was no doubt the quickest and most economical method of securing the output of 4,000 engines by March 1939, but the matter had also to be considered from the point of view of war production. It might be better to divide the firms into two groups, or three groups, each making complete engines...

Sir Herbert Austin was inclined, if there was to be any departure from the '1–7' arrangement proposed in the scheme, to favour division of the work of the seven firms into 21 parts i.e. each firm to make three sections, each section being one seventh of a complete engine. He did not himself consider, however, that the '1–7' arrangement should involve any difficulty in war, except for the risk of losing the whole output through one factory being bombed. He had, however, to hear the views of the other six firms on the point.

Apart from the expense it seemed to him a pity to multiply sets of jigs, since no two sets would make exactly the same parts entirely interchangeable.[3]

Sir Herbert Austin's views were not, however, shared with most of the other motor manufacturers. In his capacity of Director of Production, H A P Disney visited the other motor companies soliciting their opinions:

a. Captain Black of the Standard Co. stated that in his opinion the scheme of 7 would be extremely difficult to work; all his knowledge and experience told him that it was wrong and he put his views in writing to Sir Herbert on the 9th June, which letter he showed me. He was not pressing his view, as he was anxious not to cause any disturbance in what he understood to be the wishes of the Government. As a successful engineer and manufacturer, however, he was of the opinion that the difficulties of making the scheme work were almost insuperable. In common with the other leading men in the motor trade we interviewed, he wished to make complete engines.

b. Messrs. Burton and Berryman of Daimler. Here again Mr Berryman expressed the opinion very strongly that his company should make complete engines, instancing the speed and success with which they had done so in the last war on more than one type of engine. He also drew attention to the high quality of the motor car engines made by him and also the fact that he was at present making a large number of parts for Bristol engines with complete success.

c. Mr Bullock of the Singer Co. also stated that he wished to make complete engines, but his views of any subject are not worth consideration.

d. Mr Savidge of the Rover Co. expressed great doubts as to the working of the scheme, but expressed himself as anxious to do anything the Government wished.

As stated above we did not see Captain Wilkes, but Captain Black told us that before writing his letter of the 9th June mentioned above, he consulted Captain Wilkes who sent a similar letter of the same date to Sir Herbert Austin.

Mr Disney concluded:

> They refrained from pressing this point (making complete engines) of view because they think that it is the Government's wish that they should fall in with the scheme of 7 without causing any trouble; therefore they are prepared to do their best.[4]

However, as might be expected, as the threat of war increased so did the orders placed on the shadow factories.

> The recent development of the expansion program has created a requirement for further engines of the types on which the shadow factories are engaged and it has been decided to establish new shadow factories which, besides meeting this peace requirement, will also provide a substantial part of the war potential required immediately on the outbreak of war. The decision to establish these factories was taken with appreciation of the fact that to use the floor space of the motor car factories as war potential would involve the provision in advance at great expense of the bulk of the jigs, tools, and plant required for aero-engine production which would make no contribution to the Air Ministry program in peace and would take some time to install and bring into operation when the emergency occurred.[5]

The aforementioned Mr Disney also made representation to the Air Marshal later in the month.

24th June 1936

My Dear Air Marshal,

I am sending you an official minute on the results of my discussions with various executives in the motor industry. These should, of course, be read in conjunction with my remarks made to the Air Council on Monday. The fact that I feel certain that I and Mr Clegg will be asked to attend the meeting of the 7 at Bristol on Tuesday next makes it imperative that I should make one final appeal to you to allow me to abandon this scheme. As things are at present, if I go on Tuesday, I must, of course appear to give my enthusiastic support to the scheme of 7 and do my best to carry it out. However, Mr Lord, Mr Berryman and Captain Black know perfectly well that I cannot be in sympathy with it. This will probably make them help me all the more, but it will not help us to get the engines.

The prospect of obtaining approximately 12,750 engines by the 1st April 1939 does not frighten me in the least if I am given a free hand. I am perfectly convinced that the capacity is in the industry and I am just as sure that we can get the engines out of the industry by allowing certain firms to make complete engines as I am doubtful that we shall ever get them under the scheme of 7. Someone has got to run the scheme of 7 and that person is presumably myself and I shall require, as I mentioned to you the other day, an engine manufacturing expert to assist me.

I am sorry to cause you and the other members of the Air Council so much trouble and anxiety due to the attitude I am taking over this question, but I am only so persistent because I am convinced in my own mind that the scheme of 7 is a mistake. The Secretary of State told me at the meeting the other day that he was committed to the scheme of 7 and also the 4,000 engines. I therefore asked myself what would be the result of his approving of a change of scheme. As I see it there would only be one result. Mr Bullock of Singers would be disgruntled and the others would heave a sigh of relief and get on with the job.

I want to assure you once more, although I hope such assurance is unnecessary, that my attitude in this matter is dictated only by the fact that I am convinced that the Air Council is making a fundamental mistake in tackling the engine problem in the way they have. If the decision is finally for the scheme, I need hardly assure you that I and Mr Clegg will do our very best to make it work, but I would make this last appeal to you and the Secretary of State to change the scheme.

Yours sincerely,
H AP Disney
Director of Production
PS Mr Clegg has read this and is in entire agreement with me on every point.[6]

The introduction mentioned Lord Nuffield was initially reluctant to engage with this initiative. The following is part of an undated memo to Lord Weir documenting that Lord Nuffield was coming round to taking an active part in the shadow factory scheme. However, rather than join in with the production of aero engines, Lord Nuffield was tasked with producing Spitfires at a new factory in Castle Bromwich.

To: Lord Weir
I have just spoken to Sir Herbert Austin on the telephone. He told me that the result of his interview with Lord Nuffield was that Lord Nuffield was now prepared to come into the scheme and produce his allotted parts. Sir Herbert Austin said that Lord Nuffield would probably put up a proposition that we should take over a building of his in Coventry and equip it with machinery from Lord Nuffield's aero-engine factory in Birmingham. I said that we should of course have to be satisfied with two things:

1.   That the building was suitable.

2. That the machinery was suitable.[7]

Of the seven motor manufacturers involved in the initial shadow scheme, it was to Lord Austin that everyone's thoughts turned.

15th July 1936

86 Petty France SW1
To: The Rt. Hon. Sir Thomas Inskip MP

Dear Sir Thomas,
I venture to send you one or two statements which have been given to me confidentially by the Austin Works, as I think you know, I have been doing my best to keep in touch with them with regard to the future aircraft activities of the firm. They have very kindly given me this information. I told them that I should be passing this on for your consideration, but they would like me to stress that the outstanding points have now been settled between themselves and the Air Ministry and the work is going ahead. But I am sending you these observations in the hope that they may be of some service.

Yours sincerely,
Ronald Cartland.

Air Manufacture by Austin Motor Co Ltd

1. Discussion with the Air Ministry by the Company first began in February of this year and it is the general opinion that these discussions could have been concluded within a month. It is reckoned that there was an avoidable delay of nearly three months, partly due to discussion as to the rate of profit on the contract and also on the question of management expenses (which took a month to settle).
2. Up till last Monday no contract had ever been received by the Company from the Air Ministry. There had, of course, been verbal communications and telegrams and it was on a telegram that the Company was going ahead in the placing of sub-contracts. No details had been settled as to how these sub-contracts were to be placed, whether in the name of the Company or in the name of the Air Ministry. Details such as to who was to meet the cost should estimates be exceeded were still outstanding.

    Austins, about four months ago, took steps in the purchase of land the detailing of staff for the factory designing. But the delay as to the contract has resulted in missing the best months for excavating and building operations. It is estimated that the factory will not be ready until March of next year.

3.   With regard to air frames, I understand that there are nearly 4,000 plans which have to be sent to them from Bristol. A negligible quantity of these have been received so far, and, of course until they are received, it is impossible to go full steam ahead with regard to planning and designing. It is estimated that by next March one aeroplane may be ready and after that delivery will take place, but of course at a very slow rate at the start; and it is extremely unlikely that the 900 a year which Austins are to turn out can possibly be reached in time for the full program to be completed by 1939.

4.   With regard to the engines, I understand that none of the other firms have done anything at all, but this apparently will be a fairly simple matter to start work on. There is bound to be delay for the other firms in the purchase and excavation of land and buildings being erected.

With regard to the proposal that Austins and one other motor firm should put the engines together after construction, it was suggested by the Air Ministry that they should only work on day shifts in order to allow for possible extension in case of war. This decision of the Air Ministry was only announced on July 2nd at the meeting at Bristol and took the firms entirely by surprise. I also understand that the number of engine firms having been reduced from seven to six has led to complete alteration in the allocation of contracts.

5.   There was a very general feeling that there was some difference of opinion at the Air Ministry as to the roles of the technical side and supply side. At the Bristol meeting there was quite a controversy between Disney and Major Bullman (who is, I think, the technical officer).

Austins are prepared to go full steam ahead now and the only thing they fear is the delay which may result from the receipt of the plans from Bristol for the Aircraft frames and any delay that may arise from the fact that the Air Ministry have not yet worked out the details as to how contracts are to be placed and the relations between the Air Ministry, the main contractors, and the sub-contractors. The company desire me to stress that no obstacles are being placed in the way of the company by the Air Ministry but they did feel very strongly at first that the lack of co-ordination between the various departments of the Air Ministry was delaying them unfairly.[8]

The text above and Appendix IV mention the agreements between some of the early shadow factories and the Ministry of Production. It might be worth reviewing some of the comments from the Director of Contracts (A) as the agreements were being finalised within the Ministry.

20th November 1936

Treasury Inter-service Committee Shadow schemes – Insurance

1. The firms acting as managers of factories under the shadow scheme have asked to be informed as soon as possible of the particular insurances that are to be undertaken by them on behalf of the Air Ministry, and of the insurances that are not to be undertaken.

2. The risks which the Bristol Aeroplane Company normally covered by insurance are as set out in the statement attached.

3. The Air Ministry propose that in accordance with normal Government practice the firms should be told not to insure in respect of the following:
   a. Fire.
   b. Accidental damage (including damage to aeroplanes in flight and to engines undergoing tests).
   c. Transit risks.
   d. Theft.

4. Risks in respect of workmen abroad do not arise.

5. It is considered that insurance in respect of the following risks should be taken out by the firms:
   a. Workmen's compensation. Although it is understood to have been the general practice of the Ministry of Munitions not to insure against workmen's compensation risks in agency managed factories, it is considered undesirable to follow this precedent in the case of the shadow firms. It may well be that there will be transfers of individuals between the firms' own works and the shadow factories, and in some cases of injury it might be a matter of considerable difficulty to determine where the liability to compensate lay; further additional staff at the Air Ministry would undoubtedly be required to deal with the cases that would arise. It is proposed to instruct the firms to take out an ordinary commercial insurance policy in this respect. This is considered to be in consonance with the underlying policy of the scheme under which the managers undertake the normal functions and responsibilities of manufacture.
   b. Flying risks (i.e. risks to pilots, technical and mechanical staff and third party risks from flights). The necessity to cover these risks is equally clear.
   c. Boiler Insurance. It is already standard practice to insure boilers in Air Ministry establishments.

6. Motor transport (third party risks). The extent to which motor transport will be used by shadow firms is not clear but it is proposed to instruct the firms to insure against third party risks where mechanical transport is acquired.

The concurrence of the Committee in these proposals is sought.
Air Ministry[9]

A memorandum concerning insurance was issued some years later:

January 1942

Shadow Schemes Memorandum on Insurance

1. It is not desired that property of the Ministry of Aircraft Production, such as building and plant, should be insured.
2. Insurance should, however, be effected in respect of the following:
    a. Liabilities under Workmen's Compensation Acts, Employers' Liability Acts, Fatal Accidents Act, and at Common Law in respect of manual workers, regardless of earnings and of non-manual workers whose earnings do not exceed £350 per annum.
    b. Liabilities under Fatal Accidents Act, at Common Law in respect of non-manual workers whose earnings bring them outside the scope of the Workmen's Compensation Acts (i.e. those earning over £350 per annum).
    c. If not covered by (a) and (b) risks to pilots, technical etc, staff arising from flights and/or compensation on engine running.
    d. Risks to third parties arising from flights and from the use of motor transport specially purchased for the shadow factory.
    e. Boilers. The policy should however, be limited to:
        i.   High pressure of steam systems.
        ii. Steam pipes during their manufacture only, air receivers during their manufacture and subsequent use.
    f. Damage to buildings hired, only if insisted upon by the lessors.
3. Except as indicated in the case of boilers, the policies taken out should conform to normal commercial practice.
4. The Ministry of Aircraft Production will accept liability in all cases not coming within the scope of paragraph (2) above. In the event of any claim arising it should be referred with a complete statement of the circumstances to the Secretary, Ministry of Aircraft Production PS8, Millbank. Nothing in this memorandum shall relieve the Company from its duty to the Minister to exercise the same care in the selection of its servants and agents and in the management of the factory as the Company in fact exercises in the management of its own business.
5. If any insurance already effected is not in accordance with paragraph 2 above, steps should be taken immediately, if practicable, to modify the cover as may be necessary (with appropriate adjustment of premium where cover is reduced, unless the saving involved is trivial). Where amendment of the policy would result in a trivial saving only, suitable action should be taken when the policy expires.

6. Special attention is detected to the following cases in which insurance is <u>not</u> required:

    a. Buildings in course of erection.

        The Ministry will bear only the risk of loss or damage by fire from King's enemy risks to buildings in the course of erection to materials properly on the site. All other risks to such buildings or materials, and all risks (including risks of loss or damage by fire or from King's enemy risks) to temporary structures erected on or to tools, plant, machinery and equipment brought on to site by the building contractor are to be borne by him, and the building contract should accordingly so provide.

        The term 'loss' includes destruction and the term 'King's enemy risks' has the meaning assigned to it by section 15(i)(a) of the War Risks Insurance Act 1939 and any order made thereunder.

    b. Goods in transit.

        Goods in transit other than by transport specially purchased for shadow factory should be either at the risk of the carrier or of the contractor supplying them.

    c. Goods shipped from overseas.

        Where delivery <u>under the contract</u> is f.a.s. or f.a.b. and onwards conveyance is arranged by the shadow factory, no insurance should be taken out to cover loss or damage during transit even though no risk is borne by the carrier.[10]

28th June 1937

Shadow Factories Workmen's Compensation

Apart from general observations two particular questions are asked, the first being whether workmen employed in shadow factories are, for the purposes of workmen's compensation, in the employment of the agent firms or the Department on whose behalf the agent is acting. In my view workmen employed in shadow factories are, for the purposes of workmen's compensation, in the employment of the agent firms. The workman's contract of service is with the agent firm, and moreover by Section 5 of the Workmen's Compensation Act, 1925, which defines the term employer, where the services of a workman are temporarily lent or let on hire to another person by the person with whom the workman has entered into a contract of service, the latter is, for the purposes of the Act, deemed to continue to be the employer of the workman whilst he is working for that other person.

The second question is whether, if these workmen are the agent's employees, the employee can take legal action against the Department under Section 6 of the Workmen's Compensation Act, 1925, as the contractor's principle. It may be convenient here to point out that by Section 33 the Act is stated to apply to workmen employed by or under the Crown other than to persons in the Naval, Military or Air Services of the Crown, and by Rule 95 of the Workmen's Compensation Rules 1926, provision is made for proceedings where the Crown is a party.

By Section 6(1) where any person (the principal) in due course of, or for the purposes of, his trade or business contracts with any other person (the contractor) for the execution by or under the contractor of the whole of any part of any work undertaken by the principal, the principal is liable to pay to any workman employed in the execution of the work any compensation under the Act which he would have been liable to pay if that workman had been immediately employed by him, and by Section 6(2) the principal who has had to pay compensation to a contractor's workman may claim an indemnity against the contractor.[11]

Whilst all aero engine companies were of importance, some developed engines which were used in a variety of aircraft. For example, the various types of Merlin engine were not only used in Spitfires but also used in other aircraft such as the Lancaster bomber. Even before the war broke out, it was apparent that Rolls-Royce would be unable to manufacture sufficient engines to service the needs of all aeroplane manufacturers. Of course, Rolls-Royce had spent untold funds developing this engine and were initially reluctant to release the design specifications to other manufacturers.

12th October 1937

To: AMSO

It became apparent to me some considerable time ago that some steps would have to be taken to have Rolls-Royce engines made elsewhere than at Rolls-Royce works, at any rate in war.

I referred to the old papers on the subject and found that Rolls-Royce have always strenuously opposed the manufacture of their engines by any other firm. I set out slowly but surely to break down this attitude. I was greatly assisted in this by a change in the management at Rolls-Royce. The present manager, Mr Hives, is young and very progressive and is very much more long-sighted than the previous manager. He fully appreciated the necessity for having Rolls-Royce engines made elsewhere and the result of all my talks to him and Mr Sidgreaves have now culminated in Mr Sidgreave's letter of the 8th October.

You may think that the Private Office should be informed of this letter from Mr Sidgreaves as I know it has been the impression of other members of the Air Council that Rolls-Royce would strenuously oppose any effort on our part to arrange for their engines to be made elsewhere.

DAP[12]

In a follow-up letter the next year, the Air Council Committee on Supply allocated some funds allowing for the expansion of the Rolls-Royce factory and for the shadow engine factory at Crewe. Additionally, as mentioned in the previous chapter, Packard in the United States also made some Merlin engines for the British shadow factories.

26th July 1938

To: Rolls-Royce Limited

Gentlemen,

I am directed to inform you that the Air Council Committee on Supply have had under consideration the estimates prepared by you of the scheme to increase your manufacturing capacity at Derby and to provide a nucleus shadow factory at Crewe, and they agree that the total expenditure under these headings may be increased from £1,000,000 to £1,220,000 made up as follows:

Derby (including plant for sub-contractors)	£245,923
Crewe	£970,006
Total	£1,215,929

Say £1,220,000

Air Ministry letter of 14th June 1938 should accordingly be read as though this latter figure were substituted for £1 m wherever it occurs.

The Committee also agree that the extensions to your engine erecting shop (K1) at Derby estimated to cost £7,000 may rank for consideration under the provisions of the capital clause.

With regard to the provision necessary to meet the ARP requirements, I am to confirm that the arrangements outlined in your letter of the 23rd July, addressed to Sir Wilfred Freeman, are acceptable to the Committee. They understand that the total of £1,220,000 mentioned will suffice to cover these requirements.

I am to add that a decision will be conveyed to you in due course regarding the schemes outlined in your letter of 3rd July 1938 for further increasing the size and capacity of the Crewe factory.

I am Gentlemen,
Your obedient servant
Signed H Russell
Secretary of the Air Council Committee on Supply.[13]

Many shadow factories required new building. Perhaps the search for a relevant plot of land and the subsequent purchase for the shadow factory at Crewe might serve as an example for all of the other shadow factories.

2nd June 1938

Sites at Crewe
Rolls-Royce Shadow Factory

In accordance with your instructions I have inspected two sites situated at Crewe and beg to submit the following report. On these inspections which took place on the 1st instant, I was accompanied by Messrs H Hives (Director), W G Phillips (Architect) and T S Haldenby representing Rolls-Royce and The Mayor, Town Clerk, Borough Surveyor and several members representing the Crewe Town Council (the owners of the sites).

Later in the day Captain W A W Hallam visited the site which, as the result of the earlier inspections had been considered to be the more suitable for the purpose intended.

Site 1

This site which comprises 70 acres or thereabouts is situated at the south-east extremity of the Borough of Crewe, with extensive frontages to Weston Road and abutting upon the North Staffordshire railway line throughout its western boundary. The utility of this site for the purposes of a factory is materially affected by the proposed aerodrome scheme of the Crewe Corporation, as the site for such aerodrome is situated on the opposite side of Western Road and the greater portion of the proposed site is subject to stringent limitations as to the height of buildings to be erected thereon.

Apart from the foregoing, this site has other disadvantages, namely:
1. It is inconvenient in shape, being long and very narrow.
2. It is not well drained and at times is known to be waterlogged.
3. The price required by the Crewe Corporation is excessive.

Having regard to the foregoing disadvantages it is the opinion of the representatives of Messrs Rolls-Royce and myself that it would not be advisable to proceed further with negotiations for the acquisition of this site.

Site 2

This site is situated at the extreme west of the Borough of Crewe.

The site is bounded on the north and west by public highways, on the south by the LM & S railway line, Crewe to Holyhead, and at the south-east corner has access to a main road known as West Street which passes through the Borough of Crewe. The area of this site is 58 acres or thereabouts. Its surface is uniformly even with the exception of a mound in the south-west corner which has evidently been formed by deposit when the railway cutting was formed. There is a gradual and slight fall from north to south.

The railway line which forms the southern boundary is in a cutting 15ft or so below the site level and the provision of sidings would undoubtedly prove costly.

It is understood that the provision of a railway siding is not essential to the successful development of the site.

The land is strong in character with a clay sub-soil and it is understood that this clay extends for a very great depth.

The owners are the Crewe Corporation and the Corporation also farm the land. It is a distinct advantage from the purchaser's point of view, as no disturbance of a sitting tenant will be necessitated, with the consequent payment of compensation etc.

The land is in grass with the exception of 17 acres planted with potatoes.

If the site is acquired by the Air Ministry the Crewe Corporation have agreed to accept payment at the rate of £5 per acre for the land planted with potatoes, if the development of the site precludes them from lifting and marketing the crop. With the foregoing exception there will be no compensation payable for tenant-right or otherwise, and possession of the site can be obtained immediately.

The Crewe Corporation purchased this site several years ago for the sum of £5,762, and if this site is required by the Air Ministry, the Corporation is prepared to sell the same at the price mentioned, which works out at slightly less than £100 per acre. In my opinion the site is well worth this amount.

Upon reference to the plan (Figure 3.1), it will be seen that to the west of the proposed site and on the other side of the road known as Pyms Lane are two other fields. The land verged in bold which comprises 7.119 acres or thereabouts belongs to the Crewe Corporation and is available for purchase at the price of £1,068, which works out at £150 per acre, and is the price actually paid for the same by the Corporation.

The other piece of land comprises 6.75 acres and although this land does not at present belong to the Corporation it is understood that the Corporation can secure an option on the same, and if required for the Air Ministry's scheme it is anticipated that the land would be available at the price of £150 per acre.

In connection with the layout of the proposed factory the representatives of Messrs Rolls-Royce say that the acquisition of this additional land is essential, for the purpose of providing recreational facilities and probably for the erection of test houses.

If it is agreed to include this additional land I would recommend that negotiations be immediately opened for the acquisition of the area in bold as the price for this particular field will undoubtedly be increased if the proposals of the Air Ministry become publicly known.

Conclusion

I am of the opinion that this site is an admirable one for the purpose intended. It is provided with good means of access, road frontages, water and electricity services and facilities for a railway siding. The Corporation's main sewer crosses the land from south to north, and it is understood that access to this sewer is available if required.

Lands officer[14]

Looking through some of the other National Archives folios, this procedure seems to be fairly common. By that I mean looking at two or three suitable sites from which a decision was then made. In some cases, there was an airfield nearby, in others land to build one needed to be taken into account. Some of the airfields built around this time still survive as airfields today or were airfields until redeveloped in the more recent past. Further details appear later.

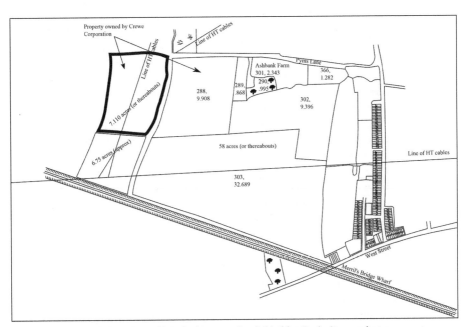

Figure 3.1 Sketch showing the field. (Author's diagram)

Having evolved the process of site selection to a point where it was routine, some thoughts turned to establishing a standard system of contracts. As already mentioned, the early contracts were workable but in some cases open to more interpretation than they needed to be. This sentiment is reflected in the letter below.

Note that this letter was written some four years after the early discussions with the car manufacturers!

16th August 1940

D of C
DCF
Deputy Secretary
Attached is a model draft Shadow Factory Agreement which ADC(D) had drawn up for current use in guiding new firms on procedure and weaning old firms from such early hotch-potch of compromises as went to make the first engine and air-frame agreements. We were proposing that all new agreements and extension agreements should generally be on this uniform basis.

Remuneration conditions would need to be added in each case.

It is for consideration whether to regulate management activities on special points, e.g. output bonuses, high salaries and wages etc. we should rely on Clause 24, which has been adapted and strengthened for the purpose, or whether we should attempt to cover such matters by more specifically restrictive clauses.

DDC1 has scrutinised the draft at various stages and F8 has assisted in the erection and equipping clauses. DDC1 presses strongly for reference to the Treasury Solicitor and I suggest a copy should go to him for information and comments. While normal departmental procedure might serve for short Heads of Agreement in the first instance, leaving Treasury Solicitor to throw these into the legal form at leisure, I feel that we cannot resist pressure from firms and from other Departments of the MAP for fuller details of what constitutes a Shadow Agreement and for a guide on detailed procedure.

The managing firms need something more clear and straightforward than the very confusing first engine agreements, and the Treasury Solicitor is inclined to use the clauses of those agreements as models for later agreements. I suggest writing to Mr Speed semi-officially forwarding a copy of the draft and saying that we are using this for guidance of firms and virtually as heads of agreement, and adding that if he had any criticism of the clauses, most of which are derived from his earlier efforts, we should be glad to have them.

D of C (A)[15]

Incidentally, in most cases these letters are addressed to a job title or a department as in the case of F8 mentioned above. This approach allowed the post holders to move without needing to re-write the letters when post holders changed. To further strengthen the administration and procedures adopted by the Ministry of Supply, a few months after establishing the above template for the shadow factory agreements, it was proposed that a department be created just to oversee administration connected with shadow factories.

5th May 1941

To DGF

It is suggested that for the adequate supervision of agency factories, many of which are now coming into production, the setting up of a supervisory organisation within the Ministry of Supply should be considered, not only as a convenience, but as a necessity. It may be that the DOF would be the proper person to take charge of this question; or that a joint organisation would be found more appropriate. But it is submitted that the need is plain, and that Finance should press the question without delay.

1. That the existence of such an organisation would be a convenience is apparent if the problem is considered merely from the aspect of capital assistance.

    Attached is a draft form of agreement for agency cases. Clauses 1, 4 and 5(b) of this draft, illustrate the underlying conception, namely that the manager of an agency factory is a trusted servant of the Department, is given a considerable measure of discretion, and a corresponding measure of responsibility, and is subject to two duties: one, to draw the Minister's attention to questions which ought to be decided by the Minister; the other, on all matters on which the Minister gives directions, to carry out those directions.

    For failure in either of these criteria, the draft makes the agent responsible.

    a. This responsibility is much more likely to be accepted by agents if they are assured that there is a standing organisation, readily accessible, to whom reference can be made on points of doubt or difficulty.

        The acceptance of responsibility on these lines will be an incentive to efficiency and good management.

    b. The fact that the agent knows that his activities are being watched by an organisation whose special duty it is to do so, will be a further incentive and encouragement.

    c. No form of agreement can codify once for all the line to be taken in dealing with particular day-to-day problems, in regard to some of which the interest of the agent may be at variance with the interest of the Minster. Clauses 6 and 7 of the draft are illustrations of the extent to which a codification can be attempted, and of its weaknesses. If the agent's own factories are the most convenient and economic source of supply of materials required for the agency factory, it is better that source should be used; but it immediately becomes convenient for the agent to have a supervisory body who can authorise the terms upon which the supplies are to be taken. Without such authority, the agent is interested on both sides of the account, and abuses may be discovered only after the event.

    d.   Even if the agreement went into enormous detail, it would still be impracticable to settle every point in advance. Great simplification is achieved if the general principles are agreed, and the details left to be settled by subsequent decision in light of experience. This is facilitated by the existence of a supervisory board.

2.   It is undoubtedly true in many cases that no effective supervision is at present achieved. It is submitted that his stage of affairs ought to be remedied, and that the establishment of a special organisation, which will be a convenience for the reasons given in (1) above, is also a necessity.

    a.   No agreement can codify all future events.

    b.   An agreement on general principles is desirable at as early a stage as possible, and can be reached on some such lines as those of the attached draft, but only if it can be assumed that some subsequent control will be exercised in practice.

3.   The object of this minute is primarily to raise the point for consideration, secondly to illustrate the part which the contract itself can play and the limitations to which any legal document is necessarily subject, and thirdly, to show the necessity for, and the convenience of, a controlling organisation. It is probably outside the scope of this minute to make suggestions as to how the organisation should be composed, but it may not be out of place to pursue the point to this extent.

4.   It is submitted accordingly:

    a.   That a supervisory Board would be a convenience from the point of view of simplicity and effectiveness in the negotiation and framing of the contract.

    b.   That the supervisory Board is, in fact, a necessity as well as a convenience, to secure effective control.

    c.   That it should be representative of all the aspects of the problem, not excluding the commercial aspect.

    d.   That it should be sub-divided so as to give individual supervision to convenient groups of factories.

DDGF(S)[16]

The need to create a government department followed that of the pressure placed on Lord Austin some years earlier during the formation of the No. 1 Engine Group.

9th June 1937

To: The Rt. Hon. Lord Austin

There is a distinct danger in my opinion that the engine shadow factories will get out of balance due to lack of co-operation between the companies and unwillingness to assist each other in the balancing of machine tools. I would, therefore, ask you once again to appoint this sub-committee and empower it to deal with manufacturing questions and to make the necessary arrangements for the exchange of information between factories. You are, I understand, holding a meeting of the Aero Engine Committee on Monday, the 14th instant, and I would be grateful if you would bring this question of the technical sub-committee forward at that time. Should you wish to discuss this matter with me during the next few days, I will arrange any time to suit your convenience in London or shall be only too pleased to come up to Birmingham and see you.

Yours sincerely,
H AP Disney[17]

Finally, with the adoption of a standard form of agreement and an overseeing department able to keep track of the shadow factories, which incidentally by this time had grown in number considerably, the system had some measure of stability and control. Of course, the whole system was initially conceived to manufacture parts for the Battle airplane. It is interesting to note that by the time the above agreements were in place the Battle was essentially a redundant airplane! Just for completeness, Figure 3.2 is of a Battle which is on display in the RAF Museum. The text that follows is reproduced from the information board adjacent to the airplane.

Although lacking in speed and defensive armament and therefore totally unsuitable for unescorted daylight operation, the Battle will always be remembered for the heroic attacks on the bridges at Maastricht and Sedan following the German invasion in May 1940.

The Fairey Battle was one of the most promising aircraft chosen for the rapidly expanding RAF in the 1930s. When introduced into service in 1937 it could carry twice as many bombs over twice the distance of the Hawker Hart and Hind bombers it replaced.

By 1939 it was obsolete but due to the lack of more modern types it remained in front line service. Battles of No 226 Squadron were the first RAF aircraft to be sent to France on the outbreak of war ... removed from operations in September 1940, the Battle was subsequently used in training in Britain and Canada.[18]

Figure 3.2 A Fairey Battle. (Author's photograph)

Expansion of the Scheme

Inevitably, the advent of war and in addition to the need to produce aircraft other than the Battle led to an expansion of the shadow scheme. The second tranche of shadow factories are shown below in Figure 3.3.

Firm	Supply
Rolls-Royce	Engines
Plessey	Engines, starters, pumps, etc.
Vickers-Armstrong	Airframes
No. 2 Engine Group (Rootes, Rover, Standard and Daimler)	Engines
British Thomson Houston	Magnetos
Cossor	Radio sets
General Electric Company	Radio valves

Figure 3.3 Second tranche of shadow factories.[19]

As the shadow scheme expanded, so did the interests of the major motor companies; however the Austin Motor Company was always at the vanguard of the expansion scheme. Lord Austin was involved in many ways including the administration of the scheme and in aircraft repair, see later. By this time Lord Nuffield was busy building and initially operating the Spitfire factory at Castle Bromwich and managing other activities connected with the Ministry of Supply, and so was not involved in further expansion of his shadow factory interests at this time.

The National Archives, therefore, have more paperwork and agreements for the Austin Motor Company compared with any of the other motor manufacturers. I have chosen to reproduce the agreement to produce Spitfires (see later chapters and Appendix V) because by that time not only the contracts were more standard but also there was more interest in the manufacture of Spitfires compared with Battles (of course, this agreement was between Lord Nuffield and the Secretary of State for Air).

The interested reader can find the main contract for the Austin Motor Company to manufacture Fairey Battle planes in the National Archives folio AIR 19/5, and the extension to the agreement, dated 20 October 1945 in AVIA 15/320. A copy of the Austin contract dated 10 December 1937 for engine parts manufacture is in AIR 2/1823, where the other contracts for the No. 1 Engine Group can also be found. The shadow factory definition of accounts, assets, liabilities and expenditure is a long document (greater than 60 pages!) detailing the assets needed to be taken into account is filed in AIR 20/2396.

It is difficult to appreciate from photographs but the Fairey Battle shown above in Figure 3.2 is a relatively small airplane. The move to manufacture larger aircraft prompted an expansion to the buildings and in some cases runways of the relevant shadow factories.

27th October 1938

Austin shadow factories – proposed extensions

> Mr Russell reminded the committee that during the recent crisis expenditure of a sum of £6,500 to provide for extensions to be made to the Austin Airframe Shadow Factory to enable the B12/36 to be produced, had been approved, subject to confirmation later at a full meeting of the committee, but that DAP had withdrawn the item from consideration at a previous meeting because he had been under the impression that the scheme related to an entirely different matter, viz, housing of Air Ministry accountants. Revised details had now been put forward to DGP by Lord Austin who now asked for authority to proceed forthwith with the plans at an estimated cost of £13,350. Authorisation was duly given by letter dated 3 February 1939.[20]

B12/36 was a prototype bomber designed by R J Mitchell. There were only two prototypes, the concept being cancelled early in the war. Nevertheless, the buildings needed modification to accommodate the relatively large prototypes. Expansion of the component manufactures' buildings in the shadow scheme also took place; in the example below, it was more about increasing capacity rather than the component dimensions.

6th October 1939

Capacity of BTH Magnetos

In order to meet the expanded program as understood on the 1st October last, we shall need to have a capacity of at least 7,000 BTH major magnetos per month with light magnetos, hand starters, distributor heads and other equipment in proportion. The present plant with new extension due to come into operation in March next, will, when engaged on a two-shift day, ensure a supply of 5,000 major magnetos per month together with proportionate other equipment. It is, therefore, recommended that a shadow factory should be set up, having a capacity of providing 2,000 major magnetos (with other equipment in proportion) on a single-shift basis. This will then leave a reserve to meet any expansion in the aircraft program and/or contingencies arising from enemy action.

Magneto work calls for a large number of skilled workmen which may not be easy to obtain. The BTH Co. is exploring some sites in Nottingham, a district approved by the Ministry of Labour.

In a scheme which they drew up a year ago, it then appeared that the capital cost would be of the order of £200,000 for the building plus £300,000 for equipment. These figures will probably be affected by the outbreak of war.

Can authority please be obtained for the BTH Co. to take immediately whatever steps are necessary to carry out the above suggestions.

ADAEP[21]

The comment concerning appropriate skilled labour was one which faced many fledgling factories, especially when large work forces were needed for multiple organisations. For this and other reasons, including that of relevant accommodation, the Ministry of Labour was frequently consulted.

19th December 1939

The circular letter at 1A is addressed to a number of Departments. Concurrently, the Coventry branch of the Engineering Employers' Association were in communication with the Minister for the Co-Ordination of Defence on the same subject, as a result of which they were invited to send a deputation to the Ministry of Labour on the 15th instant. DGP attended this meeting on behalf of the Air Ministry and I was also present. A copy of the statement presented by the employers is enclosed temporarily at 2C. It will be seen that the main points of their argument are as follows:

1.   There has been a phenomenal growth in the population of Coventry since the last war. The present figure is 234,000 and it is estimated that not

less than 37,000 additional work people must be imported in the next 12 months to meet the demands for armament work; the chief demand relates to the shadow factories for the Air Ministry. We accept their figures as a true picture.

2. For practical purposes there are no unemployed in Coventry. The latest figures published by the Ministry of Labour show, however, that there are 1,400,000 unemployed in other parts of the country. The employers ask what steps it is proposed to take to provide recruits for Coventry from this pool.

3. Most of the new recruits will require training for munition work. What help can the Ministry of Labour give here?

4. Can any assistance be given on the question of dilution and relaxing the provisions of the Factories Act so that women and young persons can work at night?

5. Finally, imported labour will require housing accommodation on a considerable scale. The possibilities of meeting this demand are lodgings, hostels and the erection of houses. What action is proposed on this and the related problems of transport and general services, such as water, electricity etc.?

6. Etc…

DPWP[22]

The reply to some of these points was:

24th January 1940

Housing in Coventry

The probable needs of the future relate to the absorption into the factories in the Coventry area, engaged on government work, of additional work people, estimated by the Coventry branch of the Engineering Employers' Federation to amount to 37,000. This estimate is in close agreement with that of the Coventry City Council of Officers. The majority will be required by firms engaged on direct Air Ministry contracts, particularly in the new shadow factories.

It is anticipated that 9,000 of these might be females, and in the opinion of the local authorities a considerable amount of additional local labour is available, estimated by them at 16,000 although at present it is not clear how many of the 9,000 women just mentioned may be included in this figure.

It is evident that upwards of 20,000 work people not at present resident in the area may have to be accommodated, and the nature of this accommodation is being considered under the headings of:

i.   Lodgings.
ii.   Existing houses vacant and available.
iii. New houses.
iv.   Hostels for single men.

Lodgings and existing vacant houses form the subject of a survey which the local authorities have agreed to undertake in conjunction with the local officials of the Ministry of Health. Director of Planning War Production has agreed to co-operate in this survey, and is awaiting the completion of the preliminary arrangements. Various estimates have been given of the amount of such accommodation available, none of which can be relied upon pending the result of this enquiry.

New Houses The Ministry of Health has authorised the completion of 968 houses, forming part of the pre-war town planning scheme of the Coventry City Council. The Council estimates that a further 4,000 houses will be needed. The correctness or otherwise of this cannot be accepted, pending the result of the survey already referred to, although it appears probable that the 968 houses mentioned above will not suffice.

There is a possibility of further building by private enterprise. A deputation of the local builders was received at the Ministry of Health and was asked to prepare a statement of their proposals, indicating what materials and finances would be involved. When this statement is received the Ministry of Health will consider in what direction and to what extent they may be prepared to give their support.

Hostels for single men This form of accommodation will only be considered when it is known to what extent, if any, the availability of existing houses and lodgings, and the number of new houses authorised, will leave a residue of workers still in need of accommodation.

From the foregoing it will be seen that the extent of the measures necessary to meet the problems in Coventry created by the anticipated labour expansion cannot be estimated until the results of the survey of existing accommodation is known. This is in the hands of the Ministry of Health.

It appears desirable that the Supply Committee should be aware of the present position.

DPWP[23]

Whilst this expansion was being considered in Coventry, other parts of the country were considered in order to spread the risk and also utilise available local labour. Of the many schemes that could be used as examples, that of the de Havilland factories in Watford and Aldenham may be of interest, not so much for the use during wartime but for the way in which the land is now used in Leavesden, the site chosen just north of Watford, more of which later.

6th March 1940

DDGP1

A memorandum for submission to the Supply Committee on the new factory to be erected at Watford and taking over existing buildings at Aldenham and Western Avenue in connection with a scheme for Messrs de Havilland to produce Halifax aircraft under some shadow arrangement, is enclosed for your approval.

A brochure is attached, and F7 have had an opportunity to see the brochure and to discuss the scheme with representatives of Messrs de Havilland in a general way.

You decided that if possible this matter should come before the Supply Committee on Saturday March 9th and that representatives of Messrs de Havilland should be asked to be available to the Supply Committee on that day. Accordingly, Mr Lee Murray will attend the Supply Committee as requested by S8.

DAP[24]

The work needed for this shadow factory was further detailed in the following:

Modifications to Leavesden Aerodrome buildings for assembly and test of Halifax aircraft production

In March 1941, it was proposed by the Ministry of Aircraft Production that London Aircraft Production should utilise a proportion of the Leavesden aerodrome for Halifax assembly and test. The Board accepted this proposal on the 31st March and Instructions to Proceed with the work were finally received from the Ministry of Aircraft Production on 26th May under contract reference 1085.

The lay-out of the assembly shed, known as No 1 on the aerodrome was examined in relation to the handling of the Halifax and a production scheme planned, which was subsequently approved by the Ministry of Aircraft Production. The changes necessitated in the aerodrome and buildings may be dealt with broadly under the following headings:

1. The rear wall of bays no 3 and 4 of No 1 shed to be removed and steel doors provided, in order to permit a flow production system to be utilised.
2. A flight shed to be erected on the south-west side of the aerodrome.
3. Equipment to be purchased for production purposes in No 1 shed and the flight shed.

4. Modifications to the air raid precautions arrangements to accord with the above changes and the latest practices.
5. Increases in boiler capacity and modifications to drainage.
6. Canteen furnishing and equipment.[25]

Figure 3.4 shows the two sites. Of course, the land at Leavesden Aerodrome is now used as a film studio and is where the Harry Potter series of films were made and is now the venue of the Harry Potter theme park.

Expansion of the shadow scheme led to some interesting issues relating to security. On the one hand, there was the need to ensure that the factories were as safe as possible from air attacks. Using a distributed system of factory locations helped. Additionally, there was also the need to ensure that only those who needed to know what took place in the factories were told. Of course, it was impossible to keep this knowledge from locals if aircraft were being produced, for as soon as test flights were initiated all the locals were immediately aware! Of increasing concern was the use of modified letter-headed notepaper on the part of participating firms. You could perhaps suggest that they should have known better than to advertise their involvement. Nevertheless, the following highlights the problem.

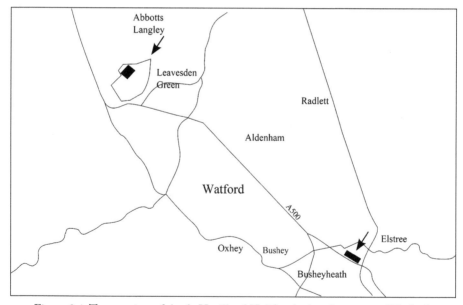

Figure 3.4 The two sites of the de Havilland Halifax shadow factory near Watford.
(Author's diagram)[26]

12th August 1941

Mr Curzon

The secretary has remarked that many of our contractors – presumably contractors managing shadow factories – have their notepaper endorsed *For and on behalf of MAP*. The Secretary has seen instances in which contractors have corresponded with the TUC using notepaper so endorsed and have even corresponded with this Department on similar paper.

He has asked me for a note indicating the origin of this practice and the authorities which have, in fact, been given to contractors in this connection.

Will you please turn out the papers and let me know the position.

In another note, the same issue is discussed.

The Secretary has seen; he would be glad, however, to see the papers containing the correspondence with Messrs Ford regarding the use of the formula. In particular, the Secretary would like to know whether the circumstances in which the formula may be used were defined. It was Fords, for example, who wrote to the TUC using the formula.

A further letter included the following:

The correspondence about the Ford shadow factory is probably not a complete record of the discussions which took place when the scheme was initiated ... it will be seen that in particular it was agreed at the company's request that the name Ford should not appear in the name of the works, or in its letter headings.

The Company were so incensed at the Department's refusal to allow them to adopt the type of factory construction which the company desired that they said that they could not allow the name of Ford to appear in correspondence precisely on the point raised in minute 4, but it is unquestionable that Ford's held strong views on kindred questions, and it is most likely that the matter was mentioned in conversation when the Department would have no hesitation in agreeing to extend to Ford's practice then and still current with managing firms, the use of the formula by shadow factories being time-honoured, and on the accounting side frequently approved by the accounts branch when the method of signing cheques is settled. The shadow factory managers are our agents, and in general as the letter from Treasury Solicitor shows, we cannot prevent them, especially at this time of day, from saying so if they wish.

Here is another note.

Shadow factories Notepaper Heading

I have discussed this matter with Mr Robinson, PS14 and a legal member of his staff, who have demonstrated to me that:

1. The use of the term *for and on behalf of the Minister of Aircraft Production* by the shadow factories is inevitable. It is true that we have an agreement with the managing firm which binds us to indemnify them, but only against charges properly incurred, and up to reasonable amounts of which we are the judge. The shadow factories, therefore, will insist that the Department should be bound by their original transaction. The best example is, perhaps, contracts for the supply of gas. We are not bound under the Shadow Agreement to reimburse the managing firm the cost of any amount of gas which they may use, but only the cost of the amount of gas reasonably required by them to fulfil their agreement with us. Similarly, there are contracts the fulfilment of which may extend over a number of years, e.g. for the erection of a railway halt which the railway company may require us to maintain, say, for 40 years. It would, of course, be unreasonable to expect the managing firm to undertake any liability in such cases.

Moreover, there are certain contracts, e.g. for the supply of machine tools and, I believe, gas, where the Government gets certain rebates if the contract is made in the name of a Government Department.

2. We cannot devise any amendment of the wording which would limit the use of the phrase in question to proper occasions. Indeed, since the Shadow Agreement requires the managing firm to engage and manage labour, but at the same time to give effect to such directions as the Minister may give with regard to wages and conditions of employment, it may be quite proper for the managing firm to correspond with the TUC on occasions for and on behalf of the Ministry.[27]

As if the use of letter-headed notepaper was not enough, the issue of intellectual property also came to the fore. Basically, the need to consider patenting new ideas and the utilisation of existing and protected ideas was a concern to many. One of the advantages of patents is the right to exclude others from using your ideas unless they pay a licence fee.

15th October 1941

PDDC Mr Jenkins

We have been giving consideration to the standard clause in the shadow agreements giving the Minister free use of the managing company's patents etc., which has formed the subject of a number of exchanges between ourselves and Mr Pryce, and on which you sent us on 7th September a general minute arising out of the Integral Auxiliary Equipment case. We understand your position to be that in the case of manufacture by companies in their own factories of their own patents, the Royal Commission have very rarely allowed royalty payments in addition to profits and you are in consequence generally able to dissuade manufacturers from making a claim. You seek to extend this procedure to shadow factories under the management of the holder of the patent and to obtain recognition of the waiver of claim by means of this clause. If, however, the clause were not there the position would still be intact and it would still be open to you later on to dissuade the managing companies from making, and if necessary to contest, any claim.

While we have admittedly managed to get this clause accepted in a number of, mainly minor, cases (e. ICI, GEC, Cossor, Lucas, M&Pd Depot Hadfield, Phillips & Powis and de Havillands, Lostock), we have in other cases met with strenuous resistance from companies (e.g. Vickers, BSA Guns, Integral Auxiliary Equipment, Napier), who are either not prepared to accept the clause or will only accept it with important limitations. It is also quite certain that resistance will be encountered in certain future negotiations, e.g. with Bristol Company, and with de Havillands in respect of the Watford shadow.

The reply from the legal department was as follows:

PS14

The view we previously put forward, based on the assumption that remuneration for shadow management was comparable with commercial remuneration after allowing for the different origin of the capital, was that it is reasonable to look upon shadow manufacture, when undertaken by the design-owning company, as an extension of their commercial manufacture and that it then became illogical to admit in the one case a royalty claim that is not admitted in the other.

You now state that no such analogy is tenable, since present-day management remuneration is more akin to reimbursement of out-of-pocket expenses. We must therefore modify our view, and say that if a company is unwilling to accept the free user clause after being pressed to do so and you consider that the proposed remuneration justifies their objection, the Department cannot very well do other than submit (I am unable to say whether the Ministry of Supply and Admiralty hold the same view). The eventual financial effect may, however, be considerable. I would, however, like to say that it appears strange to us that a firm like Napiers, which has been almost wholly supported by the Department, should reject what firms like GEC, ICI, Cossor and Lucas have accepted, but this may perhaps be explained by differences in their management remuneration. We are also reluctant that Napiers should be in a better position than Rolls-Royce.[28]

Without wishing to labour the point. In continuing the patent discussion, the following letter also mentions the activities of the Bristol shadow agreements which is interesting.

27th June 1942

To: DPAO

In connection with minute 26 on Sec. Fin. 18406 and our conversation of yesterday regarding the patent clauses in Bristol Shadow Agreements, I subscribe a statement of the factories and the supplies on which they are engaged:

1.   No 1 Engine – the assembly of Bristol engines and the assembly of Rotal airsrews.
2.   Weston – Beaufighter production.
3.   Accrington – Bristol engines, Bristol exhaust rings, repairs to engines and Merlin carburettors.
4.   Corsham – Bristol engines and probably Dowty undercarriages.

    It will be appreciated that we endeavour to secure in the management agreement the widest possible undertaking by the Company to manufacture whatever supplies the Minister may require.

S Robinson[29]

The Beaufighter was a twin-engined night fighter, the prototype of which flew its maiden flight just before war was declared.

In October 1938, the Bristol Aeroplane Company submitted a proposal for a twin-engined night fighter, heavily armed and equipped with A1 radar, to the Air Staff. Specification F.17/39 was written around the proposal and an order placed for 300 Beaufighters, as the aircraft would be named. The first of four Beaufighter prototypes (R2052) flew for the first time on 17th July 1939, powered by two Bristol Hercules I-SM engines (the forerunner of the Hercules III). By mid-1940 Bristol had received a second contract, for 918 Beaufighters.[30]

Figure 3.5 shows a Beaufighter TF.X RD253 which was actually built by the Bristol Aircraft Company at Oldmixon and delivered to the RAF in November 1944.

Figure 3.5 A Bristol Beaufighter. (Author's photograph)

But what of the costs of these expansions? Chapter 4 discusses in detail the costs of setting up the shadow scheme. Perhaps, it is more appropriate to present the expansion costs here. In both cases, the costs are larger than one might imagine, especially so once one realises that domestic houses could be built for far smaller sums than are mentioned below!

14th January 1942

Air Supply Board
Capital expenditure on extensions of capacity

In accordance with the agreed procedure whereby capital expenditure for extensions of capacity, not exceeding £50,000 may be authorised departmentally, the following commitments are reported for the information of the Board.

1. **Austin Motor Co Ltd, Birmingham**. Adaptations to premises and plant for the Horsa production, £5,000.
2. **Vickers-Armstrongs, Blackpool**. Adaptations necessary in connection with dispersal of Wellington production (two adaptations) £13,730 and £6,400.

3. **Burtonwood Repair Depot**. Adaptations to premises, heating of shops, plant and fire-fighting equipment, £5,005.
4. **Austin Motor Co Ltd, Birmingham.** Excess expenditure to that approved for provision of additional machine tools for production of balloon cable cutters and anvils, £6,301.

It is suggested that the Board need only note this expenditure but call for such further information as it may desire in any particular case.[31]

Cost overruns on building works have been the norm for many years, and continued to be so in wartime. However, the number of factories involved in the scheme at this time, and the amounts involved, prompted the following. As far as can be determined, the amount of paperwork now involved in just running and improving the factories was beyond the remit of the Ministry of Aircraft Production. It made more sense at this time to consider transferring the responsibility for the construction and maintenance to the Ministry of Works.

27th February 1943

Ministry of Aircraft Production Office Memoranda 16-20/43

The Directorate-General of Aircraft Production Factories will be transferred to the Ministry of Works on the 1st March 1943, and the following arrangements will then apply:

1. The MAP will retain responsibility for final decisions on the nature of the schemes whether involving buildings and works services only or plant and equipment only or both buildings and plant and equipment, including approval, in the light of advice received from the Ministry of Works, of estimates of costs and of major variations.
2. The MAP will continue normally to employ managing firms as agents and in such cases will look to the Ministry of Works for advice on such matters as:
   a. The reasonableness of the estimates of cost of building work, services, plant or equipment submitted to the MAP by managing firms.
   b. The suitability of sites from the building aspect.
   c. The layout and design of buildings and works in terms of constructional design and economy in the use of labour and materials.
   d. The selection of architects and of contractors to be invited to tender, paying due regard to the wishes of the managing firm by whom the commissions or contracts will be placed.

    e.   The terms and conditions of the contracts for works and services to be entered into by managing firms.

    f.   The relative merits of tenders received.

    g.   The progress of the work both of buildings and services and of the construction and installation of plant and equipment.

3.   In cases where the MAP decides not to employ the managing firm as agent, the MAP will continue to be responsible for the merits of the scheme but the Ministry of Works will, subject to meeting MAP production requirements, be responsible for:

    a.   The preparation of estimates of cost of buildings, services, plant and equipment, layout plans, etc.

    b.   The selection of contractors to be invited to tender, and the receipt, examination and acceptance of tenders up to and including the settlement of contracts.

    c.   The supervision of works in course of execution.

    d.   Approval of variations to building contracts within the limits of the normal delegated authority granted to the Ministry of Works.

    e.   Payment of periodical advances to and settlement of accounts with contractors.

4.   The MAP will retain responsibility for the purchase, leasing and requisition of land or buildings.

5.   The Ministry of Works will as from the 1st March 1943, take over and assume responsibility for the work and staff of DGAPF as a running concern. It is contemplated that, save insofar as this would conflict with the general organisation of the Ministry of Works, the present set up of the Directorate-General will not be disturbed.

6.   The staff will retain on transfer their existing rights as regards pay and conditions of service. The transfer did not involve any immediate change of accommodation for the majority of the staff concerned.

7.   Salaries, wages, subsistence and travelling expenses, etc. will be borne against the MAP vote up to the 31st March 1943 inclusive.

8.   The D of C will assist the Ministry of Works in carrying to completion certain contract work in connection with contracts for works services let by him prior to 1st March 1943.[32]

There followed a series of paragraphs relating to the administration of transfer, issuing new headquarters passes, the transfer of sensitive information on the location of the factories.

The concept of transferring the duties of building maintenance and management to the Ministry of Works was generally met with approval. The issue of concern to some other members of the Air Ministry was that the Ministry of Aircraft Production should retain responsibility for maintenance of RAF airfields.

29th November 1943

Austin Motor Co Ltd – adaptions to final assembly and flight sheds
at Elmdon for production of Lancaster Mk I and introduction
of Lancaster Mk IV

On 20th May 1943 the Board gave approval for the expenditure of £244,428 in connection with the changing over from Stirling to Lancaster production by the Austin Motor Co; which included £8,700 for re-arranging the Elmdon assembly line at right angles to the original layout as used for Stirling. Further adaptations have now been found necessary at Elmdon in order to meet the program for Lancaster Mk I.

Assembly shop
Owing to the different methods of erecting the Stirling and Lancaster fuselages, it will be necessary to level the floor of the main assembly shop. The Stirling fuselage is assembled at the Austin main works at Longbridge and transported complete to Elmdon for final erection. The Lancaster fuselage will be transported on cradles in separate parts for assembling at Elmdon, and as the assembly shop floor is of varying levels it is considered both impracticable and dangerous to attempt assembly of the Lancaster fuselage without bringing the floor to the same level throughout.

Flight Shed
The present flight shed has accommodation for four Stirlings or four Lancaster MkI, but it is necessary for standing room to be provided for seven aircraft in the flight shed to enable the company to maintain the MAP program. It is, therefore, proposed to dismantle two Bellman hangers adjacent to the flight shed and to erect on this site an additional flight shed giving accommodation for four more aircraft.

The dismantled Bellman hangers will have to be re-erected, one for the use of the RAF Training School alongside their existing buildings and the other adjacent to the main factory for storage by the Austin Company.

Lancaster Mk IV.
The introduction of the Lancaster Mk IV at this factory necessitates alterations being carried out to the existing flight shed by increasing the door openings owing to the increased wing span.

In order that this work may be done without interrupting production of the Mark I Lancaster, it is essential that arrangements be made for the work to be carried out during the summer of 1944, when the company considers that they can manage temporarily without using the flight shed. Steel allocations must be obtained at an early date in order that the necessary steel work may be fabricated and delivered, and the approval of the Board is sought for the work proposed.

DGAPF has given consideration and approval to the project.

The proposals will not involve any additional labour above that already allocated to Austin for the production of the Lancaster aircraft.

The approval in principle of the Board is accordingly sought for the provision of these facilities at an estimated cost of £80,000.

Note by DGAP[33]

Modifications were also needed to engine manufacturing facilities as well as those proposed for aircraft manufacturing facilities. In some cases, engine design changes or indeed newer engine types necessitated changes to the physical factory layout. In others, it was the number of engines needing manufacture at the same factory.

28th February 1944

Air Supply Board
Bristol Aeroplane Co Ltd Accrington
increase in capacity for the manufacture of Centaurus engines

Papers under the above title, were presented on the 20th May, 23rd September and 7th October 1943, and the Board approved the proposal that the scheme for the manufacture of Centaurus engines at Accrington should proceed.

As then assessed it was estimated that a total of 122 machine tools costing approximately £218,200 would be required.

On subsequent review, with the latest detail drawings available, the Bristol Company have found it necessary to revise their earlier estimate of machine tool requirements, with the result that a total of 194 machines, estimated to cost £467,805, will be required to achieve the Centaurus program of 150 engines per month plus spares at the Accrington factory.

In revising the machine tool estimates, improved methods of manufacture, the use, wherever possible, of special-purpose machines will have the effect of conserving labour, and it is also probable that a substantial number of standard machine tools will ultimately be released from this factory.

In order to complete the partial change-over in manufacturing capacity at Accrington, the approval in principle of the Board is sought for the further expenditure of machine tools, estimated at £249,605, subject to detailed technical and financial examinations.[34]

The need to upgrade machine tools to cope with newer engine types was not new. Of increasing concern as the war progressed was how best to utilise those obsolete machines stripped out during the refurbishment work. I am reminded here that the original concept was to minimise the production of machine jigs, tools and gauges by instructing the original engine shadow factories to only make part engines, here we are eight years later with obsolete equipment!

3rd May 1944

Notice to managers of MAP shadow factories No 18A Disposal of redundant and obsolete jigs, tools and gauges

1. Managers are reminded that the retention of redundant and obsolete jigs, tools and gauges in works not only absorbs valuable storage space, but also withholds from the war effort a substantial weight of steel and other materials. Redundant stocks of usable tools and gauges should be disposed of through channels which will make them readily available to other users.

2. Jigs, tools and gauges which are no longer required on orders for main equipment or 'spares' production, or which cannot be utilised for new production, should be reported to the Directorate of Regional Organisation (Gauges, Jigs and Tools Division) MAP, Harrogate, or, in respect of sub-contract supplies, to the ordering firm. Three copies of the list of redundant tools are required and should include the following particulars:

   a. Order number(s) under which the tools were provided or against which they were used and the description of the RAF equipment concerned.

   b. Location, description, quantity, size or approximate weight.

      i. Jigs, fixtures and press tools briefly described and classified as (a) main assembly; (b) major component; (c) minor component; (d) detail and press tools.

      ii. Special cutting tools and gauges.

      iii. Standard cutting tools and gauges.

   c. Cause of redundancy.

   On receipt of the above information the Department will decide whether any further use could be made of the redundant equipment.

3. The Department will issue disposal instructions and may, in suitable cases, authorise the manager to sell at fair and reasonable prices through channels approved by the appropriate control.

4. The list of standard cutting tools and gauges at sub para 2(b)(iii) above will be referred by the Department to the Machine Tool Control who will advise the manager as the disposal. No cash payment will be made by the Machine Tool Control for any tooling equipment which they take over, but the items will be priced and the manager will despatch the tools with Despatch Notes or Issue Vouchers which will be receipted by the Machine Tool Control.

5. The register of jigs and tools maintained at the shadow factory in accordance with normal practice must be properly annotated as regards all disposal whether made under the above arrangements or transferred to other users on MAP instructions.

6. Managers are requested to survey the tooling position of each item which has gone out of production and to write to the Directorate of Regional Organisation (Gauges, Jigs and Tools Division) MAP, Harrogate, giving their proposals. This survey should also cover redundant jigs, tools and gauges lying at the works of your principle sub-contractors.

7. This notice cancels section (A) of Notice to Managers of MAP Shadow Factories No 18.

Director of Contracts[35]

The number of factories involved in the shadow scheme continued to increase during the war – at least until late 1944. By this time, manufacturing techniques had been honed and refined and a move to more productive mass production techniques introduced. It is worth recording here that a compiled list of shadow factories appears in Appendix VI and has been generated to reflect the increased number of factories.

4

Finance and Administration

The introduction of a government-backed scheme into an established industry, albeit to produce different materials, led to many interesting discussions, even in the run up to and during the war. Whilst every motor car manufacturer was keen to support and work with the government, each business leader was also interested in the financial implications perhaps more so than the government might have wished.

There were several issues and included (in no particular order) the following:

- Timescales.
- Cash flow.
- Set-up cost.
- Return on investment.
- Management fees.
- Reporting lines and administration.
- End of war wrap-up.

After all the motor car manufacturers in the main were individuals who had started their respective businesses from scratch and were motivated by the normal financial management practices of their industries. That is not to say that they did not care to help the government. Some of the individuals worked on government committees without any financial remuneration. Indeed Lord Austin worked his shadow factory at no profit to himself. It is just to say that their normal modus operandi was to consider practical and financial matters when looking at new business proposals. The other issue was that these industrialists still had their 'day job' of running large motor manufacturing companies. Indeed, it has been estimated that during the war, the motor manufacturing companies manufactured over 900,000 military vehicles and other commodities. These were busy people with demanding 'day jobs'. Shadow factories were an addition to their normal lives. Understandably, they were keen for the administration to closely match their normal working environment.

The same was the case for the aircraft industry who were now being asked to part with their drawings, intellectual property or in some cases their staff (for limited periods). The leaders of these companies were in many ways like their counterparts in the motor industry. The government staff were, therefore, on a steep learning curve in their discussions with both sectors now being asked to work together. Perhaps, the following was one of the earliest pre-meeting discussions held in government offices which addressed the issue of strategy when dealing with groups of individuals from the two industry sectors.

9th June 1936

To: The Secretary of State

I believe that Mr Fairey intends to raise the question of finance with you at this meeting on Thursday next. But I think it would be a good thing if it were made clear to him the services which we expect this Company to render. These are:

1. To supply Messrs. Austin with copies of all workshop drawings necessary for the manufacture of the Battle as soon as they become available.
2. To supply drawings of all jigs and tools used by the Fairey Aviation Company for the manufacture of this machine. (Messrs. Austin may not use all these drawings but they will be a help and a guide to them).
3. To complete and maintain a complete set of master tracings constituting the design of the Battle aeroplane.
4. To supply Messrs. Austin with all the blue prints or photographic copies of these master tracings that they require for the purposes of manufacture. (It would be unfortunate if Messrs. Austin made a set of master tracings of their own for this aeroplane as this would bring into existence another type of aeroplane, namely the Austin Battle. Messrs. Faireys should be able to supply Messrs. Austin with all copies of drawings required).
5. To supply Messrs. Austin with copies of all alterations made to these master drawings at the same time that they are supplied to Messrs. Faireys' own workshop.
6. It is thought that Messrs. Austin should not be permitted to make any changes in the design of this aeroplane without the concurrence of the Fairey Aviation Company: indeed, from a technical point of view, it would be a great convenience if Messrs. Austin did not attempt to alter the design in any way. (It may easily be that more time would be wasted in discussing and approving such alterations than would be saved in manufacture).
7. To help and advise the Austin Company on all detail questions requiring special knowledge in the manufacture of aeroplanes such as the handling and treatment of light alloys and the special steels used in construction.

AMRD[1]

The meeting with Mr C R Fairey took place shortly after the above, on 11 June 1936.

> Mr C R Fairey opened by saying that he felt it necessary to bring the position of his company to the Secretary of State's notice. By spending more than £838,000 in new buildings and new equipment, which had necessitated using up all their reserved and liquid assets, the Board had put themselves in a position in which their action might well be called in question by the shareholders.
>
> He had assisted Sir Herbert Austin to the best of his ability in his preparation for shadow manufacture, and he was anxious to do all that he could to further the success of that scheme. The offer of remuneration made to him was, however, altogether incommensurate with the sacrifice he was making, and he felt that an exaggerated idea of the company's profits was held in the Air Ministry.
>
> The Secretary of State insisted that profits were entirely irrelevant. He had simply to determine a reasonable remuneration for what the company were being called upon to do having regard to comparable past transactions with other firms. If the terms offered were not acceptable, arbitration would be available…
>
> The only course open to him, however, so far as he could understand, was to wait for arbitration at the end of the contract.[2]

A further meeting with Mr C R Fairey followed on 26 June 1936.

Shadow Scheme remuneration

> The Secretary of State began by recalling the arrangement reached with Mr Fairey on 11th June that the remuneration to be paid in connection with the shadow manufacture of the Battle by the Aviation Company should be decided by arbitration. He had since made a similar proposal to the Bristol Company (who were, of course, concerned in regard to engines as well as airframes), and in the course of discussion the suggestion that arbitration would have to be deferred until experience had been gained of what 'servicing' would be involved had been properly considered. The proposal he now wished to put to the Fairey Aviation Co. was that arbitration might take place at once. The 'servicing' element, which had seemed to make some deferment inevitable, consisted in part of the salaries of staff who might have to be allotted by the parent company for liaison duties at the shadow factories … it had been agreed with the Bristol Company that, in their case, the arbitrator should be a man of wide practical experience and that the arbitration should be informal, without representation by council. After various suggestions had been made and considered, it was decided to propose that Lord Justice Greene should act as arbitrator, if he were available and willing to do so.…
>
> Mr Fairey referred the disorganisation which the shadow manufacture would involve in his works. The whole staff were working long hours and at

high pressure, and the training of the personnel of the Austin shadow factory (who were newly engaged without any experience either of airframe manufacture or of the Fairey methods) would place a very great strain on his organisation. He thought it only fair to make it clear that his company could not accept any responsibility for the output of the shadow factory. There was, he feared, a possibility that they might be blamed for delays which were outside their control. The manager whom the Austin Company had appointed for the shadow factory was, for example, already asking for drawings of jigs etc. which were not yet ready.[3]

The costs of creating a workable factory into which the engineering equipment could be delivered and brought to operational efficiency were also somewhat taxing. In some cases, these were over half a million pounds (Figure 4.1, and the letter immediately after the table).

Factory	Expenditure on Buildings and Plant		Actual Expenditure £	Remuneration during Construction of Factory £
	Original Sanctions £	Revised Sanctions Including Extensions £		
Austin engines	720,920	701,000	668,227	24,000
Bristol engines	389,786	390,873	384,023	20,000
Daimler engines	579,841	764,244	696,939	24,000
Rootes engines	542,700	936,959	752,250	24,000
Rover engines	708,221	842,424	796,945	24,000
Standard engines	610,000	889,804	627,908	24,000
Austin frames	958,510	1,010,000	971,670	50,000
Rootes frames	1,411,850	2,251,411	1,804,886	50,000
De Havilland screws	572,000	943,500	656,151	25,000
Hobson carburettors	103,000	216,158	171,341	5,150
Standard carburettors	261,500	282,620	293,805	10,000
Machine products, bombs (Plesseys)	189,620	306,000	287,059	10,000[a]

Note:
a Increased by £3,000 on account of revised sanctions.

Figure 4.1 Statistics relating to the 12 shadow factories in production.[4]

24th June 1937

To: Captain W Hallam
For the Director of Aeronautical Production

Dear Sir,

Shadow Industry Aeronautical Production

With further reference to your letter of the 3rd instant relative to the expenditure on our aero engine and airframe sections, we enclose a statement showing the estimated requirements for the completion of this work compared with the brochure sent to you on the 29th January 1937.

The total estimated expenditure, as you will see, is now shown as £1,802,831 against the brochure figure of £1,690,155 which includes all contingencies. In the £1,802,831 there is £14,143 for a clearing press which we were instructed to purchase out of the Shadow Contingency Fund, but which, we were informed, would be afterwards deleted from that account and charged to some other account. This would make a total expenditure of £1,788,688 showing an excess of £98,533.

We wish, however, to draw your particular attention to the plant and tool equipment for the Airframes Section, which has a total of £653,086 as against the estimated expenditure of £472,000.

At the time the brochure was issued we believed that we had received, or knew of, all the drawings of the Fairey Battle Machine. Since then, however, we have received no less than 996 new drawings, and besides this have had 1992 modifications of the old drawings, and in this connection we may mention that since we commenced operations, when we were informed that there would be about 4,000 drawings, we have actually received to the present nearly 7,000, and the total modifications amount to approximately 6,700.

Also, when the original estimates were made we were not aware that Messrs. Fairey did not themselves manufacture such articles as fins, rudders, ailerons, tanks, oleo legs, hoodings and a very large quantity of small parts, nuts etc. all of which we are, under instructions, making ourselves and which require very heavy expenditure in jigs and tools. We must also inform you that our figures will absorb all the contingency fund, and, judging by what has already occurred by reason of modifications and alterations to design, etc. that at least another £50,000 should be sanctioned to meet further unknown possibilities.

Yours faithfully
For and on behalf of the Austin Motor Company Limited[5]

Such was the strategic importance of the aero engine shadow factories the Air Ministry arranged the following one year before the outbreak of war.

25th September 1938

Gentlemen,

I am commanded by the Air Council to inform you that they have under consideration the effect upon production of aircraft, aero-engines, armament and aeronautical material which might result from the withdrawal from manufacturing firms of Royal Air Force Reservists, in the event of such Reservists being recalled for Service during an emergency.

The Council have decided that, should an emergency arise in which Royal Air Force Reservists are recalled for Service, your firm shall be authorised in the interests of preventing any interruption in the delivery of aircraft, aero-engines, armament and aeronautical equipment to the Air Force, to retain for the time being and pending further investigations any Air Force Reservists so recalled whom you employ and whose withdrawal would have a prejudicial effect upon deliveries in question to the Royal Air Force.

The Council desires me to convey to you also the authority to authorise any firms with whom you have placed sub-contracts, similarly to retain for the time being and pending investigations any Air Force Reservists whose withdrawal would be likely prejudicially to affect your deliveries to the Royal Air Force by reason of affecting adversely supplies to you by your sub-contractors.

I am to request that you will acknowledge receipt of this letter and also inform this Department and the Officer-in-Charge of Records, Royal Air Force Record Office, Ruislip, Middlesex, of the names and nature of employment of any Royal Air Force Reservists retained for the time being by you or by sub-contractors indicating, in the case of retention by sub-contractors, the names and addresses of the firms concerned.

As you will appreciate the aim of the Council in granting this authority is to make the best use of available personnel from the point of view of the requirements of the Service. The Council rely upon you, therefore not to retain any Royal Air Force Reservists whose retention is not essential.

I am Gentlemen,
Your Obedient Servant[6]

I mentioned at the start of this chapter that the industrialists involved in the shadow scheme had business principles ingrained in their every action. The issue of efficiency bonuses is another case in point. Having set up their respective factories and worked on the issues surrounding unfamiliar blue prints, training their new workforce, etc., they were keen to ensure that any bonus due to them was recognised by the Ministry and paid in line with the agreement.

15th January 1940

To: The Under Secretary of State for Air, Air Ministry

Dear Sir,

Efficiency Bonus

The Committee have instructed me to forward to you the enclosed particulars of the costs of the first four batches of 100 Mercury Engines manufactured and delivered by the factories of the No 1 Shadow Group, for the purpose of agreeing with you the basic price for calculation of the efficiency bonus payable to the Committee in the terms of the Supplemental Agreement of the 10th December 1937. The amounts shown in the enclosed statement have been arrived at by taking the ascertained costs of each of the engines in the order of their delivery in equal numbers by the two assembly factories.

Yours faithfully, The Secretary
Aero Engine Committee No 1

Figure 4.2 shows details of the last 100 engines of the series, by way of an example.

	50 ex Bristol	50 ex Austin	Average of 100
Austin parts	221	239	230
Daimler parts	177	198	188
Rover parts	257	316	286
Rootes parts	410	532	471
Standard parts	262	552	507
Spares ex all part factories	7	4	6
Main assembly and test	269	362	315
	£1,803	£2,203	£2,003

Figure 4.2 The fourth hundred engines.

The reply to the above letter was written less than a week after submission!

20th January 1940

Dear Lord Austin,

As promised I have inquired into the progress of the consideration which is being given to the general question, affecting a number of departments, of remuneration in wartime for the management of shadow factories. As I explained at the meeting on Wednesday, the 17th instant, pending the outcome of the deliberations on this question we have not a free hand at the Air Ministry to conclude terms for future agreements, and I fear that it may be some weeks before we shall be able to proceed.

I have noted very carefully the representations made by yourself and Mr Geoffrey Burton and will see that they are given full weight when the time comes to reopen negotiations. I should like again to assure you that there is no misapprehension at the Ministry, or lack of appreciation, of the magnitude of the task which has been accomplished at the engine shadow factories, nor have we any misgivings in regard to the way in which our future requirements from these factories will be met. I hear that your Committee have now formally accepted the terms of the contract for the year to June 1940, and I am naturally delighted that it has been possible to conclude the protracted negotiations on this point.

Yours sincerely,
Kingsley Wood[7]

Note at the end of this letter the statement concerning the agreements, the first draft of which was drawn in 1937.

This letter was from the accounting department, adding their thoughts to the discussion.

5th March 1940

1. Following Sir Harold Howitt's visit to the Austin Shadow Factory, and his recommendation that in view of the virtual breakdown of the cost accounting arrangements there, the provisions in the agreement for the calculation of bonus payments for Battles should be abandoned, and the agreement amended to provide for an alternative scheme, detailed costing has ceased, and the costs will be taken out in two 'blocks' – one of the first 128 aeroplanes and one of the remainder.

2. The company recommended (see their letter of 5th December) that a target cost should be based on the technical estimates taken at a point immediately following the first 128 machines. This is quite impractical.

3. By its own failure on the cost accounting side the company has made any calculation of bonus on the ascertained costs of a particular batch of aeroplanes, as was provided for in the agreement, impossible. I do not think it can be argued that as a consequence payment of bonus can be ruled out of consideration. The spirit of the agreement was that a bonus should be paid in addition to the fixed fee of £200 per aeroplane, if the Battles were produced at a reasonable cost. The batch costing system having failed, it remains to find a standard by which to measure what is a reasonable cost and to derive the bonus therefrom.

4. The concurrent manufacture of Battles by the Fairey Company at Stockport affords a standard of comparison which could be used for the purpose in view.

5. We know the actual costs of only the first 60 Battles manufactured at Stockport. The remainder have been paid for at fixed prices, and although we could probably make a fairly close estimate of the costs of these also, it seems to me that the further we can get away from estimates and the more we can rely on facts in this matter the less room there will be for argument and the greater prospect of a satisfactory solution. I therefore suggest we should work from the prices actually paid for the Fairey Battles. This will necessitate some allowance being made for wear and tear and depreciation of plant and buildings at the shadow factory, and also for interests on the capital cost of the factory and plant. If these, together with the fee of £200, are added to the actual cash expended on labour, material and overheads at the Austin factory, we shall get a figure which is nearly comparable with the price paid for the Fairey machines. The difference, which should result in an overall figure in favour of the shadow factory, is Fairey's profit in excess of £200, and the various elements in the Fairey overheads which do not apply to the shadow factory.[8]

As if the government departments had nothing else to do, ICI which produced a range of chemicals at several factories, see Appendix VI for example, were also concerned with operating fees.

Imperial Chemical Industries Limited Millbank London
Secret

14th November 1939

To H C Gordon Ministry of Supply

Fees for the operation of plants on behalf of the Ministry of Supply

Dear Mr Gordon,
With reference to the conversation we have recently had regarding the above, the matter has now been discussed and I write to give you the terms on which we are prepared to operate factories on your behalf, subject of course to special terms in connection with certain contracts already made between us.

Before going into details I should say that the matter has been reviewed from many points of view, but in all of them, with the exception of the basis now brought forward, we have found that certain objectionable features present themselves.

We are, for example, averse from basing our remuneration on the tonnage of material produced, as this lays us open to the attack that we are interested financially in the prolongation of hostilities.

The same attack can be made if we are interested in the turnover of the plants or in the cost of production. In the latter case there would be two flaws, namely, that we could run the plants wastefully and obtain more remuneration or that the output was increased for national purposes with the same result.

An endeavour has therefore been made to base such remuneration as we ask in the first place upon something for which you alone take responsibility, and secondly, which will not vary from time to time with increase or decrease in production. For this reason we have adopted as a basis the capital sum spent by you on fixed assets in each individual plant erected.

Although it is true that we have actually constructed the plants, I think it is correct to say that 90% of the expenditure has been approved by you prior to commitment, and when each plant is completed you will have approved every pound spent. For this reason we regard such capital expenditure as arising from your actions only and entirely your responsibility.

In view of the fact that you have provided all the capital you would normally be entitled to the full profits or benefits from such capital expenditure, but as you are unable to supply the necessary skilled staff and management and we can do so, it is obvious that you must forego to some extent the benefits which accrues to your capital. Such amount of profit as you agree to give up to reward us for our services can reasonably be quoted as a percentage of the money you have spent, (as the expected yield on any capital scheme is normally quoted this way) and this percentage we wish to put on a very low basis. Furthermore, we suggest that the low figure at which we start should be scaled down for the larger jobs undertaken and should be treated as a fixed fee ascertainable once and for all regarding a given plant as it stands at the time we commence to operate it.

I will give the details of our suggestion in paragraphs (a) to (f) below. We shall merely ask for a round sum fee. You will be able to check it by reference to to (c).

a) In respect of the whole or any part of the first £1,000,000 of fixed capital you pay us a fee at the rate of 1.5% thereon per annum.

b) In respect of the whole or any part of the second £1,000,000 of fixed capital you pay us a fee at the rate of 1% thereon per annum.

c) In respect of the whole or any part of sums in excess of £2,000,000 of fixed capital you pay us a fee at the rate of 0.5% of such excess per annum.

d) The fee for each factory to be payable quarterly in advance.

e) The fee is to be payable for any quarter after completion of construction unless the factory has formally been put by you on a care and maintenance basis, irrespective of the rate at which it is working.

f) You will pay to us at the commencement of each month a round sum approximating the expenditure at each factory during such month, in order that we shall not be called upon to have our own funds outstanding by reason of the operation of such factories.

g)   Overhead expenses will be charged in accordance with a scheme to be agreed between us.

The only point to which I wish to draw special attention in connection with the above paragraphs are that our services in connection with operation start some time before production, such as in the choosing and training of staff, as you agreed at one of our talks, our operating services do not stop immediately production ceases, as it might take upwards of six months to close down and protect a large factory and get it on to a case and maintenance basis. The second point I wish to make is that in several of our agreements in which operation appeared to be likely we reserved the right to charge our overheads on the same basis as we would have done had the plant belonged to us. This can be dealt with when I see you.

Yours sincerely,
H D Butchart[9]

Written in 1940, there was a determined effort to resolve some of the issues with ICI.

PPAO (Mr Price)

As you are probably aware, the conclusion of operation agreements regulating ICI shadow factories is long overdue. For this Ministry they manage at present only the shadow factories of Gowerton (light alloys), Kilmarnock (incendiary bombs etc.), Runcorn (ethyl chloride), Widnes (monomer) and Rawtenstall (Perspex), but there is a very large number of agency factories which they manage for the Ministry of Supply involving £50 of capital. Tripartite negotiations between the two Ministries and the firm were recently undertaken with a view to agreeing upon a master agreement for each Ministry, each as nearly as possible identical with the other, covering all the projects managed for each Ministry. We have throughout recognised that the Ministry of Supply's interest was so much greater than ours that the conduct of the negotiations should fall primarily upon them and that it would be necessary for the MAP to fall in with the wording agreed between the other two parties wherever it was possible to do so. The document which we hope will result, while covering the same ground as, will bear little superficial resemblance to, the ordinary form of MAP shadow agreement.[10]

Unfortunately, not all of the arrangements ran smoothly. In the case of the agreement for Rover Company Limited to manufacture and repair Cheetah engines, the Government decided to provide a standard contract and not create a new shadow factory. This led to a totally different cost position for Rover compared with the aero engine shadow factories. It is provided here as an exemplar of the different ways of obtaining engines used by the Ministry of Aircraft Production.

11th June 1940

Manufacture and repair of Cheetah engines

Gentlemen,

With reference to the negotiations which have taken place relating to the manufacture and repair of Cheetah engines by your company, I am directed by the Minister of Aircraft Production to set out below the terms which have been agreed for the carrying out of this work.

You will adapt in accordance with the requirements of the Department that portion of your works which has been allocated for the purpose for the manufacture of 100 and the repair of 40 Cheetah engines per week working double shift. For this purpose you will:

i.   Remove and store any car equipment in the part of the works to be adapted not required for the manufacture and repair of engines or other supplies ordered by the Air Ministry from the company; re-arrange, as necessary, the remaining equipment which may be useful for this work and install such new plant and machinery as you may be authorised to manufacture or purchase.

ii. Manufacture as far as possible the necessary jigs and tools required to carry out the work involved in the contracts; any such items which cannot be manufactured by you shall be purchased in the most economical manner, the prior approval of the Department to be obtained to the scale of provision.

The Air Ministry will reimburse the company in respect of the expenditure incurred under the above paragraph as follows:

i.   For jigs and tools purchased by the company, the net invoice cost.

ii. For jigs and tools manufactured by the company, and the work for adapting the factory, the net cost of materials, the actual wages paid plus appropriate overhead charges thereon. Such overhead charges shall comprise establishment expenses which are solely and properly applicable to the work of adapting your works, and the agreed apportionment of other expenses as are properly attributable to the aero-engine production and repair and the company's other business. They will not include any expenses which can be regarded as appropriate solely to the company's other business.

iii. Etc.

Signed J T Cottom
Director of Aircraft contracts.[11]

Whilst this approach seemed to be reasonable, there were nevertheless some companies who wanted to directly charge the Ministry for fuel costs. The letter below is one such which mentions the use of an imprest account. This type of account is mentioned in several other unrelated letters which appear below. It was an audited account held by each shadow factory from which they could draw expenses, and into which fees were payable from the various government departments.

13th October 1940

To: The Central Electricity
Board East Horsley

Gentlemen,
I am directed to refer to your letter WGR/5700/6 dated 8th October 1940, in which you claim £10,531.9s.10d in connection with the supply of electricity to the Bristol No 3 Engine Shadow Factory at Accrington.

It would be convenient to the Department if payment in this and future cases could be made through the imprest account operated by the Bristol Aeroplane Co Ltd who manage the factory for and on behalf of the Minister of Aircraft Production. On the assumption that you will raise no objection to this procedure, instructions are being sent to the Bristol Aeroplane Co. to make payment accordingly, and you are required to address future claims to the company at Accrington.

B Davidson[12]

The somewhat chaotic financial arrangements, particularly in the early days of the shadow scheme, led to one or two moments where the motor companies almost ran into cash flow problems, particularly those instances where the government departments tried to order aero parts from traditional motor companies on a contract basis. Perhaps this was to be expected given the will on the part of the motor industry to make a success of the shadow scheme and help in any way they could.

Notes of meeting held at Coventry, 30th October 1940 arranged by The Minister of Aircraft Production to discuss future arrangements for financing the Company's aero production

Present: representatives of the Rover Company and the Ministry of Aircraft Production.

In opening the discussion Mr Forbes asked why the company had not raised the question of their inability to finance production in the early stages of negotiation. Mr Wilks produced extracts from correspondence showing that the question of finance had been raised from time to time by him and that as early as September 1939 letters had been written to Sir Kingsley Wood, Sir Wilfred Freeman and Major Bulman on the subject and that again in April the company, in writing to Mr Pickles, had expressed concern about the future financial outlook.

Mr Wilks said that although the letters written in September 1939 only mentioned finance in connection with conversion, he naturally had in mind the general financial position, but at that time expected that any progress payment scheme adopted would take care of production. This, unfortunately, did not prove to be the case with the result that an alternative method had got to be found for dealing with the problem. Mr Forbes said that it appeared to him to be a question of purely temporary accommodation and that the Ministry's view was that the company should obtain the necessary accommodation from the banks and stated that the banks were, under such circumstances as this, prepared to provide the necessary working capital on overdraft. Mr Wilks said that such an arrangement was very probably the proper one in the case of an ordinary aircraft manufacturer but pointed out that his attitude had always been that the Rover Company were in an entirely different category from firms whose normal business was to do aero work and said that throughout the whole negotiations he had insisted that the company must safeguard its position in order to enable it to get back into the car business after the war and that the Board were, therefore, not prepared to pledge their assets to the bank...

Mr Forbes then summarised the position as follows. That the company had undertaken a contract comprised in correspondence which they were unable to carry out and that the Ministry's view was that they should go to the bank for accommodation but the company were not prepared to take this step. He understood that it had been suggested that some form of reimbursement on imprest for expenditure similar to that adopted by the shadow factories might be a solution but the Ministry were anxious to keep the work on a commercial basis which involved agreeing and working to a fixed price. He therefore, asked what available capital the company were prepared to put up. Mr Wilks, in replying, said that he did not consider that a contract had been entered into and, in fact, he had at all times avoided signing a contract pending settlement of this financial question...

The meeting then adjourned leaving Mr Forbes, Mr Wilks and Mr Graham to discuss the question of recent correspondence from Mr Pickles.[13]

The financial problems did not go away.

29th April 1941

There are now coming into production a fair number of shadow factories concerned with the production of materials, metals or parts such as oleos and hydraulic pumps not commonly issued on Embodiment Loan. In other words, the products will be sold either to the industry or to other shadow factories. It will be necessary to decide what is to be done with the proceeds of the sale and an early decision is required, since the shadow agreements now in active negotiation should presumably cover the point.

There appear to be three alternatives:

1. That the proceeds should be paid into the imprest accounts.
2. That they should be paid to the Ministry and regarded as Appropriations-in-Aid.
3. That they should be paid to the Ministry but should not so far as possible be treated as Appropriations-in-Aid.

If the decision on File Sec.Fin.1222 regarding payments by Rolls-Royce for purchases from the Hillington Factory is followed, (3) would doubtless be the alternative selected. That decision, however, appears to relate to sub-contracting work and probably was not meant to embrace the routine sale of complete products.

There would seem to be a good deal to be said for alternative (1) which not only strikes the lay mind as the natural and tidy way of handling the matter (since to say that the Government by means of these shadow factories is not virtually involved in trading activities seems mere evasion of an unpleasant truth), but would make it possible from resulting profit and loss account readily to ascertain how far any one factory was being economically conducted. Against this must be set the objection that it is desirable that the balance of the imprest account should be kept as low as possible in order to obviate extravagance on the part of the managing firm.

If, however, I am right in thinking that a weekly statement of the balance is made by the managing firm it should always be possible to call in some of the balance should it grow too great, without the money lying idle for more than a week. Moreover, these cases seem to me clearly distinguishable from the Rolls-Royce and sub-contracting cases, in that the latter dealt with what may perhaps be called windfalls. The proceeds of the sale of the products of the shadow factories in question will of course be regular income which can be foreseen and it should to a large extent be possible to anticipate it when payments are made into the imprest account without any danger of an overdraft.

It should also be pointed out that in at least one alloy melting case – and there will doubtless be others – the position is complicated by the fact that it has been arranged to follow the procedure known as 'melting on toll' i.e. the Adderbury shadow will not buy virgin aluminium from the Northern Aluminium Company and then sell the alloy back to it, but there will be a single transaction by which the company will pay the shadow for processing its material. This sort of thing cannot properly be reconciled with any procedure under which the proceeds of the sales are credited direct to the Ministry.

We should be glad to learn as soon as possible what procedure it is proposed should be followed in general at the factories in question (and whether there will be any exceptions) and whether you agree that the point should be covered in the appropriate shadow agreements. I assume that there will be adjustments to cover transactions between shadow factories.

PS14[14]

The decision of which of the various options to adopt was:

We are prepared to accept your proposal regarding the disposal of the proceeds of sales of shadow factory products. Unless you see any objection we shall provide in the relevant agreements that the proceeds shall be credited to the Minister in accordance with directions given by him from time to time. It will be for you to issue the detailed instructions in the cases concerned about the collection of the debts and the method of crediting them to the Ministry, though we should be glad of some general indication of the method which you propose. I have no doubt that you will bear in mind the desirability of making the procedure as simple and as uniform as possible. Doubtless also you are prepared to deal with the multiplicity of receipts, possibly quite small, which may result if each debt from sales is separately credited to the Ministry after collection by the shadow manager.[15]

In some cases sales of goods from one shadow factory to another was straightforward and in others more complex. Figure 4.3 shows some examples of shadow factory sales.

	Example
Buildings or building material	Trimpell
Plant	General – to other shadow factories
Jigs and tools	Austin Shadow – Battle – to Fairey Parent Company Rootes Shadow – Stirling – to Austin Shadow Fairey Shadow – Beaufighter – to Rootes Shadow Rootes Shadow – Stirling – to Short Harland
Scrap and swarf arisings	General – to scrap merchants
By-products	Castner – Keller – hydrochloric acid on commercial market
Surplus raw materials and semi-manufacturers	Austin shadow ex Battle to Fairey and Redwing Parent Co Hadfield 'bomb castings' to Jarrow
Products below inspection standard	Rolls-Royce Glasgow – Merlin parts built into tank engines – to Ministry of Supply GEC wireless valves – to Post Office

	Example
Manufacture of complete parts or components (not including work as a member of a group)	Lockheed – undercarriage parts to parent company Rolls-Royce Glasgow – engine parts to Ministry of Supply for tank engines BMARC – gun parts – to parent company and others BSA (Guns) Ltd – gun parts Rolls-Royce Glasgow – engine parts to parent company
Manufacture of a complete product or one requiring further processing	ICI (Rawtenstall) – Perspex – to contractors Leyland Motors Ltd – carburettor castings – to Hobsons, parent company of Shadow or Standard Shadow
Loaned labour	Austin Shadow to Castle Bromwich and Boulton Paul
Engine parts ex USA	Rolls-Royce 'Pool' to parent company and others manufacturing Rolls-Royce engines

Figure 4.3 A selection of sales and ledger transactions for shadow factories.[16]

The Ministry of Aircraft Production issued the following letter detailing the new financial arrangements, the distribution list for which appears in Figure 4.4.

26th June 1941

Gentlemen,

It is proposed to standardise accounting arrangements in respect of the proceeds of sales by shadow factories as follows:

1. Sales of products and parts wholly or partially fabricated, bought out parts and materials whether to the parent company or other shadow factories or commercial companies should be invoiced from the shadow factory.
2. The proceeds should, as received, be paid in at the local bank for the credit of the account of the Paymaster General (Ministry of Aircraft Production) at the Bank of England and not lodged in the Public Banking (imprest) account.
3. The proper invoicing of all such sales, the subsequent collection of amounts due by debtors and direct lodgement thereof to the credit of the department as above are responsibilities of the shadow factory management.
4. All sums paid in at the bank for the credit of the above account should be notified to the Chief Accountant (DCA2), Ministry of Aircraft Production, Ladies College, Harrogate on form DCA2/1, an initial supply of which is enclosed and a copy of each completed form should be passed to the Resident Auditor.
5. Where specific instructions are received from the Department to dispose of jigs and tools or plant by sale the proceeds should be dealt with as above.

6. The proceeds of sales of swarf and scrap together with miscellaneous receipts such as commissions, refunds or compensation payments, private telephone calls or other payments or refunds by employees should not be paid into the above account but should continue to be lodged in the imprest bank account as at present.

7. The foregoing procedure will not apply to deliveries of components between factories within the same self-contained shadow groups which will continue to be covered by the inter-factory accounting procedure already agreed.

I am Gentlemen,
Your Obedient Servant Chief Accountant[17]

PA9 Factories	Rootes Airframes
Austin Engines	Vickers Armstrongs, Castle Bromwich
Bristol No. 2 Engines	Vickers Armstrongs, Chester
Bristol No. 3 Engines	Vickers Armstrongs, Blackpool
BJH	
Daimler No. 1 Engines	**PA 11 Factories**
Daimler No. 2 Engines	JCJ Metals Ltd
Ford Motor Co.	Nobels Explosives Ltd
HM Hobson	Castner-Keller Alkali Co Ltd
Integral Auxiliary Equipment	Trimpell Ltd
D Napier and Son Ltd	Shell Refining and Marketing Co Ltd (Chester)
Rolls-Royce	Murex Ltd
Rootes No. 1 Engines	Shell Refining and Marketing Co Ltd (Teddington)
Rootes No. 2 Engines	British Aluminium Co. Ltd (Shrewsbury)
Rover No. 1 Engines	British Aluminium Co. Ltd (N. Ireland)
Rover No. 2 Engines	ICI (Plastics) Ltd
Standard No. 1 Engines	ICI (General Chemicals) Ltd
Standard No. 2 Engines	Trinidad Leaseholds Ltd
Standard Carburettors	ICI (Fertilizer and Synthetic Products) Ltd
PA 10 Factories	**PA 14 Factories**
Aeronautical and Panel Plywood	Civilian Repair Organisation (Cowley)
Airspeed (1934) Ltd	Northern Aluminium Ltd
Bristol Airframes (Western-Super-Mare)	International Alloys
British Manufacture and Research Co.	Birmetals Ltd
AC Cosser	British Aluminium
De Havilland, airscrews	High Duty Alloys Ltd

De Havilland, airframes	
Fairey Aviation	
Burtonwood Repair Depot	
General Electric	
Hadfields	
Lockheed Hydraulic Brake Co	
Joseph Lucas (Cwmbran)	
Joseph Lucas (Warwick)	
Machine Products	
Phillips and Powis	

Figure 4.4 Shadow factory sales distribution list for the letter dated 27 June 1941.[18]

The sale of goods to any factory whether in the shadow scheme or not was considered standard business practice, there were many others. I briefly mentioned earlier the need for certain types of insurance. In the early years of the war, shadow factories took out insurance policies for:

1. Motor transport.
2. Flying risks.
3. Lifts, boilers, heating, etc.

Some even needed to claim against those policies, Figure 4.5:

Factory	No. of claims
Austin Airframes and Engines	7
Daimler Co Ltd No. 2 Engines	15
Ford Motor Co Ltd Engines	6
Machine Products Ltd	1
Rootes Airframes, Speke	11
Rover No. 1 and No. 2 Engines	24
Standard No. 1 Engines and Carburettors	9
Vickers Armstrong (Blackpool)	3
Vickers Armstrong (Chester)	3
Total	79

Figure 4.5 Third party insurance claims for the year ended 31st March 1941.[19]

Under normal circumstances, motor accidents by a company was just a normal fact of life. Accidents happen. However, the situation is more complex when the vehicles are provided as free issue vehicles from central government!

18th August 1941

Shadow Factories Insurance of vehicles

A difficult position is arising owing to the fact that shadow factories taking delivery of free issue vehicles are receiving instructions from you that such vehicles must be fully insured under a comprehensive insurance policy. On the other hand, the instructions of this branch, which is responsible for the administration of all shadows, are to the effect that the shadow vehicles must be insured against third party risks only. This decision is in accordance with the shadow memorandum of insurance approved by the Treasury as applicable to shadow factories. We have no doubt that you have good reasons for your instructions, but as all instructions concerning insurance matters of policy generally should be given by this branch we would appreciate it if you kindly set out the reasons why free issue vehicles should be treated otherwise than those purchased ex imprest, so that we may be able to amend our own policy should it be decided that this is necessary.

We think that you will agree that receiving contradictory instructions from two branches of this Ministry is not helpful to shadow managers, nor is it desirable from our own internal administrative point of view.

PS14[20]

The problem of insurance was not resolved, as further correspondence was generated some two years later!

3rd November 1943

Notice to managers of MAP Shadow Factories No 20

Sir,
I am directed to inform you that in view of the special circumstances represented in your letters of the 8th March 1943 and 4th August 1943, no objection is raised to your proposals viz that the Company and managers, or the shadow factories under their management, should take out a comprehensive policy of insurance covering all risks (other than Kings Enemy Risks) to materials other than embodiment loan or contract loan material issued by those shadow factories or their sub-contractors. The policy should, however, exclude from insurance or cover, materials issued to any of the sub-contractors named in appendix (a) to *Notice to Managers of Shadow Factories No 20*, and should also exclude materials issued to other MAP shadow factories. As soon as such insurance cover has been effected the conditions attaching to all the existing relevant sub-contracts should...[21]

During all of the discussions concerning many standard financial issues, some of which are mentioned above, the shadow factories continued production. With time it became possible to compare the costs of producing identical products from several sources.

Comparison of cost of production of supplies obtained at contract and at
Shadow Factories

1.   Comparisons are now available of the costs of several shadow factories engaged on the manufacture of products which are also obtained by the Department under contract from the professional industry. The shadow factories are built, equipped and managed by firms who are responsible for the engagement of executive staff and all grades of workpeople. The circumstances attendant on the establishment of the shadow factories necessitated that the bulk of the workpeople had to be specially trained for the type of work in their new employment.

2.   In presenting the comparative costs of shadow and contract supplied, the contract prices have been adjusted to exclude the assessed profit and the overhead costs which are not applicable to shadow production. In connection with the latter it should be noted that the costs of Shadow production do not include any sums for rent, the amortisation of capital assets and the repairs to buildings. Further, the design of the product to be manufactured is supplied to the managing firm and there are also many overhead expenses normally incurred by commercial firms and recovered in their overhead charges which do not arise at shadow factories. Such expenses for example are those relating to advertisement, development and drawing office, director's fees and sales organisation.

3.   The contract prices were, with few exceptions, negotiated following estimates by the Department's Technical Costs Officers and investigations by the Department's accountants of the overhead expenses of the several firms.

4.   The following schedules are presented below:

    A.   Comparison of costs of Blenheim aeroplanes produced by the Bristol Co, AV Roe and Rootes Securities Ltd (shadow) (Figures 4.6, 4.7 and 4.8).

    B.   Comparison of costs of Battle aeroplanes produced by the Fairey Aviation Co. and the Austin Motor Co Ltd (shadow) (Figures 4.9 and 4.10).

    C.   Comparison of costs of Wellington bombers produced by Vickers-Armstrongs Ltd (Weybridge – parent company), and Vickers-Armstrongs (Chester – shadow factory) (Figures 4.11 and 4.12).

Bristol Aeroplane Co. Blenheim production

	Short Nose			Long Nose	
Quantity	150	250	250	68	220
Cost	£8,424	£5,741	£5,408	£5,793	£5,775
Adjustment for overheads	£669	£279	£235	£235	£220
Cost for comparison with shadow factory	£7,755	£5,462	£5,173	£5,558	£5,555

Notes:
i.   First contract (150) on an ascertained cost basis. Other contracts on basic costs.
ii. Costs of jigs and tools £420,379.
iii. Estimated final output 1,000 aeroplanes of which 938 supplied to the Air Ministry.

Figure 4.6   Cost of Blenheim aeroplanes made by Bristol Aeroplane Co.

AV Roe and Co. Blenheim production

	Short Nose		Long Nose	
Quantity	30	220	100	62
Price	£9,754	£7,175	£7,200	£6,950
Assessed profit	£630	£469	£470	£455
Adjustment of overheads	£377	£359	£355	£355
Cost for comparison with shadow factory	£8,747	£6,347	£6,375	£6,140

Notes:
i. Cost of jig and tools £268,451 to date.
ii. Estimated final output 1,575 aeroplanes.

Figure 4.7   AV Roe and Co. 414 Blenheim aeroplanes (contract production).

Rootes Securities Ltd Blenheim shadow factory production

	Short Nose		Long Nose	
Quantity	50	116	278	157
Cost	£11,580	£6,844	£6,123	£6,332

Notes:
i.   Type long nose after the 250th aeroplane.
ii. Cost of jigs and tools £820,000.
iii. Estimated final output 3,430 aeroplanes.

Figure 4.8   Rootes Securities Ltd, Speke Blenheim aircraft (shadow) production.

Fairey Aviation Co Ltd Battle production

Quantity	10	49	96	309	345	132	200
Price	£21,360	£8,448	£7,250	£6,600	£5,675	£5,625	£5,640
Profit	£1,468	£471	£657	£477	£370	£318	£319
Overheads (10%)	£1,807	£564	£374	£300	£213	£212	£253
Net comparable cost	£18,085	£7,413	£6,219	£5,823	£5,092	£5,095	£5,068

Average cost of the first 128, £7,703.
Average cost of the next 760, £5,430.
Notes:
i.   Cost of jigs and tools, £431,621.
ii. Estimated final output, 1,153 aeroplanes.

Figure 4.9 Fairey Aviation Co Ltd Battle production.

Austin Motor Co Ltd shadow factory production.

Quantity	128	160
Price	£10,845	£5,349

Notes:
i.   Cost of jigs and tools, £775,580.
ii. Estimated final output 1,263 aeroplanes.[22]

Figure 4.10 Austin Motor Co Ltd shadow factory production.

Vickers-Armstrongs Ltd (Weybridge – parent company).
Price of 180 Wellington Bombers
(omitting the first aeroplane).

Quantity	20	20	139
Price			£15,250
Cost	£25,190	£17,885	
Profit	–	–	£1050
Overheads	£3,090	£1,447	£1,152
Comparable cost	£22,100	£16,438	£13,048

Note:
Cost of jigs and tools £525,821. Estimated final output 1,780 aeroplanes.

Figure 4.11 Costs of Wellington bombers made at the Vickers-Armstrongs parent company.

Vickers-Armstrongs Ltd (Chester – shadow factory).

Quantity	20	30
Cost	£20,244	£17,528

Notes:
i.   The whole of production is subcontracted and the shadow factory is concerned only with the assembly of components, and erection and test.
ii.   Overheads include all preliminary expenses.[23]

Figure 4.12 Cost of Wellington bombers made at the Vickers-Armstrongs shadow factory in Chester.

The Bristol Blenheim has not been mentioned so far. Figure 4.13 shows one of the surviving airplanes and is in the RAF Museum at Hendon. The information board at RAF Hendon documents some interesting facts about it.

The Blenheim IV, with its redesigned longer nose, superseded the Blenheim I on the production lines in 1938. The original short-nose Blenheim I had been developed from a civil aircraft and was one of the first new high performance monoplanes ordered under the RAF expansion plans.

Figure 4.13 Bristol Blenheim. (Author's photograph)

After the fighting in France was over, Coastal and Bomber Command Blenheim IVs began day and night attacks against German-occupied ports and installations in frantic attempts to disrupt their invasion plans. These attacks continued through into 1941 and on 4 July Wing Commander H I Edwards was awarded the Victoria Cross for his part in a daylight bombing attack on Bremen while flying a Blenheim IV.

A number of night fighter conversions were made from early Blenheim Is and later Blenheim IVs, but their lack of speed precluded any success.[24]

Finally, at least for the financial aspects of running shadow factories, the issue of contributions to the War Fund was mentioned. A creative solution was proposed!

16th February 1945

To: F W Neden
Ministry of Aircraft Production

Dear Mr Neden,
I have received your letter dated 14th February from which I learn that MAP cannot make any contributions to the Shadow Factories' War Fund to enable payment to be continued to ex-members of the shadow factories now in the Forces.

I would, however, submit for your consideration the suggestion that we be permitted to use the balances of the Canteen Profit and Loss Accounts for the benefit of these employees.

I await the result of your consideration with interest.

Yours sincerely,
H H Norcross[25]

Management Fees and Bonus Schemes

I mentioned in the introduction the natural business stance of the motor industrialists was to run their businesses on a solid commercial basis. The issue of management fees earned for running their respective shadow factories was no exception.

11th January 1936

Management fee Bristol Aeroplane Co Ltd

Colonel Disney asked the Committee to recommend a date from which the management fee payable to the Bristol Aeroplane Co. should be paid.

The Secretary was instructed to write to the Air Ministry confirming the Chairman's recommendations that the management fee should be paid to the Bristol Aeroplane Co. as from 1st July 1936.[26]

The above letter was written at the start of the negotiations to create the shadow factory scheme. The amount payable to the members of the No. 1 Engine Group were documented in a letter later that year.

8th October 1936

The Chairman reported that the Air Ministry had agreed to the Committee's request for the division of the total amount of the management fee to be divided between the six firms instead of the original seven. The Committee then agreed that the total annual management fee of £140,000 should be divided as follows (Figure 4.14).

Shadow Factory	Amount
Austin Motor Co Ltd	£24,000
Standard Motor Co Ltd	£24,000
Rover Co Ltd	£24,000
Daimler Co Ltd	£24,000
Rootes Ltd	£24,000
Bristol Aeroplane Co Ltd	£20,000

Figure 4.14 Annual management fee for No. 1 Engine Group.[27]

The management remuneration to other shadow factories continued in the same way, for example:

11th April 1940

To: DFC

The shadow factory, Bristol No 3, the subject of this agreement, is designed to produce 400 Hercules engines a month.

The factory is estimated to cost approximately £4.5m. I understand that the cost of a Hercules engine is about £2,150 but on large production may fall to £1,800 and by the elimination of overheads not applicable to shadow factories to £2,500-£2,200. A factor in the No 3 shadow factory is that it is planned on the basis of American methods of production with the use of labour saving machine tools, and that with this objective about $0.8 m have been spent on American machine tools.

For the moment I think we can confine ourselves to the question of payments to the Bristol Company. Clause 6 provides that the company shall do their best to equip the factory within twenty four months, but it is anticipated that the factory will produce engines before the end of 1940 and will be in full production in July or August, 1941.

Under clause 19 the company propose architect's fee equal to 2% of the total cost of the factory building with work services. This is estimated at £1,387,930 of which 2% is about £27,750 which is in itself very reasonable. The proposals as to fees are:

i.   For the first year – £75,000.
ii.   For the second year and subsequently – £50,000, plus a fixed bonus of £75 in respect of each engine and a proportionate bonus in respect of spare parts.

Assuming that expectations are realised we may regard the erection period as amounting to one year only and the payment for erection as such would amount to £102,750. On full production the fee would amount to £410,000 and since the second year might stretch from first production to full production we might put the fee for that year at £250,000. All this without any incentive for savings. I understand that D of C (A) has these terms under separate consideration and that the matter is to be discussed with Bristols on Friday the 18th April. It will no doubt be considered in relation to the Ford and Napier proposals although the attitude of Bristols will be coloured by their previous experience of shadow fees. The first year's fee, i.e. the erection fee of £75,000, might, in my judgement, be reduced justifiably to £50,000. The fees for the remaining years seem much too high, particularly as they can be achieved without any incentive for savings.

You may wish to discuss with D of C(A).
S Robinson
F8[28]

There were still issues with the bonus system in May 1941.

16th May 1941

The problem of bonus payments to staffs at shadow factories, reviewed in Mr Morley's memorandum, attacks us in the now familiar two-pronged movement:

i.   What is to be our reply to an enquiry from a managing firm as to our attitude on a particular point? and
ii.   What restraint are we to attempt to place upon the judgement of the individual companies who may apply to the shadow factory the system which they accept in their own factories?

On this point it should be remembered that it is desirable that staffs should be interchangeable, it is important that no obstacle should be placed in the way of the detachment from the parent works of their key staff to the shadow, and it is impossible at the present juncture to stabilise conditions in the parent works. These display the utmost variety and every conceivable approach is made in the various parent works towards the problem.

Some award bonuses in well regulated form, others award them by special consideration of individual cases and individual merits. Some regard special payments to senior staff as derogatory, others regard them as essential. Broadly, staff may be said that the basic salary is regarded as the appropriate salary but that companies will prefer to grant increases by way of bonus, rather than by way of definite increases of salary, in order to preserve, as well as may be, the fabric of peace time scales of salary.

As regards the past I feel that broadly we must accept what has been done, and to that extent, we are prejudiced in dealing with the future. As Mr Morley suggests, consultation with Contracts may strengthen our hands on some occasions, but since the award of bonus may in some cases be regarded as payment by the company concerned out of enhanced profits, the fact that a particular bonus may be refused admission to overheads in commercial operation may not enable us to refuse to admit it as a charge against the shadow factory.

As regards the individual classes, I suggest:

1. War Bonuses.
    For the reasons given above we must accept in the shadow the war bonus system accepted in the parent works unless the shadow may be regarded as divorced from the parent works. If, however, we are asked for guidance, we should, as Mr Morley suggests, deprecate the payment of war bonuses to those who require more than £600 a year.
2. Periodic or Festival Bonus.
    This should be admitted only when the practice of the parent firm, or the practice of the district in which the shadow factory is situated, compels it. The case mentioned by Mr Morley is probably to be regarded as a commuted form of production or merit bonus the amount of which was determined by the Board of the company concerned in the light of the work done by the staff in question during the preceding year.
3. Production Bonus.
    This is the most complex. Again, if we are consulted I think that we should deprecate the payment unless dictated by the practice of the industry or parent firm. These bonuses are in some cases related to avoidance of waste, to economy of production and to other factors. Its operation is more difficult because of the accidental factors of war damage, shortage of materials and

the like. As Mr Morley says, we should aim to secure that the extension of the capacity of the factory, whether by physical extension, by straight production or by more frequent shifts does not allow the bonus to run into outrageous figures.

S Robinson
PS14[29]

So the decisions in 1936 cast a long shadow, so to speak, on the issue of a bonus culture throughout the lifetime of the scheme.

5

Building Work

Aircraft Factories

The factory at Speke is of interest for several reasons not least of which is this book cover is of the inside of the factory when in production.

28th April 1937

To: Treasury Solicitor

Speke Shadow Factory Liverpool

Arrangements have been made for the establishment of a shadow factory at Speke, Liverpool, to be managed by Messrs. Rootes in lieu of the one which was contemplated at White Waltham.

The land on which this factory is to be erected is owned by the Liverpool Corporation and the term on which the land is to be acquired by the Air Ministry are based on the recommendation of the Property Committee of Liverpool Corporation, set out in enclosure 4E which recommendations were confirmed at a special meeting of the City Council on 12th February 1937.

A draft contract has been submitted by the Town Clerk of Liverpool which is enclosed together with the form of the lease and the plan. The following observations arise on the draft contract:

a. The agreement will be entered into by the Secretary of State for Air.
b. The area of 97.23 acres and the price of £250 per acre are agreed. Much as we dislike it, the lease for 999 years is also agreed.
c. We do not propose to pay a deposit.
d. We agree that the lease shall commence as from 15th February 1937, the date on which possession of the site was handed over.

Signed
W6[1]

There are many such examples, especially in the early days of the shadow scheme. The factory at Preston was accompanied by an airfield which is still in use today. Further discussions concerning airfields appear below as several units built as part of shadow factories are still in use.

8th August 1938

To: S9

In recent meetings of the Air Council Sub-committee on Supply the possibility of placing orders with English Electric Company of Preston for the manufacture of Hampdens, and subsequently a larger type, has been considered. The scheme involves, amongst other things, erecting a shed on an aerodrome in close proximity to the works at Preston. I understand there is a municipal aerodrome in the making at Preston, which is to serve Blackpool and Preston. Will you find out from DGCAs Department if there will be any objection to the Air Ministry building an erecting shed of some 100,000 sq. ft. and to the firm using the aerodrome for test flying and delivery. I would also like to know when it is estimated the aerodrome will be ready for use.

AMSO[2]

In some cases, there was a need to extend existing factories which did not involve buying land. Figure 5.1 details the costs for two of the Rolls-Royce sites.

8th December 1938

Gentlemen,

Rolls-Royce shadow factories

I am commanded by the Air Council to refer to the extensions to your productive capacity at Derby and Crewe which are being carried out at public expense and to recent interviews with your representatives and to convey to you the formal approval of the Council to proceed with the erection of the buildings and of the provision of services detailed below in accordance with the plans and specifications submitted to the Department and within the maximum expenditure indicated.

Derby		Work	Amount (£)
	Buildings	New pattern shop	12,772
Crewe			
	Roads	Drains, fencing, car park, surfacing etc.	24,700
	Buildings	Main shop including extra work due to ponds discovered while levelling	108,100
		Annexes to main shop	10,965
		Eight test beds	14,000
		Compound wall round test beds	3,850
		Paving inside compound	3,000
		Canteen	10,000
		Works auxiliary building	4,800
		Main office block	31,711
		Stores building	16,380
		Hardening swarf, etc. lean-to	17,940
		Boiler house	7,500
		Covered ways	7,020
		Meter houses	600
		Services to above	81,000

Figure 5.1 Cost of building extensions for two Rolls-Royce sites.

2. Should it be desired to modify the plans and specifications as now approved the prior concurrence of the Council should be sought before any commitments are entered into.

3. I am also to refer to your letter of the 13th October 1938 in amplification of your letter of 7th September 1938 and to inform you that the Council have no objection to your proposals as to dispensing with competitive tendering detailed in the former letter in regard to:

   a. The provision of lighting and heating for the pattern shop, aluminium foundry and the hardening shop at Derby.

   b. The aluminium foundry re-arrangement; the pattern shop and the alterations to test beds.

   c. Preparation of the site of the pattern shop.

The Council will require, however, that you should give the necessary facilities for a post audit of the expenditure to be carried out should they so desire.

1. As regards installation charges for plant and machinery these should be dealt with in accordance with paragraph 10 of the *Notes on Procedure* forwarded under cover of Air Ministry letter of 9th September 1938.

2. A separate communication has been addressed to you in regard to the sched-
    ules of plant and equipment which will not be covered by works contracts
    forwarded to the Department under cover of your letter of the 5th November
    1938.

I am, Gentlemen,
Your obedient servant
W L Scott[3]

In most cases, the decision to build a factory, acquiring the land and undertaking
the necessary building work took a relatively short time. Sadly the Rootes Securities
shadow factory at Stoke took considerably longer. A long table (Figure 5.2) has been
reproduced in full so that the interested reader can appreciate some of the issues were
complex needing resolution by several interested parties. It is also interesting to note
the cost of the scheme.

Rootes Securities – AV Roe & Co Shadow Factory at Stoke

Date (dd/mm/yy)	
22/9/39	Proposal to erect a shadow factory at Stoke-on-Trent, using Aerodrome at Meir. Area 1,200,000 sq. ft. Day shift 10,000 people. Production, one Halifax per day. Est. cost £1,250,000–£1,500,000
29/9/39	Reported that Supply Board approved that Handley Page should be authorised to prepare plans for shadow factory in collaboration with Briggs Motor Bodies Ltd which should have the status of subcontractor to Handley Page, and would not require financial assistance
11/10/39	Proposal to erect factory in two units 1. South of Stoke 5 miles from the aerodrome (Newstead Farm) (300,000 sq. ft.). 2. On SE side of aerodrome, on site of proposed aircraft repair depot (900,000 sq. ft.).
25/10/39	Proposal that ⅓ of factory should be allocated to Briggs and ⅔ should be adjacent to aerodrome. Handley Page authorised to negotiate with Stoke City Council regarding use of aerodrome and adjoining sites (terms of proposed agreement are stated)
12/10/39	Treasury approval to erect factory at £1,500,000

Date (dd/mm/yy)	
4/11/39	Brochure estimate: a. Main building – £500,000. b. Services – £70,000. c. Levelling, roads, drains, etc. – £125,000. d. Subsidiary buildings – £80,000. e. ARP – £75,000. f. Plant – £325,000. Total – £1,175,000.
9/11/39	Reports of brochure meeting. Note: 1. It was stated that the brochure related only to the Handley Page factory. 2. Proposed to use materials already fabricated, for Briggs, at Newstead Farm. 3. Estimated total cost £1,500,000.
9/11/39	ACCS: 1. Approved proposal for erection of one factory at Stoke for Handley Page, subject to CAS approval (previously two units, apart from Briggs factory, had been considered). 2. DAMF to consider whether steelwork for Abbotsinch factory (near Glasgow airport) could best be utilised in factory at Newstead Farm. 3. Received information of facilities granted by Stoke City Council.
10/11/39	CAS agreed to erection of one large factory for Handley Page
23/11/39	ACCS authorisation for production of jigs and tools
23/11/39	Note of meeting to discuss: 1. Extension of aerodrome. 2. Brochure for Briggs factory at Newstead Farm. Reported that steelwork for Abbotsinch factory would not be used as it would be unduly expensive
29/11/39	Estimate for Briggs factory at Newstead Farm i. Buildings – £190,000. ii. Plant – £350,000. iii. Land – provided by Stoke Corporation. Briggs Motor Bodies Ltd not prepared to finance cost of factory
9/12/39	Letter approval in principle for the Handley Page factory at £1,175,000. Authority to proceed with works services as items 1–4 of brochure
5/1/40	Letter to Handley Page defining terms and conditions for management of the factory
8/1/40	Report to ACCS on progress of Stoke factory
15/1/40	Meeting with Handley Page. Reported: 1. Staffs CC would probably undertake widening of the road. 2. Stoke Corporation agreed to extend aerodrome at their own expense.
17/1/40	Handley Page declines to accept terms proposed for management of factory
24/1/40	Letter from Handley Page stating that they are unable to undertake management of the Stoke factory, as their resources, particularly of personnel, are insufficient

Date (dd/mm/yy)	
2/2/40	ACCS note that Handley Page are unwilling to undertake management of the Stoke factory
17/2/40	Handley Page report expenses incurred, to date, with references to Stoke factory ACCS considered possibility of transferring management of the Stoke factory to 1. English Electric Co. 2. General Electric Company.
29/3/40	Neither EEC nor GEC able to undertake management. Hawker Siddeley approached
11/4/40	ACCS discussion re: 1. Management of factory. 2. Possibility of producing Albermarle instead of Halifax planes.
15/4/40	Discussion with Hawker Siddeley and AV Roe & Co. regarding management of factory
19/4/40	AMF1 report of meeting with AV Roe regarding construction of Stoke factory
23/4/40	F7(c) report on financial aspect of Stoke factory. AV Roe estimate for construction of factory, with modifications, £1,095,000 against Handley Page estimate of £1,175,000. Further saving proposed on electricity supply
23/4/40	Statement of further consequences of revised plans: 1. Briggs factory at Newstead Farm (estimate £540,000) would not be needed for this scheme. 2. Production would be greater although for different type of aircraft.
13/4/40	ACCS requests Handley Page to report regarding second-hand plant which they had been authorised to purchase for the Stoke factory
1/5/40	Stated that Handley Page had ordered no plant for the Stoke plant
30/4/40	AV Roe state that, in principle, they are prepared to undertake management of the factory. Letter details proposed terms and modifications to buildings etc. They estimate £350,000 for main building against £500,000 estimate by Handley Page
9/5/40	AV Roe's revised Brochure for Stoke factory: 1. Works and services – £636,830. 2. Plant excluding installation – £345,100. 3. General equipment – £45,100. 4. Subsidiary buildings – £55,500. 5. Flight shed – £60,000. 6. Contingencies – £45,701. 7. ARP and camouflage – £49,000. 8. Fees – £37,616. Total – £1,274,847 + £5,000 for excavation of flight shed

Date (dd/ mm/yy)	
11/5/40	ASB approved: 1. That AV Roe should produce Albemarles at Stoke factory. 2. Should discuss brochure which had been submitted.
12/5/40	ASB agreed that the future of Briggs factory should be treated as a separate issue
13/5/40	Letter of approval in principle for factory, as items 1–8 of brochure (plus £5,000 for excavation of flight shed). Total excluding item 9 of brochure – £1,242,231
17/5/40	ASB informed AV Roe insisted upon abandonment of Briggs factory at Stoke in view of the labour situation
10/5/40	Report of meeting with AV Roe re erection and management fee
25/5/40	Reported to ASB that it was necessary to proceed with 'Briggs Bodies' scheme, but this should not be at Stoke
Discussion whether Stoke factory should be abandoned	
8/7/40	Proposal to complete part of the factory, for which steel had been fabricated
13/7/40	Report of a meeting to discuss whether Stoke factory should be continued
13/7/40	Report of meeting to consider commitments already incurred and what would be involved if the factory were abandoned partly constructed or wholly constructed

Figure 5.2 The protracted discussion regarding a factory at Stoke.[4]

As we saw in an earlier chapter, eventually a system was agreed to cope with sales of components from one shadow factory to another. That was not the end of the story concerning inter-factory transfers as there were instances, particularly during the construction of a site or during a change of site use, when equipment surplus to requirements was transferred from one factory to another.

13th February 1940

The Austin Motor Co Ltd (Aero Works)

To: Director of Aircraft Production Air Ministry

Dear Sir,

Warwick Shadow Factory

After the 1938 crisis, anodic treatment of sheet metal work was discontinued on 'Battle'. We removed about half of our plant, which has since been stored in our yard.

For the 'Beaufighter' which the Austin Motor Co. (parent factory) are starting to manufacture, certain anodic plant is required.

It will be a great convenience if some of the redundant plant, list attached, could be transferred to the parent company.

We understand this part of the Austin activity is considered to be part of the Warwick Shadow Factory so that the transfer will only be a book transaction.

This plant will not be required for Stirlings.

Mr Lord discussed the matter with Mr Lemon on Friday afternoon last, and it is understood that he agreed to the transfer.

Yours faithfully
The Austin Motor Company Limited[5]

One of the requirements for buying land was that there are sufficient services able to cope with the high demands readily available. Whilst this was often the case there were examples where there were potential problems.

25th April 1940

To: Sir Arthur Street,
Air Ministry
Dear Street,

Electricity supply to vital establishments and new factories

The Electricity Commissioners are concerned at the arrangements (or perhaps lack of arrangements) for consultation between them and the Service Departments, the Ministry of Supply and the Office of Works concerning the provision of supplies of electricity to new Government factories, and the safe-guarding of supplies to other industrial establishments whose operations are of vital importance in time of war.

Since the outbreak of war, the Commissioners have been consulted by the Ordnance Factory Department of the Ministry of Supply and occasionally by the Service Departments on questions concerning the provision of supplies of electricity to certain new factories and the terms and conditions on which the supplies could be obtained.

There have, however, been many cases where the Departments have not considered it necessary to consult the Commissioners, while other cases have only come to the Commissioners' notice after a decision has been reached to establish a factory at a particular place and after difficulties have arisen either as to terms or on other aspects of the matter. Difficulties have already arisen in South Wales owing to the preference shown by the Departments for new factories in this area, the prospective demand for power being in excess of the plant capacity available.

These difficulties are likely to increase and similar ones will arise in other areas unless early steps are taken to bring about closer co-ordination of planning and action between the various Departments and branches thereof.

With the great expansion of requirements which has taken place, it has obviously been difficult for those concerned in the provision of new factories for particular purposes to keep in touch with the activities of other Departments, or even of different branches of their own Departments. As a result, new factories involving large supplies of electricity are still being contemplated in areas where surplus capacity of generating plant is already largely, if not entirely, absorbed by the factories in course or erection. The Commissioners feel strongly that greater uniformity should be possible in the terms and conditions upon which the Departments are obtaining supplies than has at present been achieved as the result of their independent and unrelated negotiations.

The Commissioners accordingly suggest that there should be a small co-ordinating committee of representatives of all the Departments concerned in the erection of new factories or the extension of existing factories for which additional supplies of electricity will be required.

The Deputy Chairman of the Commissioners would be prepared to act as chairman of this committee which would meet at the Commissioner's offices in Savoy Court, Strand, and the Commissioners themselves would arrange for the necessary secretarial work.

I should be glad if you would consider the forgoing and let me know at your early convenience whether you agree with the Commissioners' suggestions, and would like to be represented on the proposed co-ordinating committee.

I have written in similar terms to the other two Service Departments, Ministry of Supply and the Office of Works.

Yours sincerely[6]

The slow build-up of the shadow scheme prior to the outbreak of war was in some ways a false dawn of the scale of factories built during the war. There were several factors influencing the speed of progress. One factor undoubtedly related to the drive for and then maintaining air superiority, another was the larger number of casualties leading to aircraft needing rebuilding or complete replacement. Additionally, there were ever increasing theatres of war needing air support. There was much to do, in part reflected in the aircraft program, Figure 5.3, which was just one of many programs.

11th September 1941

Ministry of Aircraft Production Requirements to carry out current target aircraft program of 11th September 1941 – buildings, machine tools and other plant

	Buildings		Machine tools		Other plant	
	Factory floor space in sq. ft.	Cost to complete (£)	Number still to be installed	Cost (£)	Cost (£)	Total cost (£)
Projects under construction at 11th Sept 1941						
a) Space not allocated to specific projects (principally underground).	2,590,000	2,474,000				
b) Satellite landing grounds and runways at aircraft storage units.		1,410,000				
c) Housing schemes		5,506,000				
d) General factory projects		9,212,000				
Total cost to complete		18,602,000	12,000	9,000,000	7,500,000	35,102,000
Projects not commenced at 11th September 1941						
Principal aircraft factory extensions	445,000	668,000	920	690,000	138,000	
Aircraft sub-contractors			600	450,000	90,000	
Engine works	30,000	45,000	120	90,000		
Engine accessories other than airscrews	45,000	68,000	480	360,000		
Airscrews	423,000	634,000	3,000	2,250,000	560,000	
Armaments	400,000	600,000	850	638,000	250,000	
Aircraft equipment	285,000	428,000	500	375,000	172,000	
Fabrication of materials	280,000	417,000	60	44,000	737,000	

	Buildings		Machine tools		Other plant	
Ammonia for bombs (for Ministry of Supply)					600,000	
Repair of engines and airscrews	135,000	205,000	10	8,000	173,000	
Repair of airframes	4,000,000	4,500,000			278,000	
Radio equipment	900,000	1,350,000	1,000	750,000	1,000,000	
Gas producer plant					500,000	19,068,000
Grand total (exclusive of addi- tion housing requirements)		27,517,000	19,540	14,655,000	11,998,000	54,170,000
Additional housing requirements						
Estimate in terms of para- graph 8 of the memorandum		16,000,000				16,000,000
Grand total of all projects		43,517,000				70,170,000

Figure 5.3 Some building costs.[7]

The speed at which these factories were erected must have stretched the building trade. In August 1940, a part of the Vickers-Armstrong Ltd shadow factory in Blackpool collapsed. It was not until six years later, however, the matter reached resolution.

17th October 1946

To: JD Jamieson
Ministry of Supply

Dear Mr Jamieson,
Thank you for your letter of the 15th instant confirming that a settlement of the Crown claims in connection with the collapse at Blackpool Works in August 1940 has been reached.

On examining the copy of the account which has been rendered by Sir Owen Williams for the fees due to him in respect of work carried out under his supervision, it would appear that he has omitted to include the following items of expenditure:

a.   Matron Sub-Station, £2,533.2s.3p.
b.   Work carried out at Messrs Burlinghams premises, £2,050.1s.4d.
c.   Cost of electric light and power installations for the dispersal depot, £18,716.8s.6d.

I have had a word with Mr Newman, the Quantity Surveyor, and he agrees with me that Sir Owen will be entitled to further fees for this expenditure. However, in view of the delay which has occurred in the clearing of his account of the 9th August, we are passing this on to Harrogate for payment with the request that it should be dealt with as soon as possible.

Yours sincerely.[8]

Airfields

I mentioned earlier in this chapter the need to build or extend some airfields some of which are still in use today in the civilian sector. The following details four such airfields, although the Leavesden airfield (North Watford) has since been converted into a film studio, see earlier comments.

20th April 1941

Proposals to construct runways at Brockworth, Elmdon, Ringway and Watford Aerodromes

1.   The necessity for constructing runways before next winter at those aerodromes where the flight testing and delivery of the new type of heavy bombers takes place has been under consideration recently, and a meeting was convened on the 4th April 1941, by the Chief Overseer to discuss this subject.
2.   The meeting after full consideration arrived at the following conclusions:
      i.   Necessary runways are already provided or are in hand at: Radlett, Samlesbury, Woodford, South Marston, Belfast and Yeadon.
      ii.   That runways should be constructed at the following aerodromes: Brockworth, Elmdon, Ringway and Watford.
3.   Brockworth aerodrome surface will not stand up to the severe wet periods, and difficulty was expressed in taking-off last winter; the surface is therefore unsuitable for the Stirling and Albemarle, except in good weather conditions. The construction of a single runway in the prevailing wind direction is therefore recommended.

4.   Elmdon aerodrome is used by Austins for the flight testing and delivery flights of the Stirling aircraft. A single runway in the direction of the prevailing wind is essential at this aerodrome and its construction is therefore recommended.

5.   Ringway aerodrome will be used by AV Roe for delivery flights of Manchesters and also by Faireys, Stockport, for the test flying and delivery of Halifax bombers. During winter in the Manchester area long periods of bad visibility are experienced and in consequence every short break in the weather has to be used for flight testing. It frequently happens that the wind is not in the direction prevailing for the district; during all these short breaks, therefore, one runway in the prevailing wind direction would not be adequate, and, in this instance, in view of the heavy traffic at this aerodrome, the construction of two runways is recommended.

6.   Watford aerodrome will be used for the flight testing and delivery of Halifax aircraft produced by London Aircraft Production and also probably as a dispersed aerodrome for Halifax aircraft produced by Handley Page. It is therefore recommended that a runway be constructed in the direction of the prevailing wind.

7.   It is proposed to leave DGAPF to decide whether tarmac or concrete should be used for the runways; the decision in each instance being arrived at after consideration of the local conditions etc. Only an approximate estimate of the cost can therefore be given at this stage which is as follows (Figure 5.4):

Brockworth	£45,000
Elmdon	£45,000
Ringway	£90,000
Watford	£45,000
Total	£225,000

Figure 5.4 Costs of some airfield runways

The approval of the Board is accordingly sought for this expenditure.
Note by DGAP[9]

The runway at Elmdon was subsequently extended.

30th May 1944

Air Supply Board
Austin Motor Co Ltd – Extension to runways at Elmdon

As the Board is aware, the Austin Motor Co. is going on to a program of Lancaster production including eventually the Mark IV. The first Lancaster has recently been flown at Elmdon, and the experience of that flight led to a general enquiry as to the possibility of extending the runways.

At present time there is an existing concrete runway SW-NE which is however, only 950 yards in length with poor approaches at the NE end.

There is also a runway 1,100 yards in length NW-SE which is in course of construction by the Air Ministry.

The site has been examined, and it is considered that the following improvements are necessary to enable the company to carry out their program:

1. An extension of approximately 400 yards at the NE end of the SW-NE runway, together with certain tree clearance to improve the approach at the SW end.
2. An extension of approximately 200 yards at the SE end of the NW-SE runway, together with a small amount of clearance and levelling at the NW end in order to improve the approach, and to provide a safety overrun for aircraft in case of necessity.
3. Two small connecting tracks from the main aprons to the runways.

The need for these works has been discussed with the firm's test pilots and the Overseer, and it has been agreed by all concerned that they are essential. The opinion of the Chief Test Pilot of AV Roe has also been obtained, and he too stresses the need for extensions to the Elmdon runways for flying Lancaster aircraft.

Elmdon is an RAF airfield, and the Air Ministry Works Directorate is at the moment in course of constructing the NW-SE runway. The proposed works will therefore be carried out by the Air Ministry, and after investigation they have submitted an overall estimate of £45,000.

The approval of the Board is accordingly asked for the above proposals and for the work to be put in hand immediately.

Note by DGAD[10]

Few museums are sufficiently large that they can store bombers for the public to view, an exception of which is the RAF Museum at Hendon in North West London (Figure 5.5).

It is difficult to appreciate the size of a Lancaster bomber unless you are able to see one. The information board at RAF Hendon has the following details of the Lancaster.

The industrial and military organisation needed to build and operate the Lancaster was huge. Six major companies built 7377 aircraft at ten factories on two continents; at the height of production over 1,100,000 men and women were employed working for over 920 companies. More service personnel were involved in flying and maintaining it than any other British aircraft in history...

Figure 5.5 Avro Lancaster bomber. (Author's photograph)

The Lancaster has a crew of 7, four 1280 hp Merlin XX or XXII engines, a span of 31 m, a length of 21.2 m and a normal loaded weight of 29,000 kg, which went up to 31,800 kg when loaded with 22,000 lb bombs.[11]

Unlike some of the shadow factories, those needing attached runways required large areas of land. The following, dated at a time when the earliest shadow factories were five–six years old, shows the change in attitude in buying land.

5th January 1943

Acquisition of Land (Defence) Bill your minute 30th December 1942

Apart from small cases where we should not want (or have already agreed not to try) to buy land, the serious cases are those of aerodromes.

In several cases of aerodromes belonging to local authorities (notably Speke (Liverpool), Renfrew and Meir (Stoke)), we have spent very considerable sums on the provision of runways, without being able to obtain from the local authority concerned any satisfactory 'residual value' arrangement. Although, if we had the power to do so, it is doubtful whether we should wish to acquire the freehold of an aerodrome at its unimproved value merely because we have put runways there, and, even if we did, political considerations might very well prevent the exercise of the power, it seems desirable that the right to purchase should, if possible, be secured as a bargaining factor.

The only other case of importance I can think of is the aerodrome at Leavesden, near Watford, where the bulk of the open area is on land dedicated as King George's Playing Fields. Here again, political pressure is likely to make the exercise of the power problematical, but it seems that it would be well to have it.

If it were clear that we should be able freely to use the powers when the time comes, there would be no doubt that we ought to take them now under the Bill. As, however, our ability to use the powers is doubtful, the question arises whether the effort to secure them is worthwhile. From the purely finance stand point, the answer still seems to be clear, viz, that we should attempt to obtain the powers; from the political stand point it might be argued that the political storm which might arise on the Bill would be too high a price to pay for the acquisition of a weapon of which we might be able to make little effective use.

PS7[12]

Aero Engines

The above building work has concentrated on the needs for the production of aircraft, the following are some examples of building works involving aero engines.

29th April 1938

Dear Mr Ledgard,

With reference to your letter of the 25th regarding certain items required for installation of Merlin engines, I took this matter up with the equipment people and have marked the list with the appropriate stores depot. The equipment people inform me that there should be no difficulty in obtaining early delivery of these items but should there be any delay please let me know and I will chase supply for you.

Regarding item 36DD 40001, RAE compressor drive assembly it is understood that at the moment this is not fitted on the Merlin and equipment people are awaiting a modification to determine what particular type of drive is to be fitted. Perhaps you will be good enough to have this checked up.

Regarding the AGS parts under reference 36DD 31900, priming pipes and supercharger and carburettors, these are normally contractors supply and possibly the installation operation sheets detail these as such. If this is so you will require a stock of these items for subsequent installations. If, however, these are not to be supplied by you, maybe you will be able to obtain by indenting on No 3 Stores Depot, Milton.

Your list duly marked up is returned herewith.[13]

Accommodation was a recurring theme with aero engine shadow factories, just as it was for airframes:

3rd November 1939

To: The Rt. Hon. Sir Kingsley Wood
Air Ministry

Dear Sir Kingsley,
I dare say that you will be interested to hear how we are getting on with the new factory at Hillington, near Glasgow. I enclose herewith a photograph which gives some idea of the position at the present time.

Taking all points into consideration, the project is proceeding very satisfactorily, we expect to commence installing machines in the first shop by the end of this month. There was some inevitable delay at the commencement of the war due to shortage of materials, but this has now been overcome, and thanks to the excellent weather they had in October, some of the delay has been made up.

We have taken several temporary premises and have a number of machine tools working in them training labour, we have also, by arrangement with the Glasgow Corporation, taken over the whole of the facilities at the Stowe Technical College for training.

There is one point, however, on which we may require your help, that is, on the question of houses. Glasgow and district are desperately short of houses. The Lord Provost Dollan estimated that they were 10–12,000 houses short before Rolls-Royce went to Hillington! We have had a meeting with the Lord Provost, Sir Steven Bilsland and the Commissioner for Special Areas on my visit to Glasgow last week.

They all appreciate the urgent necessity for the houses, and I am hoping that some satisfactory arrangement will be come to, without having to worry you, but if nothing happens I propose to write you and set out our case for houses.

There has been a very gratifying increase in our deliveries of Rolls-Royce engines since the commencement of the war, and we are looking forward to a further increase before the end of this year.

Yours sincerely[14]

Here is a further letter.

We spoke on the telephone today about the factory which is being established by Messrs Rolls-Royce for aircraft production at Hillington, Glasgow.

As I explained the factory will be situated in a Special Area, a short distance outside the limits of the city of Glasgow. The factory cannot function unless provision is made for housing on a substantial scale for the workers. Unassisted private enterprise cannot cope with this.

We have therefore to try to have houses put up by the government. Two alternative areas are in view.

A.   One within the city limits and already partly provided with roads and essential services with a view to a housing scheme the corporation hoped to put through with Ministry of Health assistance under the Slum Clearance and/or overcrowding provision. The estate was to be managed by the Scottish Special Housing Association, but is in abeyance through the outbreak of war and other causes.
B.   One within the Special Area, outside the city and at present virgin ground.

The following questions are submitted to you as a matter of urgency for an opinion from the legal standpoint.

1.   Would the Secretary of State be entitled under Section 51 of the Defence Act or otherwise, to take possession compulsorily of site A for houses for workers at the factory? You suggested informally that, assuming the factory to be broadly a 'government' one (which is the case) the wording of Section 51 probably does cover this power.
2.   Would the Secretary of State be entitled to take possession compulsorily of site B, and then to hand it over to the Special Area Commissioners for the erection of houses for the factory workers out of Special Area funds?
3.   If the answer to 2 is no, could the commissioners themselves acquire site B for this purpose, and are there any steps which could be taken to expedite their acquisition procedure under appendix 4 of the Special Areas Act, which I understand takes more time than we have available?
4.   As a further alternative, could the Commissioners, if agreeable, acquire the corporation housing area for us, bearing in mind that they are only empowered to carry on activities for the benefit of the Special Areas? Could it, for instance, be submitted that the purpose of the Special Areas are being served since a substantial number of the workers concerned may be recruited from those Areas?

Signed S W Warran
APS to the S of S

11th January 1940[15]

6

Research and Development

There are two engineers whose names spring to mind for their contribution to aircraft research and design and their components. R J Mitchell, for his innovative design of the Spitfire, and F Whittle FRS, for his invention of the jet engine.

The *Encyclopedia Britannica* entry for Reginald Joseph Mitchell reads as follows:

> British aircraft designer and developer of the Spitfire, one of the best-known fighters of the Second World War and a major factor in the British victory at the Battle of Britain. After secondary schooling Mitchell was an apprentice at a locomotive works and attended night classes at technical colleges. In 1916, before the age of 22, he went to work at Supermarine Aviation Works in Southampton, where he remained the rest of his life, serving as the company's director for his last 10 years. He designed seaplanes (used largely for racing) between 1922 and 1931 and by 1936 had designed and developed the Spitfire, more than two dozen versions of which were eventually created before and after his death and which was known for its aerodynamic sleekness and manoeuvrability.[1]

Tragically, Mitchell died in 1937 aged 42.

The RAF Museum at Hendon documents the full design team at the Supermarine Company as follows:

Supermarine Design Staff 1932–1945 Chief Designer's Office 1932–1937

- R J Mitchell – Director and Chief Designer.
- F Holroyd – Assistant Chief Designer.
- H J Payne – Technical Assistant.
- G Spencer – Office Administration.
- Miss V M Cross – Secretary.
- Miss B A Wood – Typist.

1937–1945

After the death of R J Mitchell in 1937 Joseph Smith was appointed Design Office Manager and subsequently became Chief Designer.

A N Clifton became Assistant Chief Designer whilst retaining his position as Chief Technician.

- J Smith – Chief Designer.
- A N Clifton – Assistant Chief Designer.
- A Millar – Secretary.

Test Pilots

- A Henshaw.
- G Pickering.
- J K Quill.
- G N Snare.
- J Summers.
- Wing Commander G Lowell.[2]

Joseph Smith and his team were an essential element in the strategy of the Air Ministry as they continued to develop the Spitfire throughout the war. The following report details some of the results of test flights. Of course, there are two obvious reasons for undertaking test flights, one as part of research and development and the other to test airworthiness of a production process. The comments below from Air Marshall Leigh-Mallory relate to the former. Some comments on test flights for airworthiness appear in Chapter 8.

10th October 1943

Spitfire Mk XIV To: The Under Secretary of State

Air Ministry ACAS
Whitehall

Sir,
I have the honour to refer to your letter dated 26th August 1943, and to state that I have again reviewed the development position of the Spitfire XIV. Trials, under CRD arrangements, have been made at Boscombe Down by the following three operationally experienced pilots:

i.   Group Captain J Rankin DSO DFC.
ii.   Wing Commander A V R Johnson DSO DFC.

iii.   Squadron Leader W A Laurie DFC.

The trials which lasted three days, took the form of a comparison between the Spitfire XIV and Spitfire VIII, in respect of fighting and handling qualities. A rough estimate of performance was made by flying one aeroplane against the other. It will be seen from the conclusions in both reports that the pilots have a very high opinion of the Spitfire XIV. This opinion was endorsed verbally by Squadron Leader Laurie. They consider that the problem of converting pilots from other marks of Spitfire would not present any major difficulty, and they would like to see the Spitfire XIV introduced into operational service as soon as practicable.

As regards performance, the results obtained by the pilots substantially bear out the estimates supplied by RDT, MAP. In round figures the Spitfire XIV appears to be 40 mph faster than the Spitfire VIII at all heights, while in climb the gain is of the order of 500 feet per min.

As regards handling, the effect of torque in take-off, and of variation in trim with change in engine power, were evident as in the Spitfire XIII, but the opinion was that pilots could soon accustom themselves to this. In point of suitability for tactical manoeuvre and fighting, the Spitfire XIV was in no way inferior to the Spitfire VIII, whereas it had the great advantage of higher performance.

There was a difference of opinion on the subject of aileron control. According to Wing Commander Johnson, the particular Spitfire tested was on the heavy side. It is believed however, that there is still considerable variation in the quality of aileron control in different aircraft of all marks of Spitfire. This question needs further attention and will be pursued separately. It is therefore not necessary to assume that on account of this criticism, Spitfire XIV ailerons will prove unsatisfactory.

From a study of the pilots' reports and discussion with them, I now adopt a more favourable view of the potential operational value of the Spitfire XIV. The increase in performance improved pilots' view, and promising handling characteristics, make it desirable that wider experience on this type under active operational conditions, Somerfelt tracks etc. should be acquired.

Consequently, provided that the operational endurance of the aircraft complies with the standard fighter specifications, and that adequate tools, repair facilities, and engine spares can be made available, I am in favour of production on a larger scale than specified in my letter of the 14th August 1943.

I should be glad to know how many aircraft of this type I can expect for the spring operations in 1944. The question of supercharger gear ratios has been dealt with separately in my letter of the 10th October 1943.

I have the honour to be Sir
Your Obedient Servant Leigh-Mallory
Air Marshall

Air Officer Commanding-in-Chief
Fighter Command[3]

All Spitfires were powered by Rolls-Royce engines. In most cases, they were powered by Merlin engines of various types; see Figure 8.11 in Chapter 8 for further details. However, some Spitfire marks used the Griffon engine (Figure 6.1).

This particular example is on display in the RAF Museum at Hendon, the information board for which reads:

> At the beginning of 1939, which was only 20 months after Whittle's first jet engine bench test, Rolls-Royce began development of the Griffon, their last piston engine to be produced in significant numbers.
>
> The engine was one of several developments which began with the earlier 1925 Buzzard and the 1931 racing 'R' series engine. In many ways it looked like a scaled up Merlin. The engine was made as compact as possible so that it could replace the Merlin in some aircraft.
>
> The Griffon was particularly successful in powering some of the later marks of Spitfire. With the addition of some advanced fuels Griffon-engined Spitfires were able to catch the small German V-1 flying bombs, although placing such a powerful engine in an airframe as small as the Spitfire resulted in some brutal handling characteristics.
>
> Later marks used by the RAF gave up to the equivalent of 29kN (653 lb) thrust at a time when jet engines could produce only half this power.
>
> This Griffon Mk 57A display engine came from an Avro Shackleton maritime reconnaissance aircraft. The last examples of this aircraft retired from RAF service in 1991, the engine having been in RAF service for forty-eight years.[4]

Fortunately, the RAF Museum at Hendon also has a Spitfire XIV on display which used a Griffon engine (Figure 6.2).

> The Mark XIV was the first full-scale production Spitfire to be powered by the Rolls-Royce Griffon engine, the 'big-brother' of the Merlin. With the Luftwaffe's introduction of the Focke Wulf Fw 190 in 1942 the RAF needed a more powerful engine for the Spitfires. The first Griffon engined Spitfire, the Mark XII, entered service in June 1943, but it was only ever an interim type, lacking performance at high altitude.
>
> Rolls-Royce focussed its efforts on refining the Griffon, whilst Supermarine modified a Spitfire Mark VIII airframe to accept the new engine. Trials were conducted early in 1943 and the new Mark XIV was approved that autumn, though further improvements to the Griffon delayed its introduction into service until January 1944.

Figure 6.1 Rolls-Royce Griffon engine. (Author's photograph)

The production FR XIVe variant had a cut down rear fuselage with a bubble canopy, greatly improving the pilot's view, port and starboard camera ports, an additional rear fuel tank, and clipped wing tips for improved roll-control at low altitude. The FR XIVe proved a successful fighter and ground attack aircraft performing armed reconnaissance operations over northwest Europe in the last year of the war.[5]

Such was the activities at Rolls-Royce that over 3,400 people were employed on research and development. This report of a visit to the Rolls-Royce factory has more details.

24th July 1943

Reference: visit to Rolls-Royce on 23rd July 1943
Rolls-Royce Merlin and Griffon Engines

Visits were made with Lt. Colonel Hitchcock to the Rolls-Royce installation and power plant establishment at Hucknall and to the Rolls-Royce factory at Derby to discuss Merlin and Griffon engine developments. Discussions were held with the following (Figure 6.3):

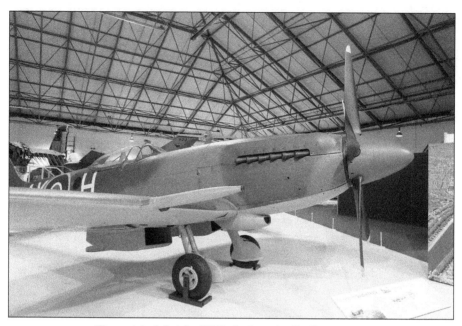

Figure 6.2 A Spitfire XIV which used a Griffon engine.

Location	Discussions held with	Position
Huchnall	Mr Dorey	Manager
Derby	Mr Sidgreaves	Managing Director
	Mr Swift	Manager – Aero Production
	Mr Hives	Director and General Manager
	Mr Lovesey	Chief Experimental Engineer
	Mr Morris	Fuel Engineer
	Mr Reed	Chief – Engine Performance Section

Figure 6.3 List of people visited at Roll-Royce.

At Hucknall we were shown the mock-up of the Rolls-Royce fighter proposal with a Mustang wing and a Griffon engine mounted back of the pilot, similar to the Bell Aero-Cobra. We also saw the Griffon powered Spitfire with the 5 bladed propeller (Hydulignum) and were told that changes were being made to the vertical tail surfaces of this airplane to improve stability.

At Derby Messrs Hives and Lovesey described the development of the Merlin 66 which has passed special category acceptance tests at 2040 hp at 3,000 rpm at 25 lbs boost, and the Merlin 14SM which has passed a 15 minute combat period bench test at 2,300 hp at 3,300 rpm at 30 lbs boost. The Merlin 66 tests were run with 100 octane fuel to which 5½ cc of tetra-ethyl lead per imperial gallon have been added (making a total of 11 cc per gallon) and the 14SM tests were run with 140 grade fuel (OPC3) and extra tetra-ethyl lead.

Mr Hives mentioned the urgent need for a supply of improved fuel to make it possible to operate at these higher powers with the Merlin, particularly in fighter aircraft, and stated that the practical limitation of the Merlin 66 with the presently available 100 octane fuel is 1,750 hp at 18 lbs boost. The engine dry weight at this rating is about 0.95 lbs per brake horse power, whereas the 14SM at 2,300 hp using improved fuel has a dry weight of only about 0.7 lbs per brake horse power. He is very interested in the possibilities of producing mono-ethyl aniline in sufficient quantity in the US to make available 160 grade fuel for the operation of the Merlin 14SM at 2,300 hp.

In general it is expected that the Griffon development will lead to a 24% greater power expectancy in that engine than has been demonstrated in the Merlin with comparable fuels. To date the Griffon has been tested up to 21 lbs of boost. Mr Hives emphasised the advantages of liquid cooling in making it possible to obtain these substantial power increases and described the improved efficiency of cooling at the higher powers, where the 50% increase in power has only required about 25% increase in cooling.

One of the most interesting developments is the new Rolls-Royce Governor Controlled Fuel Injector, of which the prototype has successfully completed its 100 hour test on the 14SM. A small quantity of these new injectors is now being built in the experimental shop at Derby for further tests and complete data have been forwarded to Mr Eller (now at Packard) and to BAC in Washington. This new injector seems to be showing up better than the previous Rolls-Royce SU Injector type 6,000 and, in addition to replacing a heavy carburettor it will make possible a simpler arrangement of air intake for either up-draught or down-draught or side intake.

Other studies and tests are being made to determine better methods of utilising the approximately 700 hp lost in the exhaust of which only about 150 to 250 hp is usually reclaimed through high speed jet effect. The present proposal is to run the exhaust through a turbine which is geared to the engine crank shaft and thereby transmit the larger portion of the exhaust energy back into the airplane propeller, at the same time getting the usual jet effect at the exhaust outlet. It is further proposed to add another gear driven blower at the rear of the engine, ducted to feed into the front of the exhaust collector to cool the exhaust before entering the turbine. There is some thought that the size of this additional blower might be prohibitive as sufficient air must be fed into the exhaust both to complete the combustion of the unburnt fuel and to cool the exhaust. With improved fuels the combustion will be more complete and this problem some-what simpler, and in the 2-cycle engine with which they are experimenting it is not thought that the additional blower will be necessary as the scavenging air will result in a cooler exhaust.

Mr Hives mentioned the advantages of extremely close liaison with Packard so that developments at Rolls-Royce may go ahead concurrently in the US and recommended a very capable Packard representative be planted at Derby permanently to transmit information and recommendations to the Packard development engineers. He is hoping to visit the US in August or September and will go into this proposal further at that time.

The recommendation made some time ago that the Griffon be put into production in the US was then discussed briefly and the Rolls-Royce representatives recommended that Packard should undertake such a job in preference to any other American manufacturers who are unfamiliar with Rolls-Royce and their manufacturing methods. It was estimated roughly that the Griffon could be in production in the US somewhere between 15 and 18 months.

After inspecting several of their latest developments in the experimental factory we are given the following figures on the number of employees in the reciprocating engine research and development establishment at Derby and the installation establishment at Hucknall (Figure 6.4).

	Derby	Hucknall
Project engineers and technicians	164	65
Designers and draughtsmen	219	165
Shop employees and pilot production	1200	1300
Laboratory staff and development testing	217	40
Test pilots	–	8

Figure 6.4 Number of employees involved in research and development.

In addition to the above there are 67 metallurgy experts and development men at Derby, making a total of 3436 employees in the Rolls-Royce development and pilot production section. Pilot production, which consists of the actual fabrication of the first 100 or 200 sets of new types of equipment utilises about 1000 of these employees, so the total number on strict research and development is about 2436.

Edwin C Walton[6]

Provision for Jet Engine Research and Manufacture

Born on 1 June 1907 in Coventry, Sir Frank Whittle OM CBE CB FRS has the following entry in the *Encyclopaedia Britannica*.

The son of a mechanic, Whittle entered the Royal Air Force (RAF) as a boy apprentice and soon qualified as a pilot at the RAF College in Cranwell. He was posted to a fighter squadron in 1928 and served as a test pilot in 1931–32. He then pursued further studies at the RAF engineering school and at the University of Cambridge (1934–37). Early in his career Whittle recognized the potential demand for an aircraft that would be able to fly at great speed and height, and he first put forth his vision of jet propulsion in 1928, in his senior thesis at the RAF College. The young officer's ideas were ridiculed by the Air Ministry as impractical, however, and attracted support from neither the government nor private industry.

Whittle obtained his first patent for a turbo-jet engine in 1930, and in 1936 he joined with associates to found a company called Power Jets Ltd. He tested his first jet engine on the ground in 1937. This event is customarily regarded as the invention of the jet engine, but the first operational jet engine was designed in Germany by Hans Pabst von Ohain and powered the first jet-aircraft flight on August 27, 1939. The outbreak of the Second World War finally spurred the British government into supporting Whittle's development work. A jet engine of his invention was fitted to a specially built Gloster E.28/39 airframe, and the plane's maiden flight took place on May 15, 1941. The British government took over Power Jets Ltd in 1944, by which time Britain's Gloster Meteor jet aircraft were in service with the RAF, intercepting German V-1 rockets.

Whittle retired from the RAF in 1948 with the rank of air commodore, and that same year he was knighted. The British government eventually atoned for their earlier neglect by granting him a tax-free gift of £100,000. He was awarded the Order of Merit in 1986. In 1977 he became a research professor at the U.S. Naval Academy in Annapolis, Maryland.[7]

Sir Frank died on 8 August 1996 in Columbia, Maryland, US.
Following the successful flight of the Gloster E.28/39 mentioned above, a meeting later that year discussed a new factory from which to further develop the jet engine.

15th October 1941

Power Jets Ltd Revised proposals for provision of a new factory at Whetstone, Near Leicester, complete with machine tools and necessary services

At their meeting on the 8th August the Board considered the provision of a new factory for Power Jets Ltd just outside Leicester. This proposal was refereed back for DGAPF to be consulted with regard to estimates of cost and DL with regard to the availability of labour. It was however, pointed out that the possibility of moving away from Lutterworth had been accepted, and it was difficult to believe that an existing building of 120,000 sq. ft. could not somewhere be found for the project.

Since the above meeting consultations have been held between Power Jets and representatives of DGAPF, DST, DL, Finance and DF1 in which close consideration has been given to the factors involved in using:

a.   The most suitable existing building recommended by DF1 viz, Martins Ltd Apperley Bridge Bradford, and
b.   The new factory just outside Leicester, situated at Whetstone.

In favour of the factory at Bradford is the saving in cost (about £31,000) in building materials.

In favour of the factory at Whetstone are:

a.   The technical advantage of being able to start work (partly, but without dislocation) within 3 months, as opposed to having to wait for at least 9 months until the factory at Bradford is ready for occupation.
b.   The advantage of the proximity of Whetstone to Lutterworth and Leicester where the bulk of the employees now reside.

On the subject of supply of additional labour, the Ministry of Labour are of opinion that there is more chance of obtaining skilled men in Bradford, and that, whereas in Leicester the concentration of industries has been carried out to a considerable extent, this process in Bradford has not proceeded so far.

In the matter of accommodation both Bradford and Leicester are considered by the Ministry of Health as capable of absorbing work-people into lodgings or billets but separate houses were not to be expected in either town.

With regard to the time factor, it is considered that the Bradford scheme would take equally long, if not longer, to complete than the Whetstone scheme, primarily because of the need for removal and re-installation of the heavy presses, machinery and numerous networks of large steam pipes now in the building.

In view of the high priority and urgency attached to the Whittle engine it is considered that the quickest results will be obtained by providing the new factory at Whetstone, and it is the purpose of this memorandum to submit revised proposals for the provision of such a factory, complete with machine tools, plant and services.

The area of the site at Whetstone is 25 acres and the cost is estimated, by the Inland Revenue Authorities, at £2,500.

Particulars of 1) floor space, 2) costs of buildings and services, and 3) machine tools required, as set out in appendix a, involve a total estimated expenditure, including 10% for contingencies of £237,930.

1.   The total working space now found to be necessary is 136,000 sq. ft.
2.   The cost of the buildings and services has been carefully checked and found to be in the region of £152,000.

3.   The number of machine tools and plant items required is 73, the cost of which is estimated at £62,000. The list has been examined by MT3 who have certified that the prices are fair and reasonable and that satisfactory deliveries of the tools can quite confidently be realised.

The approval of the Board is accordingly sought for the scheme to proceed involving expenditure within a maximum of £237,930.[8]

List of tenders received and opened at Thames House on Thursday 16th October 1941 at 4 pm for Power Jets, New Factory at Whetstone, in the presence of Captain Hallam, T Bedford Esq and A Orr (Figure 6.5).

Contractor	Amount (£)	Time
John Laing and Sons	125,460	22–30 weeks
MJ Gleeson	132,097	20–35 weeks
Bosworth and Co Ltd	133,000	32–52 weeks
Holland Hannen and Cubitt	133,206	20–34 weeks
William Moss	144,000	24–40 weeks
Chapman and Sons Ltd	145,900	28–44 weeks

Figure 6.5 Tender details for the new Power Jets factory.[9]

The need for accommodation was also discussed.

16th March 1942

With reference to the attached papers, the Department must of course provide adequate shelter accommodation for the staff of Power Jets Ltd working at Lutterworth. We are naturally anxious to keep this expenditure at Lutterworth to a minimum in view of the fact that a complete new factory is being erected for the company near Leicester, and it would not be unreasonable to ask the staff at Lutterworth to put up with possible overcrowding for a few months if expenditure on building shelters could thereby be cut down to a minimum.

I do not think your fourth point in your minute 12/3 is a good one. We do not know who will occupy these works when Power Jets vacate, but we should think it extremely probable that the works will be de-requisitioned and revert back to their owners, the BTH Company, who will presumably be under a liability themselves to provide such accommodation as they require.

C R Malcolm
PS8a[10]

Almost two years after a new building was first muted, the accounts were still not settled.

18th March 1943

To: Power Jets Ltd
Whetstone Leicester

Gentlemen,

I am directed to inform you that the Department is anxious that the contract for the construction of the Whetstone factory be brought to a conclusion as soon as possible and the various contractors' accounts finalised. It is assumed that the buildings already provided will be in general sufficient for your Company's purposes, and if any small ancillary buildings or minor alterations are found necessary arrangements can be made for fresh contracts to be placed. I am to request therefore that you will expedite any instructions which may be outstanding in respect of work already authorised by the Department.

It is understood that you have given instructions for certain work to be done in the machine shop by way of re-arrangement of plant and removal of partitions, and for this purpose have instructed some outside building and electrical contractor. I am to point out that no financial approval appears to have been obtained from the Department for this work upon the Department's property, and that the Department will not bear the cost of any work for which it has not given approval in advance. Any orders of this nature are therefore given upon your Company's sole financial responsibility.

I am gentlemen,
Your obedient servant[11]

With the accommodation for further development in place, the scene was set for further development of the engine.

The Jet Engine

At first sight, one might ask the question why would the development of the jet engine be included if the work was undertaken by a privately run company. The answer lies in a memo written in 1941.

19th May 1941

FUS

At enclosure 23A the Rover Company suggest some amendments to our record of the meeting on the Whittle scheme (at enclosure 17a). I certainly understood that Mr Wilks assented to your proposition that financial difficulties might arise under development work other than a shadow basis. But do not think we need quarrel with the impression Mr Wilks wishes to leave on more mature reflection, and I think that we can accept the remaining alterations which involve an undertaking that acceptance of the shadow basis is dependent upon arrangements being concluded whereby the Rover Company receive commercial rights in production after the war and whereby the Ministry <u>will</u> give the company first refusal of the equipment, if the Ministry desires to dispose of it.

PS14[12]

This led to the full involvement of Rover cars in a shadow agreement the following year.

12th September 1942

Rover Shadow Agreement and development of Whittle type by the Rover Company

On a loose minute dated 5th May 1942, you gave me details of statements made to Mr Wilks of the Rover Company in connection with the production manufacture of the Whittle engine by that Company and the development work related thereto. These statements related to discussions at a meeting on 25th April 1941, when the Deputy Secretary said that as regards the work to be conducted <u>in the development part of the shadow factory</u>, the Department realising the peculiar nature and urgency of the project, the agreement would be so drawn as to give Mr Wilks substantially a free hand as to the nature and extent of the work to be carried out in this respect. He would not require to refer to the Department for financial approval for conducting experiments along lines which he believed to be promising, although he would, of course, be keeping in touch <u>from time to time</u> with the technical officers of the Department.

As far as RDE are concerned, we have assumed that the above discussion and agreements related to developments associated with the production manufacturing technique and such alterations so related thereto, covering financial authority for which was subsequently arranged by the issue of contract c:/eng/1271/28(b) dated 18th November 1941.

In order to control and expedite this design development work and the financial expenditure involved, the Department formed a MAP Technical Committee, and CRF issued a memorandum on terms of reference and procedure in connection with the same, but my representatives inform me that Mr Wilks has expressed the opinion that under the terms of the shadow agreement about to be issued, and the discussion mentioned above, that he has full authority without reference to the RDE Resident Technical or Group Supervision Officers, to put in hand such design development work as he thought desirable, including the manufacture, testing and embodiment of modified design parts.

We would appreciate your comments on this matter and an indication of whether the shadow agreement will differentiate between freedom to carry out development related to production manufacturing technique and freedom to carry out design development to improve performance and reliability to meet CRDs requirements.

DD(1)/RDE[13]

The memo below was written in response to the above.

15th September 1942

Deputy Secretary,

The point in the preceding minute is that RDE wish to control and expedite the design development work at the Rover No 6 factory but Mr Wilks claims that as a result of the arrangements recorded at 17A, when we met him, he is free to put in hand such design development work as he thinks desirable.

I think that when the arrangements outlined in 17A were made your mind was directed in the main to the financial and accounting problems, but I understood that, in expressing the Department's willingness to grant the company a substantially free hand in order not to hamper experimental work you acted in accordance with the wishes of Sir Henry Tizard FRS, who desired that the seed for the project should be scattered as widely and as freely as possible in the hope that some would fall upon good ground. It was in the same spirit that you informed Mr Wilks that he would not require to refer to the Department for financial approval for conducting experiments along lines which he believed to be promising, although he would, of course, be keeping in touch from time to time with the technical officials of the Department.

So far as the agreement is concerned, this has been delayed by the protracted discussions on the Engine Group Agreement, and by the fact that only recently have we been able to agree on the management fee for this factory. I have just sent to the company the draft of an agreement based upon the engine group draft agreement and providing, in particular, that the company shall diligently and skilfully develop and manufacture the Whittle type supercharger and spare parts therefor as the Minister may from time to time notify the company that he requires, and perform such other work as the Minister may from time to time require.

S Robinson PS14[14]

After clarifying the financial position, it then became a matter of what process to adopt in order to undertake the necessary work.

11th December 1942

Rover No 6 Engine Shadow Factory
Kingston Burner Research

To: PS14

The question has been raised by the district accountant as to whether expenditure in connection with Kingston Burner research ought to be met out of the shadow factory imprest account in view of the fact that the Kingston Burner forms an integral part of the Whittle Super Charger.

The following sums which were originally paid out of the shadow factory imprest account to Kingston Tanning Co Ltd, have been re-charged to the parent company (Figure 6.6):

Invoice date	Amount
19th July 1941 (no 3)	£398.0s.8d
1st October 1941 (no 4)	£306.16s.1d
27th February 1942 (no 5)	£283.14s.5d
Total	£988.11s.2d

Figure 6.6 Charges to Kingston Tanning Co Ltd.

A memo from Mr Farmer of the Rover Co Ltd states that this matter has already been raised by PS14 and has been discussed and cleared with them. As we have no information here on the terms of the contract for research and development work on the Kingston burner, we shall be glad of any help which you can give us in the matter.

PA9[15]

Within a year of this memo, Rolls-Royce had taken over the shadow factory from Rover Cars.

11th January 1943

Barnoldswick and Clitheroe

To: William Gairns
Deputy Chief Accountant
Ministry of Aircraft Production

Dear Gairns,
It has now been agreed that as from the 5th January 1943, Rolls-Royce are responsible for the technical direction and manufacture at Waterloo Mill, Clitheroe and Bankfield Shed, Barnoldswick.

To avoid any hold up Rolls-Royce will for the time being discharge these responsibilities through the agency of the present Rover staff. This is agreed by Rovers. Rovers will withdraw their senior people gradually to cause the least interference with the work. The change-over cannot be regarded as complete until Rolls-Royce management is installed.

It seems likely, therefore, that matters may go on the present basis for some weeks, but we will keep you advised of developments just as soon as we know of them.

Yours sincerely,
A G Hamilton-Eddy[16]

An example of an early jet engine is displayed at the RAF Museum in Hendon (Figure 6.7).

The first Whittle-designed engine, the WU, began bench trials in 1937. It remained the only British jet engine in existence until the much improved W.1X began test in December 1940.

A year earlier the Air Ministry had placed a contract for the first flight engine, the W.1. In 1940 Power Jets began design work on the improved W.2 engine to power the prototype Gloster Meteor twin-jet fighter. In turn a development of this engine, the W.2B was built in slightly different versions by three manufacturers, including Power Jets. This example is thought to be an early development W.2B/500. Although documentation is lacking there is a suggestion that this engine was flight tested in a modified Vickers Wellington bomber.[17]

From then on, and as the engine design became more reliable, other companies joined in the research and development. The position as of January 1945 is summarised below.

Figure 6.7 Power Jet engine W.2B-500. (Author's photograph)

January 1945

Research and Development position of gas turbine engines

Engines

<u>Messrs Power Jets (Research and Development) Ltd</u>

1. Flight tests with the Metropolitan-Vickers F2 unit in the Lancaster test bed are continuing in the experimental flight. In addition, W2/700 engines are being tested in a Wellington flying test bed.

2. Research work
    i. A low pressure-loss combustion chamber has been developed on the bench for use with propulsion ducts. This chamber is shortly to be subjected to flight trials in a Mustang aircraft. The principles of this design of combustion chamber are being applied to the combustion systems of gas turbine engines to effect a reduction of pressure loss and hence to improve the overall efficiency.

     ii.   To assist aerodynamic research and development, Messrs Power Jets are testing on the large turbine test plant at Whetstone, compressors of their own and other firm's design.

3.   Development work
     i.   Bench testing to improve the thrust augmentation by reheat system, already applied experimentally to the Rolls Welland engine (W2B/23), is proceeding. In parallel with this, work has gone ahead with this system on the W2/700 engine and is now to be extended to the Derwent Unit.
     ii.   Work is in hand on the injection of water at the compressor inlet. A 15% increase in take-off thrust has been obtained for a water consumption of 10 gallons per minute.

4.   W2/700
     i.   A 100 hour development test at 1950 lb maximum thrust has been completed; apart from local over-heating the engine is in good condition. Two further engines of this rating have been installed in a Meteor aircraft for tests in the Experimental Flight.
     ii.   The engine in the Gloster R28/39 aircraft continues to give good service at the RAE.

5.   W2/800
An engine which had completed a 25 hour development test at 2,100 lb maximum thrust rating has been subjected to a strip examination and found satisfactory.

6.   W2/850
This is a W2/800 engine with a larger turbine giving an increased diameter gas exit. Performance tests are progressing satisfactorily and a thrust of 2,300 lb has been achieved.

Royal Aircraft Establishment

7.   Urgent tests with the Gloster E28/39 aircraft are going ahead to investigate compressibility effects during high speed flight.
8.   Testing of the Power Jets' exhaust reheat system continues on a Meteor I aircraft and has given promising results during tests up to altitudes of 15,000 ft.

Messrs Rolls-Royce Ltd

9. W2B/23 (Welland)
   This unit, continues to give satisfactory service in the RAF squadron. Since the last report, the Meteor Squadron has completed a total of 300 hours flying with these engines.

10. Derwent
    i. Up to the present, 13 engines of this type have been delivered to Messrs Glosters for installing in Meteor III aircraft. Although a limited number of the early deliveries will give 1,800 lb., the bulk of these engines will have a maximum thrust rating of 1,900 to 2,000 lb.
    ii. The next production stage engine is the Derwent Series II. Bench development tests at 2,100 lb. thrust have been completed and two engines are being installed in a Meteor for performance trials.
    iii. Design work is in hand on the Derwent Series V unit. Although this unit will be capable of giving 3,000 lb thrust, it will be restricted to a rating of 2,500 lb. for the Meteor, as this is considered to be the ultimate power limit for this type of aircraft.

11. RB/39 (Clyde)
    The RB/39 unit is an advanced type, designed to drive a propeller. It incorporates axial and centrifugal type compressors in series driven by independent turbines. The estimated performance is 3,000 bhp for take-off plus 1,200 lb. jet thrust. The first engine is expected to be running in the Spring.

12. RB/41 (Nene)
    i. A 100 hour development test has been completed successfully on the first engine at a maximum thrust of 4,000 lb. Minor troubles were experienced with this combustion equipment but the engine performance was maintained throughout the test.
    ii. A second engine has been built and is undergoing preliminary tests. A production order for 100 of these engines has been placed.

13. H1 (Goblin)
    i. A third successful 100 hour test has been completed on one engine at a rating of 2,700 lb. maximum thrust. This engine is being prepared for further tests. One note-worthy feature about this engine is that most of its components have satisfactorily withstood some 400 to 500 hours running.
    ii. Two engines with a maximum thrust rating of 2,500 lb have been delivered to Messrs English Electric for installing on Vampire aircraft.

All engines subsequent to the fifth will have a maximum thrust rating of 2,700 lb.

iii. Preliminary development running has commenced at 3,000 lb maximum thrust and it is anticipated that this rating will be achieved without major design modifications. Design work is in hand to increase the rating still further, by incorporating modifications which will not be difficult to introduce in the production line.

14. H2 (Ghost)

The initial design of this engine is now expected to give 4,500 lb thrust. Only six engines of this design will be built, however, and the main design effort is being concentrated on a new series, which should produce 5,000 lb thrust for a smaller overall diameter and reduced weight.

Metropolitan Vickers Electrical Co. Ltd

15. F2

A new series of this engine, the F2/4, designed to deliver 3,500 lb thrust, is due to commence tests in the immediate future. The compressor has already been tested with promising results.

16. F3.

Work on the F3, ducted fan unit is still on low priority.

Bristol Aeroplane Co. Ltd

17. The 2,000 hp pilot unit is nearing completion and should be ready for tests early in March. Rig tests on the compressor have commenced.

Armstrong Siddeley Motors Ltd

18. ASX

Bench testing has been directed towards improving performance and reliability. An engine is now about to undergo a 25 hour flight clearance test prior to flight trials in a flying test bed aircraft.

19. ASP

A new unit, based on the ASX design and known as the ASP, drives a propeller and is intended to give 3,600 bhp for take-off, plus a jet thrust of 1,350 lb. Construction of one unit is well advanced, and it is expected to be ready for running tests in the Spring.

Aircraft

Gloster Aircraft Co

20. Meteor
   i.   An aircraft fitted with a trial installation pressure cabin has been flown successfully at 38,000 ft. This aircraft is powered by two W2/700 units, one of which supplied air for the pressure cabin.
   ii. A total of fifteen Meteor III aircraft have been delivered to date. The sixteenth and subsequent aircraft will have engines of improved performance; still more powerful engines will be introduced into production line aircraft during the coming months.
   iii. Messrs Glosters are continuing to concentrate their main production effort towards completing the maximum number of high quality aircraft during the next few months. To achieve this, certain improvements are having to be delayed.
   iv. A 100 gallon under-fuselage fixed fuel tank is now being subjected to flight trials. This installation will be fitted to squadron aircraft shortly.

21. F1/44
   The design and construction of prototypes is going ahead on high priority. The first prototype is expected to be completed by August of this year; it will be powered by a Rolls Nene Unit. Two of the other four prototypes will have the de Havilland Ghost engine.

De Havilland Aircraft Co

22. Vampire I.
   The two prototypes being subjected to flight trials are continuing their engine and airframe development testing. The first production Vampire is expected to be completed within the next two months.

23. Arrangements have been made for trial installation of the Rolls Nene and the de Havilland Ghost engines to be carried out in the Vampire.

Saunders ROE Ltd

24. R6/44
   Design work is proceeding with the objective of completing the first prototype by the end of this year

Vickers Armstrong (Supermarines) Ltd

25. F10/44

    The first of the three prototypes now being designed will have arrester gear installed and other improvements incorporated to enable it to be subjected to carrier trials.

Miles Aircraft Ltd

26. E24/43

    There is nothing outstanding to report. Design work is going ahead satisfactorily.

Armstrong Whitworth Ltd

27. E9/44

    Work on the design of this twin jet engine tailless aircraft is proceeding.

RSC
Ministry of Aircraft Production[18]

Perhaps, the last word should go to Churchill.

16th February 1945

Prime Minister's personal minute
To: The Minister of Aircraft Production

You wrote to me about the relation of my directive on research and development to the normal program for research and development in aircraft and aircraft engines. Certainly I do not suggest that we should slow down or abandon any such work. I had in mind rather all the relatively long-term projects now jostling one another for first claim on scientists and draughtsmen. In these, I think the general rule must hold that priority be given to munitions likely to be used in the Japanese war and that others must take their turn with due regard for the broader needs of the country.

W S C[19]

7

Forecasts and Planning

It is difficult to plan for every eventuality. Where possible, every facet can be forecast as accurately as possible; however, there are things which are impossible to predict. For example, the following is the first page of a report forecasting a shortfall of labour for the shadow factory scheme, this was predictable.

9th February 1940

Memorandum on future requirements of Supervisory and skilled staff for new aircraft and aero-engine Shadow factories

Introduction

It is the opinion of many who have had long experience of the matter that there will be a serious shortage of supervisory staff and key workers in the numerous aircraft and engine shadow factories which are being erected for the wartime aircraft rearmament expansion scheme, and which should be completed and manned towards the end of this year.

At the outbreak of war it is understood that the number of workers in the aircraft industry was of the order of 120,000, and it is estimated that to meet our requirements in about a year's time this figure will have to be raised to approximately 450,000; furthermore, to obtain aerial ascendancy in a long war an increase to 1,300,000 is believed to be necessary.

It is understood that the rationalisation of the various types of aircraft and engines, together with machine tools and plant, and the complete jigging and tooling will enable a large proportion of unskilled labour to be used for the purely production side, although it is appreciated that it is an enormous undertaking.

The object of this memorandum is to deal, not with the rank and file, but to point out that, providing all this co-ordinating work for unskilled operation is done satisfactorily, there will still be a tremendous shortage of managers, departmental heads, superintendents, foremen, key workers, toolmakers etc., in many departments throughout a factory which require fully skilled and highly trained workpeople, no matter how thoroughly the organisation has been planned for quality production.[1]

Again, the following was totally unpredictable!

30th November 1943

Prime Minister

I think that I should warn you that the very widespread and intense epidemic of influenza is having and will continue to have a most adverse effect upon aircraft production. I quote you a few of the figures (see Figure 7.1 below) of absence from this cause in some of the important factories but it is the same practically throughout the industry.

	% absent
Fairey's Heaton Chapel	13
Fairey's Errwood Park	17
AV Roe	20
Vickers, Blackpool	20
Blackburns, Brough	20
Supermarines	6

Figure 7.1 Absence through influenza.

Please note. At one of the many Supermarine dispersal factories 50% of the operatives are away ill.[2]

Among other issues that could be predicted with a high degree of certainty was the planning of modifications to various components and their introduction into production.

13th September 1938

Dear Sir Edward,

It will be recollected that during the visit of the Secretary of State for Air and yourself to the aero engine shadow factory today I was requested to write you personally in regard to proposed modifications to the AVT.95-MB carburettor which we are manufacturing in the new carburettor factory.

We have been advised to expect modifications to at least FOURTEEN parts on this carburettor, several of which are for example the carburettor body top half, boost and mixture control chamber and various cams, these being amongst the major parts of the carburettor.

We are to manufacture these carburettors in conformity with the Pegasus XVIII program, and have to be in production from early in the new year, and it will, therefore, be appreciated that although we are anxious and willing to embody any modifications which will simplify production and improve the performance of the carburettor such modifications should be in our hands during the next few days.

We are already committed to certain materials, and have ordered several items of expensive equipment which will have to be cancelled when these modifications take effect. Apart from this expense it will not be possible for us to meet the program laid down if these alterations continue indefinitely.

If you can assist us in any way by clarifying the whole position and putting a time limit when all modifications will be effected, it will assist us considerably to achieve what we have set out to do.

I mentioned to Sir Kingsley that we had not yet received the final detailed sanction of expenditure on the new carburettor factory.

In this connection I wrote to Mr Meadowcroft, Director of Contracts on 24th August 1938 when a revised sheet 3 of the brochure submitted to the Air Ministry was enclosed. This made the position perfectly clear, and we feel that it is not only necessary for the contracts department to let us have their agreement to the figures quoted on this sheet.

In conclusion I trust that Sir Kingsley and yourself enjoyed the visit, and we hope to see you again in the future.

Yours sincerely,
J P Black
The Standard Motor Company[3]

This was not the only example.

23rd September 1939

To: The Under Secretary of State
The Air Ministry
For the attention of Mr Sales

Dear Sirs,

Re: Shadow Industry Production: Mercury and Pegasus types machine tools

Please receive herewith, for your information, a copy of letter which we have today written to The Daimler Co. regarding a suggested increase of plant which is necessary as a result of modification no MS83, which introduces a flanged nut entailing additional milling operations.

Yours faithfully,
The Bristol Aeroplane Company Limited[4]

Figure 7.2 A Bristol Mercury engine. (Author's photograph)

A further letter in the National Archives mentioned a letter from The Daimler Company to Mr Sales in which the company made an application for additional funds for £10,000 for the purchase of replacement jigs and tooling equipment.

18th January 1940

Sir Kingsley Wood
Secretary of State for Air
Air Ministry

Dear Sir Kingsley Wood,
I am converting the Rover's Company factories for the production of Armstrong Siddeley Cheetah engines. The conversion will be practically completed by September.

In conjunction with Messrs. Armstrong Siddeley I have been trying for some months to secure deliveries of steel. It is now apparent that within the next eighteen months at all events, under existing arrangements, there will not be sufficient steel forthcoming even to keep Armstrong Siddeley's plant working to capacity, and literally none for the Rover Company.

I enclose a chart (Figure 7.3) showing the estimated position for the next two years.

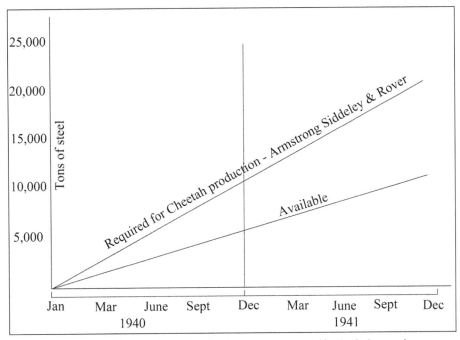

Figure 7.3 Estimated position for the next two years. (Author's diagram)

This will mean that by September next our factories which we have converted and extended at your request and at an expense to the country of approximately one and a half million pounds, will be virtually idle, unless some arrangements can be made to divert to us the steel necessary to meet your engine requirements. Your department have helped in every way they possibly can, and several meetings have been held with the Ministry of Supply, but it is now evident that without your personal interest, the necessary steel will not be forthcoming.

Yours sincerely
S B Wilks
The Rover Company Ltd
Coventry[5]

Whilst component specifications changed and machines to fabricate the modifications reached the shop floor, other directives sometimes required a complete change in the component being manufactured. Usually, this type of change was from one engine type to another. For example, the aero engine shadow factory was granted a contract for Pegasus engines, although as usual the paperwork took time to resolve.

26 July 1939

Aero-Engine Committee (Shadow Industry)

To: Sir Kingsley Wood
Secretary of State for Air

Dear Sir Kingsley,

Pegasus Agreement

We wish to thank you for giving us the facility for discussing the Pegasus Agreement, which has been over a year waiting to be finally approved.

A request for the manufacture of Pegasus engines was confirmed by the Ministry to the Committee on 23rd June 1938, for completion by 31st December 1939. In other words, it would appear that we shall finish the manufacture before an agreement is signed – a condition which we consider quite inexcusable, especially as it must obviously follow in the main the existing Mercury Agreement, which also took about a year to decide.

Numerous discussions have taken place and every effort has been made by the Committee to try and settle the amount of the management fee and the terms of the bonus.

On 29th March 1939, the Committee made an offer to the Ministry which we thought would have been at once accepted in the spirit in which it was made, viz, a keen desire to be generous and loyal, even to the extent of accepting a much less sum for management fees than was considered to be just and fair, having in mind the loss to the parent companies in diverting the attention of their management to the enormous amount of detailed supervision necessary to ensure success in the quality, number and economic cost of the engines.

Now an additional difficulty has arisen caused by the decision of the Government to include management fees of shadow factories in the operations of the Armaments Profit Duty.

Immediately the Committee knew of this additional taxation they decided to write to the Ministry, and a letter was despatched to you on 12th July, in which we seriously ask that the management fees for the Pegasus engine shall be such as will show an amount, after payment of Armaments Profit Duty, of not less than £2,000 per month, plus bonus. The receipt of this letter has been acknowledged, but in view of the urgency of the matter, and the agreement for the Hercules engine, we ask that the Pegasus Agreement shall be completed without further delay.

The payment of Armament Profits Duty out of our small fees would be out of all reason for the exceptional services we have and are rendering to the Air

Ministry. May we depend on your help to deal with this question of Armaments Profits Duty so that the Members of the Group will not be penalised?

Our request applies, of course, equally to the Mercury and Hercules Agreements.

Yours sincerely,
Lord Austin
Longbridge Works
Birmingham[6]

Appendix IV, mentioned earlier, documents the extension agreement mentioned by Lord Austin in his letter. As one can imagine, scaling up production of engines, for example, at the same time as co-ordinating upgrades to any equipment must have been a daunting task. The additional complexity in the case of Merlin engine production was that some of it took place in the United States at Packard.

26th July 1943

Subject: British and American Rolls-Royce Merlin Production Schedules
Reference: Conference with Mr Devons today

Mr Devons advised that it now appears that a total of 4,000 Merlins monthly will be required from the US sometime in late 1945, and that a decision must be made shortly as to which facilities in the US will build the 1,300 Merlins monthly over and above the present Packard schedule of 2,700 monthly. He said that it is not possible to consider an expansion in the progress here owing to the labour shortages.

He mentioned that Rolls-Royce facilities in the UK must be counted on to produce a certain quantity of internal combustion turbines which may account for a loss of about 200 Merlins monthly. This matter was taken up with General Meyers by Sir Wilfred Freeman today but no decision was reached on cabling to the US with regard to the proposed expansion. However, Professor Jewks is in Washington now on this project.

This should be followed up to determine whether Rolls-Royce might increase their Merlin production if the Meteor tank engine requirements can be reduced or eliminated by using Ford tank engines. It should also be checked to determine whether the present Rolls-Royce Meteor schedules reflect the recent reductions in the UK tank program.

Edwin C Walton[7]

A complex problem indeed, made more so because of the need to consider supplying some of the tanks with their respective engines! The bread and butter for any planning department is that of producing production schedules. In the case of completed aircraft during the war these schedules usually related to a planned increase.

8th April 1942

Additional Advanced Trainer requirements

AMSOs letter of the 1st instant seeking additional production of 40 Masters a month and 30 Ansons or Oxfords a month has now been considered.

Masters

1. Capacity for the assembly of the additional airframes could be found either at Reading or at Doncaster or at a combination of the two places. Additional machine tools would, however, be necessary, and these could be obtained only at the expense of some other production already covered in the Aircraft Program.
2. Undercarriages for Masters are made by Lockheeds. Undercarriage production generally will undoubtedly be one of our major difficulties in achieving the December program. Lockheed undercarriages will present particular difficulties: we are already suffering from lack of adequate production, particularly spares.
3. The necessary Mercury XX engines could only be obtained at considerable expense to the Hercules VI program. The cost would considerably exceed a one-for-one basis as it would be necessary to devote to Mercury production part of a factory group which is already planned and tooling up for Hercules VI production.
4. The additional Masters would add to our propeller liabilities but it is probable that the necessary production could be obtained in time.
5. In putting forward the glider program in response to the Chief of Staff Committee's latest demands, a warning was given that this program, together with that for Mosquitos and other aircraft using substantial quantities of timber, were likely to exhaust the timber supply and that it might be necessary at a later date to ask for consideration of a reduction in either the glider or the Mosquito program. If we add further Masters to the existing program, we increase our timber supply difficulties.
6. AMSO refers to the possibility of using South Marston for additional Masters production. Such a step is not, in fact, necessary to enable us to assemble the airframes and it is one which the Controller General most strongly opposes. He draws particular attention to the danger arising from the concentration in the single large Castle Bromwich factory of the major

portion of our planned Spitfire production. On grounds of sound production policy, he considers it essential that we shall establish as quickly as possible, another Spitfire assembly centre, e.g. South Marston – which in the event of damage from enemy action at Castle Bromwich, could undertake increased Spitfire assembly, etc. without delay.

Ansons or Oxfords

7. It would be easier to produce additional Ansons than additional Oxfords. We could more readily find the airframe assembly capacity and we should run into less difficulties with undercarriage production.
8. We could produce the necessary Cheetah IX engines for 30 additional Ansons a month at some expense to planned Merlin production. It is, however, probable that this additional engine production would not jeopardise our essential Merlin engine production.
9. It is not practicable, without detailed investigation, to give an assurance that the necessary additional undercarriages could be produced but it is not thought that they would present any undue difficulty.
10. Propellers could be supplied.
11. The position as to materials is much the same as in the case of the Masters. The Anson uses a considerable amount of steel, the supply of which might present difficulties.

General

12. It cannot be too strongly emphasised that the December program represents the maximum productive effort which the aircraft and associated industries can put forth with the factory space, machine tools, materials and labour which the nation can afford to dispose of for aircraft production.
13. It is the considered opinion of the Directors General of Production – with which I entirely agree – that any further additions to the aircraft program cannot be made with any real hope of achievement.
14. In order to live up to the December program, we have to obtain large additional supplies of machine tools, labour and materials. All the present indications are that there will certainly be delays in obtaining these essential facilities for production and that in certain directions – particularly some critical classes of machine tools – our requirements will not be met.
15. It is felt that the Air Staff do not appreciate that it is impracticable to exchange a given number of, say, Hurricanes, for a given number of advanced trainers. It is only in certain factories that we can hope to produce aircraft of a given type with reasonable economy and in a reasonable space of time. We were able to add Hurricanes to the December program because the Hawker Aircraft Company is now working with much higher efficiency than it was

some time ago and because there has been a marked improvement in both the actual and prospective output of Merlin XX engines. In particular, we can now place greater reliance on anticipated deliveries of Merlin engines from America than we could when the December program was drafted. We could not, however, make any substantial contribution in advanced trainers, from the Hawker Aircraft for a very long time to come, and Merlin engines, which would be released if the Hurricanes were not made, could not be used for advanced trainers of existing types.

16. In his letter of the 1st April, AMSO refers to his anxiety regarding trainer allocations from the USA. The cablegrams on this subject make it clear that the US authorities are far from satisfied that the Air Ministry's advanced trainer requirements have been properly calculated. If the US authorities can be satisfied on this point, it is difficult to believe that the increased production necessary cannot be obtained far more readily from the greater – and, at present much less tapped – resources of the US than from this country.

17. While the shipping point is appreciated, it should be practicable to have advanced trainers shipped in parts for assembly and flight testing in this country. Shipment in this way would materially reduce the shipping space involved.

Deputy CG[8]

The interested reader will find a picture of the Hercules and Merlin XX engines in Figures 7.4 and 7.5.

First bench tested in 1936 it was put into production and along with the Rolls-Royce Merlin it was one of the standard British aero-engines of the Second World War. By 1945 production had exceeded 57,400 and it had been used in many aircraft including some marks of Stirling, Halifax, Lancaster, Beaufighter and Wellington. The Hercules XVIII engine was used in Beaufighter and Wellington aircraft serving in Coastal Command and differed from the earlier marks in having cropped supercharger impellers, giving an increase in power at take-off and low altitude work.[9]

The Merlin XX was designed as a replacement for the Merlin X from which is was derived.

More than 28,000 were built at Rolls-Royce's Derby, Crew and Glasgow factories, and by Ford at Manchester.

The engine was used to power Halifax and Lancaster bombers, and Hurricane and Defiant fighters.[10]

Figure 7.4 Bristol Hercules engine. (Author's photograph)

Figure 7.5 A Merlin XX engine. (Author's photograph)

As with Merlin engines mentioned above, there was also a joint program, mentioned in Chapter 2 under the section on lend–lease, concerning the planned aircraft output. Figure 7.6 shows the total number of aircraft in both the British July 1941 programme and the USA 8E programmes.

All Operational Types (Excluding Fleet Air Arm)						
1941	**July**	**Aug.**	**Sept.**	**Oct.**	**Nov.**	**Dec.**
British	1,304	1,363	1,368	1,352	1,364	1,391
USA	366	396	421	437	493	538
Total	1,670	1,759	1,789	1,789	1,857	1,929
Trainers						
British	580	617	640	657	662	662
USA	103	122	128	131	137	142
Total	683	739	768	788	799	804
All Types (Including Fleet Air Arm)						
British	2,019	2,166	2,150	2,146	2,164	2,187
USA	469	518	549	568	630	680
Total	2,488	2,634	2,699	2,714	2,794	2,867
1942	**Jan.**	**Feb.**	**Mar.**	**April**	**May**	**June**
All Operational Types (Excluding Fleet Air Arm)						
British	1,396	1,449	1,481	1,509	1,503	1,453
USA	606	647	699	702	755	915
Total	2,002	2,096	2,180	2,211	2,258	2,368
Trainers						
British	625	605	550	531	515	515
USA	116	55	55	55	3	–
Total	741	660	605	586	518	515
All Operational Types (Excluding Fleet Air Arm)						
British	2,157	2,195	2,158	2,135	2,110	2,078
USA	722	702	754	757	758	915
Total	2,879	2,897	2,912	2,892	2,868	2,993

Figure 7.6 Planned aircraft output.[11]

Two months were allowed for sending across American aircraft. Below is a letter of support for an increase in the number of advanced trainers.

12th May 1942

To: Col J J Llewllin MP Ministry of Aircraft Production

My Dear Minister,
I have for some time been owing you a reply to your letter dated 22nd April 1942 about advanced trainers. The matter has, from my point of view, been somewhat complicated by the discussions that have recently been going on with the Air Staff in regard to a revision of our target towers.

I was delighted to hear that you had given instructions for an increase in Anson production from 100 to 125/130 per month. This, I think, will meet our requirements in twin-engined trainers.

I do not think that I should be justified in pressing my original proposal that the production of Master trainers should be continued at 40 a month from October 1942 onwards. We have a good stock of Masters at present and these, (provided the propellers now deficient are found for them) together with current production, should meet requirements until the middle of next year. On present calculations it seems probable that we shall then need further supplies of single-engined advanced trainers, and that we could obtain our needs from Canadian Harvard production, provided we are prepared to accept the shipping commitments.

You have been in correspondence with the Secretary of State about target towers, and I agree with you that it will be undesirable to obtain further supplies from British production at the cost of operational types. Most of our additional requirements are likely to be in Canada, and it will obviously be desirable to find a suitable American type for target towing. What I would suggest therefore, is that the conversion of the Harvard (or some similar American type) for target towing should be at once investigated. As soon as the conversion has been cleared, we should require production arrangements to enable some 30–40 aircraft a month to be converted.

Yours sincerely,
Air Ministry[12]

There were also tables comparing the various programmes.

26th October 1944

Prime Minister

Comparison between August, September and October Aircraft Programs

1. The August 1944 Aircraft Program was based on the War Cabinet decision that the MAP labour allocation was to be reduced from 1.75 million to 1.62 million by the end of 1944, and made no assumptions as to the end of the German war (i.e. planned production as if it would continue indefinitely).

2. The September 1944 Program, on the other hand, was influenced by the assumptions, authorised by the War Cabinet, that the German war would not continue beyond 31st December 1944 and that the Japanese war would last eighteen months beyond that date. This program therefore provided for overall reductions made possible by the ending of the European war, as soon as they could be made effective, and at the same time allowed for the special requirements of the Japanese war, for example it advanced and increased production of some Fleet Air Arm types at the expense of some RAF fighters, and planned the change-over of certain heavy bombers to transport versions. This program was not issued to firms.

3. The program approved by Cabinet on the 16th October was a modification of the September program. It has now been put into force and is known as the October Program. It delays the change-over from stage 1 to stage 2 requirements in respect of certain types but without disturbing the general pattern of the program.

4. The following tables (Figures 7.7 through 7.12) give, for four particular months, the monthly deliveries due under each of the three programs. It will be appreciated that little change could be made in the deliveries of aircraft by the end of 1944, and the programs only begin to diverge substantially in 1945.

	August Program	September Program	October Program
Heavy bombers	457	453	435
Medium bombers	162	159	161
Light bombers and fighters	879	870	870
General reconnaissance	95	97	97
Transports and ASR	71	71	83
Naval	243	242	240
Trainers	115	115	128
Total	2,022	2,007	2,014

Figure 7.7 Monthly deliveries – December 1944.

	August Program	September Program	October Program
Heavy bombers	512	323	425
Medium bombers	133	107	129
Light bombers and fighters	953	772	867
General reconnaissance	82	77	82
Transports and ASR	84	161	106
Naval	243	251	254
Trainers	99	100	98
Total	2,106	1,791	1,961

Figure 7.8 Monthly deliveries – March 1945.

	August Program	September Program	October Program
Heavy bombers	549	255	355
Medium bombers	96	46	76
Light bombers and fighters	1,025	685	795
General reconnaissance	68	67	75
Transports and ASR	56	133	86
Naval	257	267	272
Trainers	114	90	88
Total	2,165	1,543	1,747

Figure 7.9 Monthly deliveries – June 1945.

	August Program	September Program	October Program
Heavy bombers	550	205	240
Medium bombers	72	–	–
Light bombers and fighters	973	610	592
General reconnaissance	63	64	66
Transports and ASR	34	136	101
Naval	276	338	339
Trainers	90	65	70
Total	2,058	1,418	1,408

Figure 7.10 Monthly deliveries – December 1945.

Figure 7.11 shows, for each program, the aggregate number of aircraft due between 1st October 1944 and 30th June 1945.

	August Program	September Program	October Program
Heavy bombers	4,396	3,274	3,710
Medium bombers	1,272	1,103	1,212
Light bombers and fighters	8,409	7,138	7,581
General reconnaissance	758	756	787
Transports and ASR	549	1,072	832
Naval	2,225	2,272	2,284
Trainers	1,013	966	976
Total	18,722	16,581	17,382

Figure 7.11 Aggregate number of aircraft due between 1 October 1944 and 30 June 1945.

Figure 7.12 illustrates (by reference to the same four months used above) the difference between the three programs in terms of the manpower they require.

	August Program	September Program	October program
December 1944	1,623,000	1,520,000	1,600,000
March 1945	1,623,000	1,250,000	1,450,000
June 1945	1,623,000	1,180,000	1,200,000
December 1945	1,623,000	1,170,000	1,170,000

Figure 7.12 Manpower predictions for the three programmes.[13]

The whole issue of trainers both in their supply and in their type had implications to delivery of aircraft needed for operational, as opposed to training, purposes, for example.

8

Parts Manufacture and Aircraft Assembly

Figure 8.1 shows the shadow factories in existence on 6 October 1936, often know as No. 1 Engine Group, which was mentioned in the introduction and indeed in earlier chapters. This table summarises the parts they initially contracted to manufacture.

Motor Company	Aero Engine Part(s)
Austin	Crankshafts, reduction gears etc. Engine testing and assembly
Standard	Cylinders
Rover	Connecting rods, pistons, valves, cams (plus tappets)
Rootes	Blower and rear cover etc. (plus petrol pump)
Daimler	Crankcase, oil sump, air intake etc. (less tappets, less petrol pump, plus rocker gear)
Bristol Aeroplane Co.	Engine assembly and testing

Figure 8.1 The No. 1 Engine Group parts production in 1936.[1]

From this modest beginning, many other factories were created such that even before war was declared in 1939, there were companies involved in producing an ever expanding range of engines (Figure 8.2).

Firm	Location	Engines in Production		
		Type	No. delivered	No. to be delivered
Armstrong Siddeley Motors Ltd	Parkside, Coventry	Tiger VIII	101	136
		Cheetah X	356	186
		Cheetah IX	16	194
		Genet Major	0	16
The Bristol Aeroplane Co Ltd	Filton, Bristol	Mercury VIII	723	111
		Mercury IX	0	26
		Pegasus VI	132	24
		Pegasus XXII	125	37
		Pegasus XVIII	11	781
		Pegasus III	18	154
		Perseus X	0	500
		Perseus XII	79	375
		Taurus TEIM	0	126
		Taurus TEIS	0	171
		Hercules HEIM	0	55
		Hercules HEISM	0	180
De Havilland Aircraft Co Ltd	Stag Lane, Edgware	Gypsy Queen	65	9
		Gypsy King	4	371
		Gypsy Major	56	184
Napier & Sons Ltd	Acton	Rapier Dagger VIII	71	4
			0	222
Messrs Rolls-Royce Ltd	Derby	Merlin	990	2441
The Shadow Industry[a]	Various locations[b]	Bristol Mercury VIII	22	3478

Notes:

a   The Austin Motor Company, the Bristol Aeroplane Co Ltd, the Daimler Co Ltd, Messrs Rootes Securities Ltd, the Rover Co Ltd, the Standard Motor Co Ltd

b   Longbridge Birmingham, Filton Bristol, Radford Coventry, Coventry, Acock's Green Birmingham, Coventry

Figure 8.2 Pre-war aero engine manufacture.[2]

Similarly, there was a corresponding increase in the types of airframes and companies involved in aircraft manufacturing (Figure 8.3).

Firm	Location	Type	Aircraft in Production	
			Delivered by 7th May 1938	To be Delivered
Airspeed Ltd	Portsmouth	Oxford	26	300
Austin Motor Co Ltd	Aero Works, Longbridge	Battle	0	863

Firm	Location	Type	Aircraft in Production	
			Delivered by 7th May 1938	To be Delivered
Blackburn Aircraft Ltd	Brough, East Yorks	Skua Botha	0 / 0	190 / 242
Blackburn Aircraft Ltd	Dumbarton	Botha	0	244
Boulton Paul Aircraft Ltd	The Airport, Wolverhampton	Defiant	0	450
The Bristol Aeroplane Co Ltd	Filton House, Bristol	Blenheim Beaufort	228 / 0	590 / 350
De Havilland	Hatfield, Herts	Don Queen Bee Oxford Tiger Moth	0 / 11 / 0 / 0	50 / 49 / 200 / 50
Fairey	Hayes, Middlesex Stockport, Cheshire Hamble, Hants	Swordfish Albacore Battle Seafox	196 / 0 / 159 / 40	76 / 262 / 496 / 24
Handley Page Ltd	Cricklewood, NW2 Radlett	Hampden Halifax	0 / 0	430 / 100
Sir WG Armstrong-Whitworth Aircraft Ltd	Whitley, Coventry Aerodrome, Baginton	Whitley Wellington	70 / 0	278 / 64
Gloster Aircraft Ltd	Brockworth Aerodrome, Gloucester	Gladiator Henley Wellington	0 / 0 / 0	378 / 200 / 200
Hawker Aircraft Ltd	Kingston Brooklands	Hurricane	34	966
AV Roe	Newton Heath, Manchester	Anson Blenheim Manchester	6 / 0 / 0	582 / 350 / 200
Phillips and Powis	Woodley Aerodrome, Reading	Mentor Magister Kestrel T	1 / 66 / 0	44 / 402 / 500
Rootes Securities	Speke, Liverpool	Blenheim	0	600
Saunders-Roe Ltd	East Cowes, I of W	London Lerwick	5 / 0	1 / 21
Shorts Ltd	Rochester	Sunderland B12/36	1 / 0	23 / 100
Short Harland	Belfast	Hereford Bomba B12/36	0 / 0 / 0	100 / 80 / 100

Firm	Location	Type	Aircraft in Production	
			Delivered by 7th May 1938	To be Delivered
Supermarine	Woolston, Hants Hythe, Eastleigh	Walrus Stranraer Spitfire	79 7 0	89 10 510
Vickers	Weybridge	Wellington	0	300
Westland	Yeovil	Lysander	0	283

Figure 8.3 Early airframe production from shadow factories.[3]

Figures 8.4, 8.5 and 8.6 show three of the aircraft from Figure 8.3 as these aircraft may be less well known to some readers. They are all exhibited at the RAF Museum at Hendon.

The pre-war government faced some interesting challenges in the late 1930s. War seemed inevitable and therefore the need to increase aircraft production the only sensible strategy (I am only discussing RAF requirements here). The issue was how many of each type should be produced and stockpiled? It led to some factories with spare capacity, at least in late 1938.

Figure 8.4 Airspeed Oxford trainer. (Author's photograph)

Figure 8.5 A Tiger Moth. (Author's photograph)

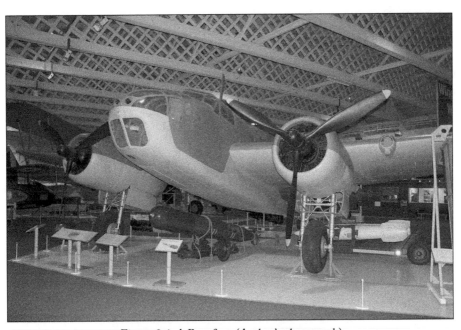

Figure 8.6 A Beaufort. (Author's photograph)

30th November 1938

To: Sir Kingsley Wood
Air Ministry

Dear Sir Kingsley Wood,

Our Alcocks Green Shadow Factory, working to the latest schedule we have had from the Ministry, will reach the peak of its production in January next year, after which production will fall away until by June it will be down to less than half the capacity of the factory – which will of course necessitate turning away a lot of skilled personnel that we have trained.

We should have to know in the very near future if this break in production is to be avoided, otherwise it would be too late to obtain materials in time.

The Shadow Factories are still 'news', and I am concerned because I fear that if I turn men away from our factory at a time when the Government are increasing production facilities and raising additional finance, the fact may be made use of politically, and I want to be sure, therefore, that you appreciate the position before it is too late to alter it. Fortunately, as you know, we are not operating the shadow factory on a profit basis, so that I can bring the matter to your notice without fear of being accused of having ulterior motives.

Yours sincerely
S B Wilks[4]

By this time the concept of the shadow factories was well known, at least in broad terms as the scheme was announced in the press during its launch in 1936. Of course, Churchill came to power only after the war had started; however, he did provide his thoughts on production on more than one occasion. Churchill wrote this letter in 1941; he made other comments, some of which appear later.

13th July 1941

Action this day: Prime Minister's personal minute

1. I was deeply concerned at the new programs of MAP which show a static condition for the next twelve or eighteen months in numbers of aircraft. No doubt new production would be bent on in the later phase. I asked that these figures should be subject to the test of man-hours involved in each type of machine. This certainly shows an improvement of about 50% in the British field by the twelfth month from now. The American figures improve the calculation both from the number of aircraft and the man-hours standpoint, and one might almost say that the output for July 1942 would be to the present output as 1 to 1.75.

2. I cannot feel that this is enough. Our estimate of German monthly production by numbers is 2,100, which is the numerical level at which we stand up till July 1942, and indeed thereafter, apart from new projects. We must assume that the Germans also would derive comfort from translating these numbers of aircraft into man-hours. They may, or they may not be making a similar expansion in size and quality. Broadly, from the figures put before me the impression would be one of equality for the next twelve months, so as far as British and German construction is concerned, leaving any increase to be supplied by our share of the United States production. Moreover, this takes no count of MAP's caveat that their estimates may be reduced by 15%.

3. We cannot be content with the above situation which excludes all possibility of decisive dominance indispensable for victory. I wish, therefore, these programs to be re-examined, and the following three methods of expansion, together with any others suggested, to be explored by the highest authorities concerned. The three methods are:

    a. An improvement in the existing figures by speeding up and working the machine tools longer, or by any other measures taken in the sphere of MAP production.

    b. By construction of new factories and assembling plants, or by the re-occupation or full occupation of plants vacated for the sake of dispersion. This may well be justified in view of our increasing command of the British air by day, and the improvement of night-fighting devices.

    c. By re-classification of the bomber program so as to secure a larger delivery from well-tried types in that period. Fighter aircraft must continually strive for mastery, and rapid changes of design may be imperative. But a large proportion of the Bomber Force will in the next twelve months be employed under steady condition, and within ranges which are moderate. While all bombers required for long distance or great heights or daylight action must be the subject of intensive improvement, a large proportion of the Bombing Force will be carrying their nightly load to (say) the Ruhr, or other nearby targets. It would seem that the Air Staff could divide their activities into near and far, and that on this basis some good lines of production, which have not yet reached their maximum, could be given a longer run at the peak, with very definite addition to numbers. This would, for instance, seem to apply to the Blackpool Wellington which is a new supply reaching its peak in November, but only running for six months at that level. If it were allowed twelve months run at the peak, it may be that a larger delivery would be possible from November on.

4. The criterion of bomber strength is the weight of bombs deliverable per month on the reasonably foreseeable targets in Germany and Italy. Have the Air Staff plans been applied to the figures of production with this end in view? It may be that a heavier load carried by a new machine would give

better results. But a machine which is good enough to carry two tons to the Ruhr ought to have a long run in continuous production before it is discarded. There are no doubt other instances. I have asked MAP to review their programs accordingly having regard to the grievous loss on too hasty change-overs.

5.   The new program is substantially less than the March figures, and far below the October figures. However, many materials have been accumulated on the October basis. A substantial increase should therefore be possible if all factors are fitted to the optimum. The Air Ministry should show how this latest program, apart from any expansion, fits in with their pilot production for the next twelve months, having regard on the one hand to the reduced scale of losses which has been found operative by experience, and on the other hand to the much more lavish pilot establishment now said to be necessary in proportion to machines. Bombs, explosives, guns and all accessories, must be measured in relation both to the existing program and the necessary expansion. In principle, however, we must aim at nothing less than having our air force twice as strong as the German air force by the end of 1942. This ought not to be impossible if a renewed vast effort is made now. It is the very least that can be contemplated since no other way of winning the war has yet been proposed.

W S C[5]

Later in the year, Churchill was keen to ensure newly commissioned aircraft carriers were supplied with the aircraft they needed:

18th December 1941

The Prime Minister has ruled that priority is to be given to the production of Naval Air Arm aircraft of the types required to equip armoured aircraft carriers – that is, carriers such as the Illustrious as distinct from the auxiliary carriers which have been obtained by converting whalers and similar merchant vessels.

The production directorates of this department have been informed of the Prime Minister's ruling and I write to ask that you will take all possible steps to achieve the maximum practicable output of aircraft of the types in question.

You are, I know, in touch with production directors on matters relating to the manufacture of these aircraft but I hope you will write to me if there is any point in connection with which you think I can give you assistance.

Sir Charles Craven[6]

In another comment, Churchill was keen to ensure that all of the aircraft currently missing parts were completed and dispatched.

13th May 1942

To: Minister of Aircraft Production

Let me have a report on Flag C of your latest return, column 5. This shows that you have 1,797 *in preparation*. These are presumably in addition to the 649 ready, and ready within four days. The shortage of aircraft at the present moment is acute. Now is the time for you to bring forward this reserve of 1,797, which are presumably defective in this or that spare part.

Lord Beaverbrook in 1940 gained great advantages for us by a searching analysis and scrutiny of the machines in the ASUs. What we want now is more aircraft in the front line. Get at it and bite at it.

Give me therefore the following reports:

a.   The corresponding figures to 649 and 1,797, week by week, for the last two years, and
b.   Make me a proposal to bring forward into the squadrons 500 of the 1,797 by 15th July. It may well be that there are some additional spare parts with the RAF at home surplus to immediate requirements, which would make some of these machines alive. I am told the Beaufighters in particular could be brought forward, and are urgently needed. There are 280 of these on your hands. Let me have a separate return, showing what is holding back the 100 most promising Beaufighters.

I presume you have an exact record of each of these types of machines, and can say exactly what is needed to bring any one of them forward to the fighting line. If so, let me see it. If not, you ought to have. You need not give me any explanation about the 363 Wellingtons; I am already aware of it.

W S C[7]

Later in the month, Churchill was once again chasing up aircraft. Incidentally, the ACU was the shorthand term for the Aircraft Storage Units. Not all aircraft were delivered to airfields for operational use directly from the factories. Another thought from Churchill on ASUs followed in the same month.

May 1942

To: the Minister of Aircraft Production

1.   I have read your minute about aircraft in ASUs.
2.   It appears from the figures you attached that the proportion of these aircraft which are ready, or will be ready within 4 days, is now only about half what

it was at this time last year. It is important to keep the proportion available as high as possible, and I hope you will take all steps to raise it to the old level by clearing up the shortages described in your minute.

W S C[8]

Churchill received his reply within three weeks detailing some of the issues facing these aircraft.

22nd June 1942

To: The Minister
Reference attached, the position of these airframes is as follows:

1. **Beaufort (1)**. This airframe is under repair and is nearing completion, when it will be ready for the engines. The engines have been allotted.
2. **Defiant II (89)**. These are due to be converted to target towers. The conversion sets are being made by Boulton and Paul and the conversion will be carried out by two repair firms. The engines are available but not the constant speed units. It has been planned to the engineering to keep pace with the supply of constant speed units and the rate of acceptance by converting firms.
3. **Hurricane I (32)**. These airframes were robbed of wings and under-carriages to meet an overseas pack-up, together with some 50 others ex Canada now at Henlow. Those in ASUs are going to be reassembled by a repair firm at the rate of ten per fortnight, commencing two months hence, and will be engineered by the firm. The rate of assembly is limited by the rate of supply of parts and it has been arranged to supply the parts to the Canadian Hurricanes to Henlow first.
4. **Spitfires (4)**. These are under repair and require engines changed. The engines are allotted and available when the units are ready for them.
5. **Beaufighter II (49)**. These airframes are the balance of some 80 that were delivered to ASUs from the Bristol Company very incomplete over three months ago at a time when engines were short. The Bristol Co. commenced assembling them at the end of March, the work being done by the BOAC at the ASU at Colerne where they are. The original rate was assessed at five per week, the rate of supply of the engines, but progress was only about half that speed. The BOAC then withdrew from Colerne and the firm had to get new labour. During the last month progress has been almost negligible and except for a shortage of CS units it is understood the difficulties are almost entirely labour. I am pursuing the question of acceleration through DAP.

G Laing
Air Vice-Marshal[9]

With the spotlight falling on the ASUs, there was an effort to reduce the numbers of aircraft in these units.

26th June 1942

Preparation of Aircraft in Aircraft Storage Units

With reference to the Secretary of State for Air's minute to the Prime Minister, regarding the preparation of certain types of aircraft in our aircraft storage units (ASUs). The latest position is set out below:

1. **Spitfires.** There are available sufficient junction boxes to cover the deficiency of 157. Another type of junction box has been made available and this, with a slight modification, can be fitted to make good all the Spitfire deficiencies.
2. **Blenheim V's.** Every endeavour is being made to modify operationally the remaining Blenheim V's we hold in our ASUs and although there are some bottlenecks, such as tropicalisation sets and turret motors, nevertheless we are hoping that all the Blenheims to be modified will have been completed by the middle of July.
3. **Beaufighters.** Special inspections have temporarily retarded the progress of preparation on the Beaufighters. There still is, however, a need to speed up the installation of AI in order to catch up retrospectively on aircraft not fitted. There seems little prospect at present of getting CS units for a large number of Beaufighter Mark II which are deficient of these items. I suggest this matter should be referred to DGPEAE.
4. **Propellers.** I think the turning point has at last come for the propellers for Wellington Mark III and Whitley V aircraft.

DGAP in his Short Term Forecast has estimated that the following aircraft will be produced complete with propellers (Figure 8.7):

	July	August
Wellington Mark III	160	144
Whitley V	50	50

Figure 8.7 Short term forecast.

I suggest that DGPEAE should be asked to confirm that propellers will in actual fact be available for the aircraft shown above. If these propellers materialise, then a very considerable improvement will be made in the numbers of these aircraft available for operations.

E G Northway
Wing Commander[10]

We have seen earlier that Churchill thrived on understanding detailed reports and 'helping' those under him to facilitate solutions to roadblocks and problems. It has to be said once again that he was definitely the right man at the right time and in the right job. The types of reports he was sent on a regular basis contained standard production details. Whilst documenting all of them would add no value and indeed take up too much room, two might be helpful.

One concerns the production of Lancaster and York aircraft and, being too long to reproduce in the text is included as Appendix VII, the second appears below.

6th January 1944

Prime Minister
It may interest you to see the results of the year 1943 in aircraft production.

The actual output is compared to the latest program (see Figure 8.8) (September 1943) in which Lancasters and Spitfires had both been put up compared to January 1943 program, while some others, including Stirling, had been put down.

The reasons for failure to attain program amongst the more important types were the following:

i.   Stirling: Trouble at Shorts at the beginning of the year.
ii.   Halifax: Two changes of type to the IA and the III, the latter not having been anticipated in the program.
iii. Wellington: The program for Chester was fixed too high in view of the introduction of the Wellington X.
iv.   Albermarle: The many changes in purpose and mass of resultant modifications almost amounting in some cases to reconstruction.
v.   Mosquito: The multiplicity of changes of type and special purpose fittings required.
vi.   Spitfire: There has been difficulty over engines due to the change-over in type of Spitfire, and a go-slow strike seriously interfered with production.
vii. Firefly: The difficulties at Fairey's and General Aircraft which are both well on the way to solution, coupled with technical troubles with ailerons etc. which are now cleared.
viii. Barracuda: One of the firms has been behind hand but is getting straight.

	Actual	Program	Actual as a % of program
Heavy bombers			
Stirling	881	901	97.8
Lancaster	1,847	1,845	100.1
Halifax	1,824	1,928	94.6
Warwick	61	68	89.7
Total	4,613	4,742	97.3
Medium bombers			
Wellington	2,536	2,737	92.7
Buckingham	–	1	–
Whitley	95	101	94.1
Albermarle	106	170	62.4
Total	2,737	3,009	91.0
Light bombers			
Mosquito	229	243	94.2
Blenheim	147	142	103.5
Total	376	385	97.7
Fighters			
Spitfire	4,276	4,352	98.3
Beaufighter	1,641	1,655	99.2
Mosquito	923	1,110	83.2
Hurricane	2,742	2,716	101.0
Typhoon	1,137	1,202	94.6
Tempest	3	47	6.4
Welkin	5	40	12.5
Meteor	–	3	–
Total	10,727	11,125	96.4
General reconnaissance			
Beaufort	376	421	89.3
Auster	469	512	91.6
Sunderland	209	228	91.7
Total	1,054	1,161	90.8
Transport and ASR			
York	3	20	15.0
Warwick	173	187	92.5
Stirling	11	8	137.5
Albermarle	23	39	59.0
Total	210	254	82.7
Naval			
Seafire	298	310	96.1
Sea Hurricane	24	24	100.0
Firefly	53	122	43.4

	Actual	Program	Actual as a % of program
Firebrand	5	27	18.5
Barracuda	617	653	94.5
Swordfish	592	581	101.9
Walrus	97	110	88.2
Sea Otter	29	39	74.4
Fulmar	5	–	–
Total	1,720	1,866	92.2
Trainers			
Anson	1,465	1,505	97.3
Oxford	1,445	1,461	98.9
Mosquito	74	82	90.2
Master	39	39	100.0
Martinet	970	970	100.0
Moth	517	455	113.6
Queen Bee	6	26	23.1
Dominie	37	73	50.7
Proctor	256	264	97.0
Defiant	16	16	100.0
Total	4,825	4,891	98.7
Grand Total	**26,262**	**27,433**	**95.7**

Figure 8.8 Aircraft deliveries and programme – 1943.

Of course, the shadow factories were responsible for producing many of these aircraft. Equally, they produced many of the engines used in these aircraft (Figure 8.9).

	Actual Deliveries	Program	Actual as a % of program
Merlin	25,579	26,639	96.0
Griffon	403	593	68.0
Hercules	17,872	18,332	97.5
Centaurus[a]	497	774	64.2
Mercury	1,266	1,409	89.9
Pegasus	1,322	1,255	105.3
Taurus	546	545	100.2
Sabre[b]	1,151	1,519	75.8
Cheetah	7,865	8,100	97.1
Gypsy	1,438	1,469	97.9
Cirrus	40	–	–
Total	57,979	60,635	95.6

a.   New engines late in coming in owing to the usual teething troubles and too optimistic an estimate in the program;

b.   the breakdown of the Napier organisation before it was taken over by English Electric is largely responsible for this. The development of the engine was never properly carried through. It is now established and production is improving.

Figure 8.9 Engine deliveries and programme for 1943.[11]

Arguably the manufacture of Spitfires warrants a section of its own, for many reasons including the iconic status of the aircraft. Additionally, it serves as an example of a shadow factory that ran into problems resulting in a change in the management company.

Spitfire Production

Most Spitfires were manufactured at what is now the Jaguar factory in Castle Bromwich in Birmingham. A plaque on the exterior wall of the factory near the Jaguar Visitor Centre is one of the few reminders (Figure 8.10).

The story of the factory started with an offer to Lord Nuffield to build the factory and run it as a shadow factory, more of which appears in the introduction. Some of the background to the factory was summarised in the letter below.

Figure 8.10 The blue plaque marking the Spitfire factory.

27th November 1939

Up to the present date (25th November 1939) £2,373,459 has been paid by the department in connection with the building and equipment of the Castle Bromwich Aeroplane Factory. The first payment of £5,000 was made on the 17th August 1938 and £140,000 had been paid at 3rd December 1938. The agreement between the S. of S. and Lord Nuffield is dated 16th September 1938 and does not contain any date for the completion of erection and equipment of the factory. According to DAMF, the date for completion was the 30th September 1939 and on the 11th November 1939, all buildings except the final erection shop and main office were completed and 95% of the plant was installed in the machine shop.

Clause 29 of the agreement between the S. of S. and Lord Nuffield reads: *The Controller or Deputy Controller shall not be entitled to any profit or personal remuneration whatsoever for the carrying out of the terms of this agreement.*

The agreement provides for the manufacture with the utmost expedition, of 1,000 airframes of the Spitfire type and such spare parts as the S. of S. may require. Delivery dates are not specified and according to the latest DSP return, the first aeroplane will be delivered in April 1940. We have no information which would support the statement *that the plant is at least eight months behind in its deliveries.*

With regard to paragraph (4) of 1A, I am informed that one pair of wings has been delivered by CBAF to the Supermarine Company. This is the initial delivery of an order for 100 pairs of wings placed with Morris Motors Ltd on the 27th September 1938. The order was transferred to CBAF on the 8th February 1939; delivery was as early as possible.

Reference has been made to the Inspector-in-Charge, AID at CBAF. He does not agree with the statement as to the defects in the wings delivered and stated that he has accepted them as serviceable and in accordance with the contract.

A comparison with the Austin factory may be appropriate in considering paragraph (3) of 1A. The Austin factory was commenced on the 1st June 1936. The first Battle was delivered in September 1938. If therefore CBAF produced the first Spitfire by April 1940, they will have improved considerably on the Austin performance.

Deputy Director of Contracts.[12]

The agreement between the Secretary of State for Air and Lord Nuffield appears in Appendix V. The agreement specifically mentioned a Mr Oliver Boden as one of the management team. Sadly he died during the war. A meeting was called in the Secretary of State's room on the 12 March 1940 to discuss a replacement for Mr Boden as he was both Deputy Controller of the Castle Bromwich Factory and Deputy Director-General of Maintenance in the Air Ministry. At the time, the Castle

Bromwich factory was experiencing some difficulties, as described in the following meeting notes:

1. **Castle Bromwich.** It appears that the Castle Bromwich factory, which was the largest of its kind in the world, was likely to be very much behind in its forecasted production program. The reason was partly that production difficulties had been under-estimated, and partly that Mr Boden had been too busy to devote sufficient time to supervising the factory. It was generally considered that Mr Clark, who Lord Nuffield proposed to appoint in Mr Boden's place as Deputy Controller, was not quite equal to the task. It would, however, be difficult for the Secretary of State to press Lord Nuffield to make other arrangements, in the first place because Mr Clark was his own choice, and there appeared to be no satisfactory alternative within the Nuffield organisation, and in the second place because in doing so the Air Ministry would assume some degree of responsibility for the success or failure of the enterprise thereafter.

    It was eventually decided that an attempt should be made to obtain the services of Mr Westbrook of Vickers on loan as acting Deputy Controller with full powers of control, for a period of say six months, until the Vickers Blackpool factory came into production. This appointment would, it was felt, in view of Mr Westbrook's high qualities and of his experience in the manufacture of Wellingtons and Spitfires assist considerably in strengthening the organisation at Castle Bromwich and in improving output. These advantages would more than offset the decline in Vickers' production which might be expected to result from the transfer, and which was not expected to be serious since Vickers were in a good position to make satisfactory alternative arrangements for the management of their factories.

    It was decided, further, that in the first place S of S and AMDP should see Sir Charles Craven and secure his consent to the transfer, and later that S of S should see Lord Nuffield alone to put the suggestion to him.

2. **Repair Organisation.** AMSO said that Lord Nuffield proposed to appoint as joint Deputy Directors General of Maintenance Mr Ryder and Mr Seaward, but their respective responsibilities had not been so far defined. Mr Ryder was at present Deputy Controller of the Repair Organisation at Cowley and had considerable engineering experience. Mr Seaward's experience, on the other hand, had been mostly commercial. It could be arranged that Mr Ryder could be employed full time in the Air Ministry, AMSO would be quite prepared to accept his appointment without the addition of Mr Seaward, and indeed he felt that it would be difficult for the joint appointments proposed to function efficiently since the duties of the post were incapable of effective division and even if they were divided there might still be difficulties in co-ordinating the work of the two Deputy Directors General.

It was finally agreed that the Secretary of State in his discussion with Lord Nuffield should in the first place endeavour to find out exactly what was intended by the suggested appointment of joint Deputy Directors General of Maintenance. Following this he should if possible suggest that it would be preferable for a single individual to be responsible as Deputy Director-General, and to add that in the view of the Air Ministry this individual should have technical experience. He should in consequence suggest that Mr Ryder alone should be appointed and should devote his whole time to the work.

AMSO added that the post of Deputy Director-General of Maintenance was a government appointment and that the Secretary of State was therefore in a stronger position to suggest alternatives to Lord Nuffield's proposals than in the case of the appointment of a Deputy Controller for the Castle Bromwich factory.[13]

Eventually production started, the first Spitfire being flight-tested at Castle Bromwich. Details of the first test flight are recorded in the free brochure provided to visitors of the Castle Bromwich factory. The following is a first-hand account by the test pilot.

I flew my first Castle Bromwich built Spitfire, a Mark II P7281 on 15th June 1940, something all of us who were involved will always remember. I motored from Chandler's Ford with my wife to arrive at first light to find that the machine I was supposed to test was not ready and still on the tarmac, surrounded by bodies from the Managing Director down to girl cleaners, each and everyone was doing their best to help.

In spite of all their efforts, the Spitfire was not taken to the adjoining airfield until nearly nine o'clock in the evening with the sun already getting near the horizon...

The work, the worry and the trauma of getting this one aircraft ready had drained them completely (senior department heads, Sir Alex Dunbar, Chief at AID etc.). They all watched in grim silence...

My job has been easy compared with what they had had to contend with and I thought that at least I should show my appreciation before I left them. From the dive I did a series of vertical rolls and then a series of normal Spitfire aerobatics finishing with a slow roll in front of the little group so that the inverted fin of the aircraft cut a swathe through the fog only feet from where they were watching so intently.[14]

Painful as it was, the factory eventually started to produce the required number of Spitfires. In some ways though, the Spitfire was a victim of its own success as there was a seemingly unending need for variants which could go higher, turn or fly faster. The following details some of the issues needing resolution.

31st May 1941

To: Sir Henry Tizard FRS

Spitfires

The minutes of the Joint Development and Production Meeting held on 22nd May 1941 indicate that ACAST desires an alteration in our proposals with regard to Spitfire production.

The present proposals are:

1. That the Merlin XLV version should continue at Southampton and Castle Bromwich until the introduction of the universal wing.
2. The Merlin XLV engine would be replaced by the Merlin XLVI engine as soon as production became adequate to meet demands and this change over is expected, together with the universal wing, in September at Southampton and towards the end of the year at Castle Bromwich. By December all the standard Spitfire production would be Merlin XLVI universal wing type.
3. To meet the Air Staff requirement for more high altitude aircraft as early as possible, the Merlin XLVII engine has been developed and will be introduced about September 1941, in small quantities and to the extent of 100 aircraft. There would not be available another higher altitude engine until after January 1942.
4. The Merlin XLVII engine would, as soon as possible, be replaced with the Merlin XLVIII engine which would give better high altitude performance, but on the present plans we were also continuing with the Merlin XLVI version until the total production was absorbed by Griffon Spitfires. The Merlin XLVIII version was only expected to reach the figure of approximately 30 per month and it was intended to replace the Merlin XLVIII with the Merlin LX in similar quantities in the pressure cabin version.

At Castle Bromwich it was intended to continue with the Merlin XLVI until a change over to the Spitfire IV when Griffon engine was possible and this would have been towards the end of 1942.

If the Griffon Spitfire is to be deferred until the higher altitude engine is developed we must adopt one or other of the following plans:

a. To change the whole of production over to Merlin XLVIII and follow this, when possible, with Merlin LX, or
b. Substitute Spitfire VI type for the Spitfire IV type and continue with a limited number of pressure cabin versions as before.
c. Change over all production to Merlin XLVIII and Merlin LX type taking some of these as pressure cabin and some as normal Spitfires.

In each of these alterations it is necessary that we should know, as soon as possible, the numbers of each of the various types which the Air Staff require.

Another question which arises is whether the Griffon version should not be brought in parallel with the very high altitude aircraft as it gives performance, with the exception of ceiling, which is superior to the performance of any of the other types at all heights below 25–30,000 ft and is, in addition, more heavily armed.

It is the Air Staff's view that a quantity of fighter aircraft of 350 per month, all having service ceilings approximately 40,000ft will be required?

Our original understanding was that they always required a small number of aircraft with these characteristics and the remainder with the greatest high speed performance and armament at or about 25–30,000ft level. I understand that, in any case, the Griffon Spitfire will have a ceiling of over 37,000ft which is approximately the same as that for the Spitfire V and that it will be 40 miles an hour faster at 20,000 ft.

To summarise could you obtain specific answers to the following questions?

a.   Does the Air Staff require immediate plans to be made for changing over all Spitfire production to pressure cabin type?
b.   If not, do they require change over to Merlin LX through Merlin XLVIII type, some aircraft having pressure cabins and some not?
c.   If (b) is required what are the numbers of each type?
d.   Are the Air Staff satisfied to have 350 Spitfires per month, all having optimum performance above 28,000 ft and presumably having performance inferior to the Griffon Spitfire or the Merlin XLV Spitfire at 20–25,000 ft?

P Hennessy[15]

The reply makes for interesting reading as it clarified the position.

30th June 1941

Mr Hennessy,

I am sorry that there has been this misunderstanding of the Air Staff requirements in the Spitfire program. As far as the Air Staff were concerned, there has never been any question of increasing the order for a *pressure cabin* Spitfire above 350 initial order plus a subsequent maintenance trickle. They further require the Spitfire capacity, after due allowance had been made for the above, to be turned over from the Spitfire V to the Spitfire IV. The only uncertainty was the date at which it would be advantageous to introduce the Spitfire IV from the point of view of its performance vis-à-vis the development of the Griffon engine.

In order to clue up the matter, I held a conference on Sunday, 8th June. Summarised, the position can be stated as follows:

a. The development of the **Spitfire V** will be limited to a change of engine with a view to improving performance by the introduction of the Merlin 46. When this is done, it will apparently simplify the problem of engine production to introduce the Merlin XII crank case with its accommodation for the Coffman drive. The last named change has no significance as far as the Spitfire V performance is concerned but, provided it introduces no complications, I presume you will have no objection to accepting it.

b. The Spitfire IV to be introduced with the Griffon II engine (i.e. 2-speed single stage version) as early as convenient to production plans for engines and airframes. This will give an aircraft appreciably faster than the Spitfire V at all heights and having an operational ceiling with 4 × 20 mm guns in position, of about 35,500 ft. It is possible that detailed improvements in the Griffon II may better this performance before the aircraft is in service. In the design of the Spitfire IV airframe, DTD has been instructed to consider fully steps to facilitate a further change to 2-stage 2-speed Griffon engine which **might** be introduced in say two years time.

c. The **pressure cabin Spitfire** is required at the earliest possible date as interim counter to possible German high flying bombers. The numbers required are as confirmed by AMSO by separate document. The urgency of the matter leads to the probable need to introduce this Mark with the Merlin 47 engine (i.e. the Merlin 46 with the Merlin XII crank case), without waiting for the Merlin 48 (i.e. Merlin 47 + Inter-coolers). DTD has been instructed to ensure that the airframe is schemed round the additional space required for the Inter-coolers.

   As soon as the Merlin 60 engine is ready, it is desired to change-over from the Merlin 48 to the Merlin 60. This is a most awkward step since the engine is 7 inches longer. It is however one which we are bound to face owing to the improvement of ceiling and speed at top altitudes obtained thereby. DTD is considering effects of this change on the airframe structure.

I hope the above gives you a clear picture of requirements. I am of course ready to discuss the matter in detail at any time you wish.

AM[16]

The choice of engine and Spitfire Mark shows the range of potential options. Those less familiar with the details of the various Spitfire Marks might appreciate the table which is stored in the same National Archives folio as the above papers. It is included here as a reference (Figure 8.11).

Mark	Engine	Description	Production Position	Performance
I	Merlin III	Standard 8 guns	Finished	355 mph at 19800 ft. 34,000 ft ceiling
IIa	Merlin XII	Standard 8 guns as made by Castle Bromwich	Just passing out of production	363 mph at 17,000 ft. 36,500 ft ceiling
IIb	Merlin XII	2 cannon drum feed	To complete the remaining Mark II type (920)	360 mph at 17,000ft. 36,200ft ceiling
III	Merlin XX	Universal wing	Prototype flying not planned for production	382 mph at 22,000 ft. 36,300 ft ceiling
IV	Griffon	6 cannon	Under discussion prototype being built	410 mpg at 22,500 ft. 37,700 ft ceiling
Va	Merlin XLV	8 guns – interim type	Interim production now finished	375 mph at 20,250 ft. 38,000 ft ceiling
Vb	Merlin XLV	2 cannon drum feed	Production until universal wing comes in	371 mph at 20,200 ft. 37,500 ft ceiling
Vc	Merlin XLV	Universal wing. Belt feed for cannons	This type becomes standard until replaced by VIa at the end of 1941	371 mph at 20,200 ft. 37,500 ft ceiling
VIa	Merlin XLVI	Improved version of V – universal wing		382 mph at 23,500 ft. 39,500 ft ceiling
VIIa	Merlin XLVII	Interim pressure cabin version. Universal wing	100 to be made to introduce the pressure cabin type	382 mph at 23,500 ft. 39,000 ft ceiling
VIIIa	Merlin XLVIII	Pressure cabin version. Universal wing	Improved pressure cabin type at the end of 1941	395 mph at 28,000 ft. 40,500 ft ceiling
IXa	Merlin LX	Pressure cabin fully developed. Universal wing	Ultimate type mid-1942 may also be standard type without pressure cabin	408 mph at 33,000 ft. 41,600 ft ceiling

Figure 8.11 Spitfire variants.[17]

Figure 8.12 The Merlin III. (Author's photograph)

The Merlin III set the scene as it was fitted in the Spitfire Mark I. One of these engines has been preserved and is on display at the RAF Museum at Hendon (Figure 8.12).

> The Merlin III was used not only in fighter aircraft such as the Boulton Paul Defiant, Hawker Hurricane and Supermarine Spitfire, but also in Fairey Battle light bombers. More than 6,400 of these engines were produced at Rolls-Royce factories at Derby and Crewe.[18]

Figure 8.11 shows a table that was written during the war and therefore contains details of the earlier Spitfire variants but does not, of course, include later Marks introduced later. It is shown here for two reasons:

- It demonstrates the variants in the Spitfire Marks, suggesting other aircraft also had many variants.
- It shows that the range of variants adds a layer of complexity when repairing aircraft for future use in battle, as the repair stations need to carry spares for the different variants. Additionally, these spares need manufacturing.

As the war raged across all the various theatres, the needs of the fighter squadrons sometimes changed. The letter below provides a small insight into the way in which orders to Castle Bromwich and Southampton (the factory owned by Supermarine, the company which developed the Spitfire) were derived.

4th May 1943

To: D. of Policy.

As a result of strong recommendation by C-in-C, Fighter Command, the CAS agreed yesterday to limit the number of Spitfire VII Squadrons in Fighter Command to 3 instead of 5, the balance of 2 being equipped with Spitfire IXs.

This will mean that we can arrange with AMSO for a further cut in the number of Spitfire VII aircraft produced, substituting Spitfire IXs. The number of Spitfire VIIs must be adequate to maintain 3 Squadrons until an equivalent number of Welkin Squadrons are in operation.

C-in-C, Fighter Command plans to use the Welkin as a night fighter aircraft with the additional day role of high altitude defence. CAS has accepted this proposition. It is therefore necessary to ensure that the Welkin is produced as a two-seater AI aircraft.

The three Spitfire Squadrons as the Spitfire VII dies out will be re-armed with Spitfire IXs in the day fighter force.

DCS Evill
Vice CAS[19]

Of course, some of the Spitfires in the fighter squadrons were destroyed by enemy action and needed replacement, some were shot down over land and may have survived or at least parts of them may have. Figure 8.13 shows the number of Spitfires produced and those brought back into use by the repair of Spitfires Mark VB and later Marks, and Figure 8.14 shows the numbers totally scrapped, both for 1943.

1943	From Production	From Repair		Grand Total
		At Works	On Site	
January	333	99	63	495
February	359	90	54	503
March	360	77	63	500
April	328	58	66	452
May	352	74	56	482
June	350	62	63	475
July	280	63	89	432
Total	2,362	523	454	3,339

Figure 8.13 Spitfire production and repair figures for the first half of July 1943.

Wastage in Fighter Command Spitfire Squadrons
Spitfire Mark VB and later Marks

1943	Written-off Cat E	Repairable Cat AC and B	Total
January	44	47	91
February	55	41	96
March	42	73	115
April	59	83	142
May	56	72	128
June	57	85	142
July	50	90	140
August (to 23rd)	40	53	93
Total for year up to 23rd August	403	544	947

Figure 8.14 Spitfire wastage for the first few months of 1943.[20]

During the same period, 2,137 Spitfires were shipped abroad for our operations in Gibraltar or Casablanca, Takoradi, India and Australia.[21]

Finally for this section, Figure 8.12 is of a Merlin III engine fitted in the Spitfire Mark 1. It is fitting that the final picture of this section should be of the Mark I, the aircraft which set the benchmark for so many other airplanes (Figure 8.15).

Figure 8.15 Spitfire Mark 1. (Author's photograph)

Recovery and Repair

Lord Nuffield was indeed a busy man. Not only was he involved in the shadow factory and in manufacturing other machinery for the Ministry of Supply but he was also appointed Director-General of Repair and Maintenance at the Air Ministry. This was alluded to in the previous chapters and is mentioned below.

December 1939

Personal and Confidential
To Mr H Dalton MP
House of Commons

My Dear Dalton,

I promised that I would put down on paper, for your own private information, what I told you in connection with the statements in the paper that you sent me to the effect that the appointment of Lord Nuffield and Mr Boden as Director-General and Deputy Director-General respectively of repair and maintenance at the Air Ministry would result in all repair and maintenance work being passed to Morris Motors, and that Morris Motors in their turn would be able to secure a profit on any work that they allocated on a sub-contracting basis.

Actually the position is as follows. Lord Nuffield and Mr Boden will be responsible for the organisation which has been established for the repair of aircraft and ancillary equipment of the Royal Air Force. Policy will be directed from the Air Ministry, but the organisation will operate through a centre, to be known as the Civilian Repair Organisation, that has been established at Cowley under the direction of an official of Morris Motors who is to be called the Director of the Civil Repair Organisation. This Director and his staff will be selected from Morris Motors and they will not become direct Government employees. Their salaries and other costs connected with the administrative services which the Civilian Repair Organisation will perform will be recovered by Morris Motors from the Air Ministry under an agreement which provides that Morris Motors shall provide the personnel, accommodation, etc. necessary to carry out certain specified services in connection with the repair of aircraft and equipment. These specified services are:

i.   To find repair capacity for all such equipment.
ii. To select repair capacity so far as possible where a minimum of works extension and capital expenditure is involved.
iii. To investigate in each instance any questions of subsequent reinstatement which may be involved.
iv. In conjunction with the Director-General of Production and the Directors of Contracts, to allocate repair work to the selected capacity.

v.   To arrange with the Directors of Contracts for appropriate contract action to be taken by them, in accordance with Air Ministry procedure.

vi. To supervise the progress of work under the consequential contracts and also under repair contracts for such equipment placed by the department prior to the inception of the Civilian Repair Organisation.

From this you will see that whilst it is the responsibility of the Civilian Repair Organisation to procure repair capacity, the allocation of work to such capacity will be made in conjunction with the Director-General of Production and the Directors of Contracts at the Air Ministry. The contracts for work so placed will not be between the firm concerned and Morris Motors, but between the firm and the Air Ministry; and the contract will be drawn up by the Director of Contracts who will ensure that the ordinary departmental safe-guards in contract matters are properly taken.

The firms which will undertake repair work will be many and varied since the Civilian Repair Organisation is to cover all RAF equipment, but the procedure which I have mentioned will be followed in every instance. Among other firms which will undertake repair work will be the Morris Motors Aircraft Repair Unit at Cowley, but as with any other firm the work to be done here will be subject to contract between the Repair unit and the Air Ministry which will contain the normal contractual safe-guards.

Yours sincerely
Kingsley Wood[22]

This confidential communication mentions the Morris Motors Aircraft Repair Unit at Cowley. The letter also states that other recovery units existed, one of which was located in Guiseley, which incidentally was near the shadow factory at Yeadon in West Yorkshire.

22nd September 1941

Ministry of Aircraft Production Schedule for the recovery and repair of parts from crashed, damaged and obsolete Bristol engines in accordance with the details hereinafter mentioned

1.   Dismantling crashed or damaged engines of the under-mentioned types and obsolete engines of various types which may be allotted to the Guiseley Factory (hereinafter referred to as *the factory*) for this purpose. Examining the engine parts, recovering such parts as may be classified as serviceable or repairable and segregating scrap material in accordance with the requirements of the Inspector-in-Charge, AID and the provisions embodied in the notes set out below.

a.   Perseus.
b.   Taurus.
c.   Hercules.
d.   Centaurus.
e.   Obsolete engines (various Bristol types).

2.   Carrying out to the requirements and satisfaction of the Inspector-in-Charge AID the work necessary to render serviceable the repairable parts (excluding carburettors) recovered at Item 1 above, in so far as such work is within the approved ability or capacity of the factory.

Note A: After carrying out work dismantling engines of current types the factory is to establish in conjunction with the Inspector-in-Charge, AID the engine category under one of the following headings:

1.   Engines of which the cost of repair and rendering fully serviceable will not exceed 75% of the cost to the Department of a new engine of a similar type.

2.   Engines of which the cost of repair will equal or exceed 75% of the cost to the Department of a new engine of a similar type.

   Engines falling under (1) above are to be transferred on the instructions of the Inspector-in-Charge, AID to the relevant current overhaul order. Engines falling under (2) and obsolete engines are to be dealt with by the factory under this order.

Note B: The factory shall at monthly intervals render lists of the articles under Item 2 of this order. The lists should state the reference number, part number, description and quantity of each item and are to be duly certified by the Inspector-in-Charge, AID and forwarded as follows:

1.   One copy to the Director of Contracts (C2(a)), Ministry of Aircraft Production, Harrogate, Yorks.

2.   One copy to the Director of Equipment (E24), Air Ministry, Harrogate, Yorks.

3.   One copy to the Chief Provisioning Officer, Master Provision Office, No 16 Maintenance Unit, RAF, Stafford.

4.   One copy to the Chief Accountant, RAF Special Accounts Section, Caldecott House, Abingdon, Berks.

1.   **Quantity**

a.   It is estimated that the quantity of engines to be covered by this order will be 50, but this estimate is for guidance only and no precise figure can be given. The Department reserves the right to vary the quantity as may be found necessary.

b.   Engines will be despatched to the factory as and when they become available and no undertaking can be given as to dates or rate of dispatch. No engine will, however, be allotted under this order after 31st March 1942.

2.   Date of Completion

The work to be carried out under this order is to be completed as soon as possible.

3.   Disposal of Parts

1.   All parts, accessories and material resulting from the work carried out under this order shall be and remain the property of the Minister.

2.   This material is to be dealt with as follows:

a.   Engine parts, assemblies or accessories (including magnetos) which are serviceable are to be placed in the MAP Bond at the factory.

b.   Repairable engine parts (excluding carburettors) will be repaired under item 2 of this order so far as the repair work is within the approved ability and capacity of the factory and after repair the parts will be placed in the MAP Bond at the factory (see Note B).

c.   Magnetos, sparking plugs and ignition harness requiring repair beyond the approved ability or capacity of the factory are to be despatched to No 7 Repairable Equipment Unit, RAF, Ruislip, Middlesex.

d.   Other parts, assemblies or accessories extraneous to the bare engine are where serviceable or repairable to be placed in the MAP Bond at the factory pending receipt of disposal instructions from the Inspector-in-Charge, AID or the Chief Provisioning Officer, Master Provision Office, No 16 Maintenance Unit, RAF, Stafford.

e.   Parts, assemblies and accessories (other than those detailed in (f) below) certified by the Inspector-in-Charge, AID as *scrap, obsolete* or *not economically repairable* are to be held on behalf of the Minister in the scrap store under the control of the factory pending receipt of disposal instructions from the Chief Accountant, RAF Special Accounts Section, Abingdon, Berks, but details of types and weights of materials need only be given when disposal instructions are sought. Parts under this heading which may be useful to the Bristol Aeroplane Co Ltd in connection with the assembly of instructional engines are to be segregated (see 3b) below).

f.   Magnetos, sparking plugs and ignition harness certified by the Inspector-in-Charge, AID as *scrap, obsolete* or *not economically repairable* are to be despatched to No 7 Repairable Equipment Unit, RAF Ruislip, Middlesex.

g.   A proportion of magnetos certified by the Inspector-in-Charge, AID as beyond economical repair may be stripped and the serviceable arisings retained in the MAP Bond for subsequent issue on embodiment loan (provided that not more than one month's supply of spares is held at one time).

h.   All carburettors whether repairable or otherwise are to be despatched to Messrs H M Hobson (Aircraft and Motor Components) Ltd, Hobson Works, Holbrook Lane, Coventry.

3.   Lists of material are to be furnished by the factory as follows:

a.   Lists detailing reference numbers and part numbers (where known) and descriptions of parts included in 2(a), (c) and (d) above indicating disposal action are to be certified by the Inspector-in-Charge, AID and forwarded to the Chief Provisioning Officer, Master Provision Office, No 16 Maintenance Unit, RAF, Stafford (copy to the Chief Accountant RAF Special Accounts Section, Abingdon, Berks).

b.   Lists of parts included under 2(e) and (f) listed in categories and weights of material – reference numbers, part numbers and descriptions need not be stated – are to be certified by the Inspector-in-Charge, AID and forwarded to the Chief Accountant, RAF Special Accounts Section, Abingdon, Berks, who will issue disposal instructions. These lists should show separately those parts which may be useful to the Bristol Aeroplane Co Ltd in connection with the assembly of instructional engines and have been segregated for that purpose. Advice concerning the type of parts which may be useful is to be sought from the Bristol Aeroplane Co Ltd, Filton House, Bristol.

Name of Factory:
The Bristol Aeroplane Co Ltd
Engine Repair Factory
Guiseley
Nr Leeds

Place at which the work is to be carried out:
Guiseley, Nr Leeds[23]

Knowing Churchill's interest in recovered and repaired aircraft and engines, the following is a report sent to him in 1941.

9th November 1941

Prime Minister,

Below are given weekly output for the week ending 8th November 1941 and 9th November 1940 for new and repaired aircraft (Figure 8.16) and new and repaired engines (Figure 8.17) and also the number of aircraft of operational types held in aircraft storage units (Figure 8.18) as ready for immediate issue and ready within four days at 8th November 1941.

Type	New		Repaired	
	w.e 8th Nov 1941	w.e. 9th Nov 1940	w.e 8th Nov 1941	w.e. 9th Nov 1940
Blenheim	9x	34xx	24	14
Halifax	5	–	2	–
Hampden	8	9	12	3
Lancaster	1	–	–	–
Manchester	3	–	–	–
Stirling	3	1	–	–
Wellington	44	27	35	19
Whitley	11	12	15	10
Beaufighter	18	6	16	–
Hurricane	60(5)	57	60	39
Spitfire	59	25	71	38
Other bombers and fighters/ General reconnaissance	22 (11)	17 (5)	29	10
Fleet Air Arm	26	23 (3)	6	4
Army co-operation	–	16	10	4
Total (Operational types)	269 (16)	226 (8)	280	141
Trainers	148	102 (-)	72	36
Miscellaneous	–	–	5	11
Grand total (all types)	417 (16)	328 (8)	357	188

Notes: x – in addition to 2 modifications; xx – in addition to 28 modifications. USA and Canadian deliveries, shown in brackets, are included in adjacent figures. New aircraft (British operational types) 269 - 16 = 253; aircraft (operational types) new production and repair 269 + 280 = 549.

Figure 8.16 Output of new and repaired aircraft.

Type	New		Repaired	
	w.e 8th Nov 1941	w.e. 9th Nov 1940	w.e 8th Nov 1941	w.e. 9th Nov 1940
All types	822	518	474	300

Figure 8.17 Output of new and repaired engines.

Type	w.e. 8th Nov 1941	Type	w.e. 8th Nov 1941
Blenheim	17	Whitley	11
Halifax	5	Beaufighter	19
Hampden	10	Hurricane	89
Lancaster	–	Spitfire	106
Manchester	–	Other types	93
Stirling	–	Total	432
Wellington	82		

Figure 8.18 Aircraft in Aircraft Storage Units (operational types).[24]

As usual, Churchill kept a keen eye on these issues.

21st September 1941

Dear Eaton Griffith,
The Prime Minister has seen the note by your Ministry dated 16th September on the repair position of day fighters, and has minuted on it:
    MAP: you are falling behind. You must make a new effort. A repaired aircraft is as good as a new aircraft. Propose the steps you will take to grapple with the growing danger and accumulation of wreckage.[25]

The turning tide of war eventually led to some closures in the repair stations, this being just one example.

4th December 1944

To: The Rover Co Ltd
Chesford Grange
Kenilworth

Gentlemen,
I am directed by the Minister of Aircraft Production to refer to the Department's letter of the 21st June 1940 addressed to your Company on the subject of the manufacture and repair of Cheetah engines, and with reference to the seventh

paragraph thereof to inform you that the Minister agrees that your Company's works at Tyseley, Birmingham, Helen Street Coventry and Seagrave Road London need not be held available for the production of supplies for this Department so soon as the contracts for which this capacity is or may be required are completed. This release does not affect your commitments to the Ministry of Supply. In that connection I am to state that it is agreed that No 1 Engine Shadow Factory at present managed by your Company on behalf of the Minister of Aircraft Production will be made available to the Ministry of Supply for the production of Meteor tank engines.

I am, Gentlemen,
Your Obedient Servant
Director of Contracts[26]

9

Visitors: Unwanted and Wanted

There is always a balancing act in war between the need to know and publicity. Those residents surrounding shadow factories producing airframes or indeed full aircraft assembly would no doubt know what was being built in the factory, especially if airplanes were taking off at regular intervals. My maternal grandfather was believed to have worked at a shadow factory in Yeadon, but to the day he died he did not discuss his war work with anyone in the family. The same was undoubtedly the case for most if not all of the other workers. Secrecy was the watch word. Yet German intelligence would have had a good idea of towns more likely to be involved in aircraft production even if the exact details were unavailable.

On the other hand, morale is nearly always boosted by visits from senior politicians and/or army personnel or indeed royalty. Most of these visits would have been kept quiet at the time, although in some cases there were press briefing notes, some of which survive. In all cases, there was a need to keep security as tight as possible.

Factory Defence

Perhaps, the most interesting question of shadow factory protection is how to protect. Perhaps, a more specific question would be what measures of protection would be deemed acceptable before the protection itself points out that a secret facility is close by. Lord Beaverbrook, suggested the formation of a police organisation.

12th October 1940

War Cabinet Home Policy Committee
proposed Aircraft Defence Police Memorandum by the Minister
of Aircraft Production

I circulate for immediate consideration of my colleagues on the Home Policy Committee a draft of a Defence Regulation which gives power to enrol a force to be known as the Aircraft Defence Police.

The purpose of this force is to afford protection to all factories employed in the production of aircraft or any part or fittings thereof and all places where the same or any materials for the production thereof are stored or kept.

These factories and places are inadequately protected at present and it is necessary to give the staffs employed there more confidence.

The War Cabinet have approved the proposal in principle.

Signed Beaverbrook

There followed:

8th October 1940

Order in Council Amending regulation 40AA of the Defence (General) Regulations 1939 (formal parts omitted)

After paragraph (1) of Regulation 40AA, there shall be inserted the following paragraph:

1(a). Without prejudice to the provisions of paragraph (1) of this regulation, the power conferred by the said section three shall extend to the appointment of persons nominated by the Minister of Aircraft Production to be special constables in, and within fifteen miles of, any premises in Great Britain which are for the time being used for or in connection with the production, storing or keeping of aircraft to be used in the service of His Majesty or any parts or fittings or accessories thereof, or for the storing or keeping of materials to be used in the production of such aircraft, parts, fittings or accessories.[1]

A few days later:

11th October 1940

To: Rt. Hon. C R Atlee
Privy Council Office

My Dear Attlee,
Following a Cabinet approval in principle, the Prime Minister and CIGC have agreed, with the following provisos, to the enrolment of a force up to 10,000 men to be known as the Aircraft Defence Police. The provisos are:

1. The force shall not be put into khaki but shall be dressed in blue in order to save khaki cloth.

2.   The rates of pay shall not be higher than those throughout the service in the War Office police.

I understand that you will put this through for me at the Home Office Policy Committee.

I enclose a draft Order in Council and a draft paper for the Home Policy Committee.

I should be glad if you would be good enough to arrange for all this to be settled at the earliest possible moment.

Yours sincerely
Beaverbrook[2]

Whilst the formation of a specific police force was adequate in the early stages of the war, as time progressed more measures were taken. The aero works at Longbridge were assigned two Hurricanes, for example.

3rd September 1941

To: The Austin Motor Co Ltd
Aero Works
Longbridge
Birmingham

Instruction Aircraft 1420/C.38(b) for the Maintenance of defence aircraft
DGE requisition of Hurricane airframe 5/E1/41.

Gentlemen,
1.   With reference to the department's letter of the 10th June last, I am directed by the Minister to inform you that two Hurricane Mark I aeroplanes have been allocated to you for the purpose of defending the shadow factory at Longbridge, and the adjacent aerodrome. The aeroplanes (of which the RAF serial numbers will be inserted at a later date) and the pilots deputed to fly them will be under the control of the Officer Commanding RAF Station Baginton.
2.   I am to request, therefore, that you will arrange for the housing, mainte-nance, and servicing of the aeroplanes. The work is to be carried out to the requirements of the Officer Commanding, RAF Station Baginton, and to the satisfaction of the Inspector-in-Charge, AID, and shall comprise:
      a.   The housing of the aeroplanes at Longbridge aerodrome.
      b.   The inspection, servicing and maintenance of the aeroplanes, including the engines, airscrews and equipment, in an airworthy condition in accordance with current Air Ministry maintenance instructions.

    c.   The execution of all necessary repairs. Details of replacements and/or repairs which you consider to be uneconomical or beyond your capacity should be notified to the department.

    d.   The embodiment in the airframes and engines of approved modifications. Where, however, such modifications are beyond your capacity, the department will issue instructions as to the embodiment procedure to be adopted.

    e.   The provision of all necessary fuel, oil and glycol.

    f.   The performance of such flight tests as are considered necessary by the Inspector-in-Charge, AID (in this connection it should be noted however, that clearance of aeroplanes for practice or operational flights should be given by your own Inspectors as ground engineers operating under AID supervision).

3.   It is desired that you shall accept responsibility for the services not called for to the fullest extent possible, but the Officer Commanding RAF Station, Baginton, will furnish:

    a.   Such information as you require for the efficient maintenance of the aeroplanes.

    b.   Such material and parts as are not available to you from other sources.

    c.   Technical assistance in matters with which you are not fully conversant.

4.   Whilst the aeroplanes are in your custody for the purposes referred to in paragraph 1 above, the Minister will accept liability for damage to the aeroplanes howsoever arising, and for all third party risks with the exception of injury to the pilot or damage to the pilot's property.

5.   The Minister will indemnify you against any action, or proceedings relating to the use of the design of the Hurricane I aeroplane and will negotiate direct with any claimants for royalty. This indemnity shall apply to this instruction only.

6.   The conditions contained in MAP forms 705 and 838 (in so far as they are not expressly overridden by the terms of this instruction) and in paragraphs 1, 3 and 4 of MAP form 2041 will apply hereto.

7.   Records will be maintained of all work carried out under this instruction and of all serviceable or repairable redundant material arising therefrom. The condition of each item should be shown, and the redundant material itself is to be returned to RAF Station, Baginton for classification. Redundant material consisting of scrap shall, however, be retained at the shadow factory and application made to the department for disposal instructions.

8.   This instruction shall be operative from the date of the first delivery to Longbridge aerodrome of either or both of the aeroplanes the subject of this instruction (the earlier of two delivery dates being regarded as the date of commencement) to the 31st March 1941 or for such other period as the Minister may determine.

9. For the purposes of this instruction the Accounting Unit shall be:
    The Chief Accountant
    Royal Air Force Special Accounts Section
    Caldecott House
    Caldecott Road
    Abingdon
    Berks

10. Further instructions will be issued by the Air Ministry with regard to the operational control of the aircraft and the conditions of service applicable to the pilots deputed to fly the aeroplanes.

11. The purpose for which the aeroplanes are allocated to you shall be regarded as confidential, and you are required to undertake that you will not disclose to any unauthorised person any information whatsoever concerning or resulting from the use of the aeroplanes for this purpose. If information is solicited by an unauthorised person an immediate report should be made to the Director of Contracts giving all relevant particulars including, if possible, the name, address and occupation of the enquirer. Your attention is drawn to the Official Secrets Acts 1911 to 1939, and to the Defence (General) Regulations 1939.

12. The agreement to be negotiated between yourselves and the department relating to the management of the Longbridge shadow factory will make provision for the services called for in this instruction.[3]

Fortunately, the RAF Museum at Hendon has a Mark 1 Hurricane on display, Figure 9.1.

Defending airfields attached to shadow factories sometimes led to interesting issues. There was always the temptation to build a flight training school next to the airfield to make use of the runways when the test pilots were not flying. Of course, the test pilots were skilled with many hours of flying. Trainee pilots were just that, novices. This sometimes led to them taxiing over grass or leaving 'skid' marks on the concrete runways should their landing be somewhat more aggressive than it needed to be.

30th December 1941

Dear Mr Carline,

From time to time instances have been put up in which the operation of Flight Training Schools (FTS) from MAP factory aerodromes has proved detrimental to the maintenance of the concealment of the aerodrome and therefore of the factory to which it was attached. Apart from such instances it is thought that MAP should consider the operation of FTS from MAP factory aerodromes as a matter of general principle.

MAP aerodromes are in the main either private aerodromes belonging to the factories or municipal aerodromes to which the factories are contiguous and in

Figure 9.1 Hawker Hurricane Mk1. (Author's photograph)

all cases the sole need from the production point of view is for sufficient space from which new machines can be taken into the air for testing and ultimately for delivery. Such space can be adequately provided by two or three landing lanes and the test flying that is carried out results in a very small number of aircraft actually taking off or landing. Fulfilling these needs produces no result that is inimicable to good camouflage, but the opposite is the case when landing lanes are extended to a complete aerodrome and when the aerodrome itself is used, in addition to test flying, by training units of the RAF. The undesirable factors which immediately arise are as follows:

a.   The training units on the landing ground prevent the limiting of test flying to lanes, and the consequent cultivation or three dimensional forms of camouflage of the remainder of the area.

b.   The constant operation of training aircraft in many cases results in scarring of the aerodrome surface which is impossible to cure thus making an easily recognisable feature.

c.   Continual flying in and out of aircraft in itself draws attention to the location.

It was recognised in the early stages of the war that the shortage of aerodromes was such that every available landing ground had to be used for operational or training purposes. During the last two years, however, very many aerodromes have been constructed and it is suggested that the time has now come when it would be reasonable that the majority of aerodromes whose primary purpose is to enable test flying to be carried out from important MAP factories should be used for this purpose only and so enable effective concealment of these most vital factories to be effected.

Photographic examples are given of some instances showing how the presence of FTS is adversely affecting factory concealment.

Please bring this minute to the attention of those concerned.

CCO[4]

The use of 'factory aerodromes' as bases for flying schools did lead to an increase in costs as well as problems of camouflage:

30th December 1941

To: Harold G Howitt
Air Ministry

Dear Sir Harold,
At its meeting on the 9th December the Supply Board was asked to consider a proposal for an expenditure of some £9,000 on repair work on Blackburn's aerodrome at Brough as a result of the operation thereon of EFTS aircraft.

I am informed that these aircraft, when leaving the hangers, have repeatedly passed from the apron in front of the hangers on to the grass surface of the aerodrome at the same point. As it may well be imagined, this has resulted in the gradual churning up of the surface of the aerodrome at this point. The muddy patch so created has now spread and extends to an area of some 12 acres and is continually growing. It has become visible from the air for a considerable distance both by day and on moonlit nights and is causing grave concern regarding the safety of the adjoining factory from air attack.

The Board took the view that the expenditure was on maintenance, and directed me to make further investigation. I am doing so, and I need not trouble you with this aspect now.

The case does, however, raise an important general question on the operation of EFTS aircraft upon aerodromes, of which Luton Airport is an example, and could, so I am informed, to a large extent be avoided if stricter measures were enforced whereby EFTS aircraft took off from the concrete apron at constantly changing points, thus obviating the heavy wear on one particular piece of turf. I do not know the size of the concrete apron usually constructed around EFTS hangers, but if these aprons are in fact too small to allow regular and frequent changes in the point of take-off, it might be well to enlarge existing aprons and to construct all future ones of a suitable size. If, however, the present size of aprons is adequate, the remedy would appear to be the issue of rigid enforcement of strict instructions as to changes in the point of leaving the apron.

If some such steps are not taken I am afraid that considerable expense and a heavy drain on maintenance and reconstruction labour may be involved at a number of aerodromes, to say nothing of the danger of the aerodromes themselves becoming sooner or later unusable.

In these circumstances, I feel that the attention of someone of considerable authority at the Air Ministry should be called to this matter, and I was wondering whether you could arrange to do this or, if not, whether you could let me know with whom you think I had best get in touch in order that the problem may be considered in the appropriate quarter and at an appropriate level.

Yours sincerely,
Sam H Brown[5]

As one might imagine, there were visits to various aerodromes and letters written by Air Ministry officials. The issues of widening the grass aprons and enforcing strict routes for support vehicles such as re-fuelling bowsers was in some ways the easier task. Of equal or even greater concern was the rubber skid marks made by aircraft wheels on landing. Clearly, novice pilots need practice in making smooth landings. In the earlier part of their training, a novice pilot may through no fault of his own make a heavy landing. These marks were very difficult to deal with as in time and with more heavy landings in the same part of the runway, they could be seen from the air.

On further investigation, the issues of flying schools based at aerodromes associated with shadow factories led to the following list, Figure 9.2. There are some familiar shadow companies on this list, each of which was thought to have an increased risk of detection or enemy action. Additionally, the Directorate of Camouflage designated most of these aerodromes of importance in resolving these issues.

Aerodrome	Factory
Brockworth	Gloster Aircraft
Brooklands	Vickers Armstrong, Hawker
Cowley	Morris Motors Ltd
Eastleigh	Cunliffe Owen etc.
Heathrow	Fairey Aviation
Horsted	Popjoy Air Motors
Longbridge	D Napier
Marwell (Southampton)	Cunliffe Owen
Radlett	Handley Page
Slough (Langley)	Hawkers
Walsall	Helliwells Ltd
Watford	De Havilland
Whitley	Armstrong Whitworth
Windsor (Smith's Lawn)	Vickers Armstrong
Woodford	AV Roe
Yate	Parnell Aircraft Co
Yeovil	Westland Aircraft
Yeovilton	Westland Aircraft

Figure 9.2 Aerodromes thought to be at risk.[6]

Several discussions followed as the Air Ministry sought to clarify current and future needs for both training and operational aircraft. A meeting of representatives of the Ministry of Home Security and the Air Ministry on 5 February 1941 sought to determine roles and responsibilities at jointly used aerodromes. It is reproduced as Appendix VIII.

Of course, applying camouflage was a passive defence measure. Although vital to the protection of the various aerodromes, there were more direct methods which were also employed. The further step was to have the Home Guards stationed on the airfields.

21st April 1942

Defence of MAP Factories

Will you please review the defence arrangements of the MAP factories listed below (Figure 9.3). The following are points which require attention:

a. The District or Sub-Area Commander should advise factory managers the number of men he considers should always be available in the factory to deal with any sudden emergency.
b. There should be sufficient numbers of rifles for each man of the duty squad to have a personal weapon available in the factory, up to the limit of one personal weapon to two Home Guards. No more rifles can, however, be provided from Command sources.
c. Compulsory powers should be exercised at factories to enrol the number of men required to ensure that (including office staff), the number of guard duties to be performed each month by each man is not excessive. The number enrolled must, however, be kept within the allotted ceiling.
d. The factory managers should be asked to provide reasonable sleeping and other accommodation in order that the duty squad may be properly housed.

Brigadier General Staff
Eastern Command

VAP Serial No.	Name and Location	VPA Class Identification	Nature of Guard
4188	De Havilland Aircraft Ltd Hatfield Herts	VP4	Home Guard
4120	De Havilland Aircraft Ltd Leavesden, Herts	VP4	Home Guard
4134	Hawker Aircraft Ltd Langley, Bucks	VP4	Home Guard
4181	Percival Aircraft Ltd Luton, Beds	VP4	Home Guard

Figure 9.3 Aero engine and airframe factories.[7]

This was followed by the introduction of AA gun emplacements:

16th January 1943

Defence of Leavesden Aerodrome To: Eastern Command

Reference E.Cent/2046/G dated 12th January 1943, also telephone conversation G3 Ops, Captain Russell, and G3 Ops and I. A visit was paid to the LDC at Leavesden, on the subject of AA emplacements be built as soon as possible as he has been informed by the MAP Authorities that the Bofor guns at present there are to be moved shortly (about 12th February). He feels therefore that between this period and the time that the RAFAA Flights take over maybe a time when the airfield is virtually undefended.

If, however, the emplacements can be put in construction forthwith, the HG, will be able and willing to man these AA. LMGs during periods of 'Alert', until such time that the RAF Regiment take over.

It is understood that a similar situation recently arose at Heathrow MAP airfield. This was taken up by London District with the RAF with the result that the emplacements were built in a very short space of time by RAF Works Services. It is also understood that in the case of this airfield, that MAP agreed to pay the costs.

HSS Aston, Major General
Command
East Central District[8]

Not every factory took delivery of its own defence aircraft! In some cases, security was less obvious, although there were times when vehicles were assigned to the defence force.

17th January 1941

Dear Sir,
I am writing to you on the subject of Beaverettes, one or more of which vehicles have been issued to you by this Ministry for your local defence.

This issue was made at a stage in the development of the war when the Home Forces were hastily re-organising and re-equipping themselves after the episode of Dunkirk and when there was grave peril of an invasion, both by sea-borne and air-borne troops descending upon us...

It has been decided by this Ministry that it is in the national interest that these protected vehicles be transferred from the MAP factories to the control of the Military Commanders in the area in which your factory is situated. The vehicles will then be added to the equipment of the mobile columns which in the event of an invasion would be operating in the vicinity of your factory and would prevent any subsequent bodies of enemy troops from reaching your factory...

The weapon mounted in the vehicles should not be released as I have decided that this weapon shall be added to the fixed defences of your factory.

Yours sincerely
Stephen King-Hall
Director,
Factory Defence Section[9]

The accompanying list of factories documents that 32 Beaverettes were deployed in MAP firms in Eastern Command and London District prior to this recall.

Earlier, I mentioned an AV Roe factory near Yeadon. In a local newspaper article written in 2012, the author Jim Greenwald wrote:

A taxiway connected the subterranean factory to Yeadon aerodrome.

Aircraft manufactured included the Bristol Blenheim (250), the Lancaster bomber (695), the Anson (more than 4,500), the York (45) and the Lincoln (25). The site itself consisted of 62 acres of which the factory took up nearly half.

Some reports say that 17,500 people worked there, others put the figure at 12,000 ... they worked in a space the size of 20 football pitches and ate hot lunches in a big canteen equipped with ovens and ten boilers. They had a doctor's surgery, a dentist's room, a telephone exchange, a fire service, 50 security guards, a Home Guard detachment and enough air raid shelter space for all.

German aircrew looking down from Dorniers or Heinkels would have seen fields, hedges, drystone walls, sheep, cattle and even ducks on a pond. Reportedly it was all fake. The farm animals were made of wood, the walls were wire and concrete and the fields were green painted cinders.[10]

Shadow Factory Visits

The Secretary of State for Air, Sir Kingsley Wood, visited the Rolls-Royce factory, the notes from which are interesting:

9 December 1938

Notes for the Press

On the occasion of the visit to the Rolls-Royce aero-engine factory at Derby by the Right Honourable Sir Kingsley Wood, Secretary of State for Air

The Rolls-Royce factory which is being visited today by the Secretary of State for Air, Sir Kingsley Wood, is one of the oldest established factories in the country engaged in the production of aero-engines. It was first registered as Rolls-Royce Ltd on 15th March 1906, and at that time was solely engaged in the manufacture of motor cars. The company entered the field of aero-engine production early in the Great War and the most famous engines produced at that time were the Falcon and Eagle. It will be recalled that two of the latter engines were fitted in the aircraft, piloted by the late Sir J Alcock and Sir A W Brown which made the first aeroplane flight across the Atlantic.

After the war the company produced many well-known engines including the Buzzard and the Rolls-Royce R engine which formed the power unit of the Supermarine S6B seaplanes which in 1933 won the Schneider Trophy outright for Great Britain and gained the world's speed record.

Production is at present concentrated of three types: the Kestrel, Merlin and Peregrine. The Kestrel first introduced in 1928 forms the power unit of the Phillips and Powis Master training aircraft which is in large scale production for the Royal Air Force. The Merlin, first produced in 1937, as used in many of the latest types of aircraft used by the Royal Air Force including the Hawker Hurricane and Supermarine (now Vickers-Armstrong) Spitfires, the Fairey Battle and Armstrong Whitworth

Whitley IV and V bombers and the Hawker Henley target towing aircraft.

The Peregrine is of very recent introduction and no details of any aircraft in which it may be utilised are at present available.

All three units are 12 cylinder V type liquid cooled supercharged motors and full details of the Kestrel (except the Kestrel CCC and special) and Merlin (except the Merlin VIII) may be published.

In the case of the Kestrel XXX and Special, Merlin VIII and Peregrine I and II the following details only may be given:

i.   The number of cylinders, type, whether geared, supercharged. The take-off, international and maximum powers, rpm, altitudes, boost pressures, bore and stroke, cubic capacity, weight and overall dimensions.

ii.   The approximate international powers of the three types are as follows: Kestrel (latest series) 700 hp; Merlin 1000 hp; Peregrine 850 hp.

A government owned factory is being erected at Crewe, which will be managed by Rolls-Royce Limited, where complete Rolls-Royce engines will be produced.[11]

The Kestrel was mentioned in Figure 8.1, one of which is on display at the RAF Museum at Hendon, Figure 9.4.

The Kestrel was produced in greater numbers than any previous Rolls-Royce engine with the 4,750th and last being delivered in 1938. The engine was used in eighty different types of aircraft and saw over eighteen years of service with the RAF.[12]

A further note to the press was issued at the same time. It was as follows:

In addition to the firms normally engaged in the production of aero-engines 6 companies are already engaged in the special production of aero-engines. They are:

1. The Austin Motor Co Ltd – Longbridge Birmingham.
2. The Rover Co Ltd – Acocks Green, Birmingham.
3. The Standard Motor Co Ltd – Coventry.
4. The Daimler Co Ltd – Coventry.
5. Messrs Rootes Securities Ltd (Humbers) – Coventry.
6. The Bristol Aeroplane Co Ltd.

The first five companies manufacture various components and the Austin Motor Co. and the Bristol Aeroplane Co. assemble the engines and test them.

Figure 9.4 Rolls-Royce Kestrel IB. (Author's photograph)

Two companies, The Austin Motor Co Ltd, and Messrs Rootes Securities Ltd (Humbers etc.) are engaged in the manufacture of complete airframes and in addition special factories are producing airscrews, carburettors and magnesium.

Press and Publicity Branch
Air Ministry
11th June 1938[13]

At some point during the war, the following briefing notes on the visit of the King and Queen to the Gloster Aircraft Company on 10 February (no year given) were written.

The Gloster Company, which is not included in the Hawker-Siddeley group of aircraft firms, was originally formed in 1916 and has designed and produced a succession of very successful types of fighter aircraft, including such biplane types as the Grebe, Gamecock, Gauntlet and Gladiator, of which the last mentioned type has just gone out of production.

The firm are now engaged on the construction of Hurricane aircraft, the well-known type of single-seater fighter designed by the Hawker Company. The aircraft is of low wing monoplane design, in which the outer wings may be either fabric-covered or stressed skin metal construction. When fitted with a Rolls-Royce engine, this aircraft has a speed of 310 mph and is armed with eight .303 inch machine guns mounted in the wings. It is anticipated that the monthly output of these aircraft by the Gloster Company will rise to 100 in October next.

The firm are also nearing completion of an order for Henley aircraft, a light bomber type adapted for towing targets.

The Gloster Company will also be undertaking the production of the following aircraft partly in their own factory and partly in a large new government factory, adjacent to their works:

a. **Albermarle**. This is a twin-engined low wing monoplane, of composite wood and metal construction, designed by Sir WG Armstrong Whitworth Aircraft Ltd, another member of the Hawker Siddeley Group, as a reconnaissance bomber.
b. **Tornado**. This is a single-seater low wing monoplane fighter of the Hawker design, fitted with one Rolls-Royce Vulture engine and armed with eight or twelve machine guns.
c. **Typhoon**. This is similar to the Tornado, but fitted with a Napier Sabre engine, which is estimated to give a speed of 464 mph.

The present labour force of approximately 3,500 is expected to increase ultimately to approximately 15,000[14]

Figure 9.5 shows a Gloster Gladiator.

Figure 9.5 Gloster Gladiator. (Author's photograph)

At the outbreak of the Second World War four home based RAF fighter squadrons were still equipped with Gladiators. Two of these units were sent to France in 1939. In just ten days of hard fighting, following the opening of the German assault on 10th May 1940, all the aircraft had been lost. In a desperate attempt to provide fighter cover for the 'little ships' involved in the Dunkirk evacuation, a detachment, known as 'G' Flight, was formed at RAF Manston in late May. A squadron of Gladiators was sent to Norway following the German invasion and they fought a rearguard action during April, May and June 1940.[15]

10

Post-war Costs/Sales of Factories

It might have taken many years to establish the full extent of the shadow factory network; however, it did not take long to start dismantling it, Figure 10.1.

Company	Factory	Date of Cessation of Production
Austin Motor Co. Ltd	No. 1 Engine Factory, Birmingham	31st Mar. 1945
Bristol Aeroplane Co. Ltd	No. 2 Engine Factory, Filton	31st Mar. 1945
Rootes Securities Ltd	No. 1 Engine Factory, Coventry	30th June 1945
Rover Co. Ltd	No. 1 Engine Factory, Birmingham	18th Aug. 1945
Standard Motor Co. Ltd	No. 1 Engine Factory, Coventry	30th June 1945
Daimler Co. Ltd	No. 2 Engine Factory, Coventry	31st Aug. 1945
Rootes Securities Ltd	No. 2 Engine Factory, Ryton-on-Dunsmore	30th Aug. 1945
Rover Co. Ltd	No. 2 Engine Factory, Solihull	30th Sept. 1945
Standard Motor Co. Ltd	No. 2 Engine Factory, Coventry	30th June 1945
Alvis Ltd	Mountsorrel	31st July 1944
Amalgamated Banket Areas Ltd	Gold Coast	30th Oct. 1944
Automotive Products Co. Ltd	Leicester	31st Dec. 1945
Birmetals Ltd	Stourbridge	31st Oct. 1944
Bristol Aeroplane Co. Ltd	Hawthorn	30th April 1945
British Aluminium Co. Ltd	Swansea	31st Oct. 1945
British Aluminium Co. Ltd	Northern Ireland	31st Dec. 1945
British Insulated Cables Ltd	High Wycombe	31st Oct. 1945
British MARC Ltd	Grantham	31st Oct. 1945
British Piston Ring Co. Ltd	Edinburgh	30th June 1945
BSA Guns Ltd	Corsham	30th Sept. 1945
BTH Co. Ltd	Leicester	31st Oct. 1945

Company	Factory	Date of Cessation of Production
AC Cossor Ltd	High Wycombe	31st Oct. 1945
Edison Swan Electrical Co. Ltd	Baldock	30th Sept. 1945
Expanded Rubber Co. Ltd	Dundee	31st Dec. 1945
Factories Direction Ltd	Lydney	30th Sept. 1945
Fisher & Ludlow Ltd	Tyburn	28th Feb. 1945
GEC Ltd	Oldham	31st Oct. 1945
Hadfields Ltd	Swinton	31st March 1944
ICI (Explosives) Ltd	St Boswells	15th Aug. 1945
ICI (Explosives) Ltd	Springfields	31st May 1945
ICI (Metals) Ltd	Gowerton	31st July 1945
ICI (Plastics) Ltd	Rawtenstall	3rd July 1945
ICI (General Chemicals) Ltd	Widnes	3rd July 1945
Integral Ltd	Whitney	31st Dec. 1945
KLG Sparking Plugs Ltd	Treforest	31st Dec. 1945
Magnesium Elektron Ltd	Lowerhouse	22nd Jan. 1945
Metal Box Co. Ltd	Apperley Bridge	30th Nov. 1945
Wm. Mills Ltd	Friar Park	1st Dec. 1945
Murex Ltd	Mossend	28th Feb. 1945
D Napier & Son Ltd	Walton	1st Oct. 1945
Northern Aluminium Co. Ltd	Adderbury	31st Dec. 1945
Rolls-Royce Ltd	Barnoldswick and Clitheroe	24th Mar. 1945
Rootes Securities Ltd	Speke	31st July 1945
Standard Motor Co Ltd	No. 1 Carburettor Factory, Coventry	31st Aug. 1945
Standard Motor Co Ltd	No. 2 Carburettor Factory, Nottingham	3rd Feb. 1945
Sterling Metals Ltd	Burton Latimer	30th June 1945
J Stone & Co Ltd	Bardsley	30th June 1945
SU Carburettor Co Ltd	Addingham	31st July 1945
United Africa Co Ltd	Gold Coast	30th June 1944
United Steel Co Ltd	Workington	30th June 1945
Vickers-Armstrongs Ltd	Blackpool	31st Oct 1945
Vickers-Armstrongs Ltd	Chester	30th Nov 1945
Wilson Lighbody Ltd	Aberdeen	30th Nov 1945

Figure 10.1 MAP shadow factories and their dates of closure.

Further factories and their proposed closure dates were also released.

Company	Factory	Expected Date of Cessation of Production
AC Cosser Ltd	Chadderton	30th June 1946
De Havilland Aircraft Co Ltd	Lostock	31st Mar. 1946
HM Hobson (A&M) Components Ltd	Oldham	16th Feb. 1946
Joseph Lucas Ltd	Cwmbran	30th June 1946
Rolls-Royce Ltd	Newcastle-under-Lyme	31st Jan. 1946
Rootes Securities Ltd	Stoke	31st Mar. 1946
Vickers-Armstrongs Ltd	Castle Bromwich	31st Jan. 1946

Figure 10.2 MAP shadow factories closing down in the near future.[1]

Ceasing production in the factories was one issue, settling accounts, and disposing of assets including the factories themselves, was something else entirely.

28th March 1945

Dear Bowen,

I see from your letter of the 13th March that your Ministry has decided to accept expenditure in connection with payment of the balance of civil pay at your agency factories in respect not only of staff but also of workpeople. As you are aware from the documents sent you previously we do not as a general rule accept extension of balance of civil pay schemes into industrial employees, as it was established here, after consideration of the matter at a very high level, that exclusion of workers from such schemes was general practice in the engineering industry. Our shadow factory managers have accepted this position, and we do not anticipate any difficulties in the future. The only field in which we are likely to have repercussions as a result of your decision, is amongst the ICI shadow factories. If repercussions do come, then we must deal with them as they arise.

I see that you have also been considering the question of the continuation of the balance of civil pay to ex agency factory employees when the factory where they were employed goes over to other management or ceases to exist. So far as we know at the moment, we are not likely to be faced with the continuation of a shadow factory on different production, but still on a shadow basis under other management. Our shadows are either being closed down altogether or are being handed over to the parent company or otherwise allocated for commercial purposes by the Board of Trade. In these circumstances we have taken the line that when the funds or imprest account from which the payments are at present being made, cease to exist, these payments must also cease. They are, of course, purely ex gratia and managements can quite well write a sympathetic letter for the cessation of the payments.[2]

In some cases, the agency company bought the factories.

6th June 1945

To: Air Ministry (through CFD3)

Standard Motor Co Ltd No 1 Engine Shadow Factory Fletchamstead, Coventry

In order to round off Crown ownership of the above premises, we have arranged for the Standard Motor Co. to purchase from them, for £1,000, the strips of land surrounding three sides of the land already purchased, which strips are at present held by you under two leases.

The Chief Valuer, who has recommended the purchase at this figure, agrees that Air Ministry should complete the purchase so that the whole site may be held in the name of the Secretary of State for Air. The price having been agreed, no negotiations would appear necessary other than those between the Treasury Solicitor and Messrs Band, Hatton & Co. who are solicitors to the Standard Motor Co. Would you please proceed to complete this deal.

We have placed a duplicate of this minute on file recording the existing leases – you will presumably treat these two leases as expired.

S F Killick
PS9[3]

It was not until September 1945 that the closure of the Austin Engine shadow factory announcement took place. Fortunately, the Austin group were able to buy the land and factory.

22nd September 1945

Austin Engine Shadow Factory Closing down

The Resident Auditor at the above shadow factory has been informed that No 2 Machine Shop has been sold to the Austin Motor Co Ltd as from 1st September 1945. The Resident Auditor has requested details of the sale and in particular details of the assets, e.g. installation of equipment etc. which are covered by this sale. Will you please let me have the necessary information?

M G Daniel
PA9.[4]

Another note in the same National Archives folio states as follows:

Austin Rover Motor Co. has by cheque letter dated 28th September 1945 paid to the Ministry of Aircraft Production the sum of £25,000 in respect of the flight shed on CC's land at Longbridge (Figure 10.3).

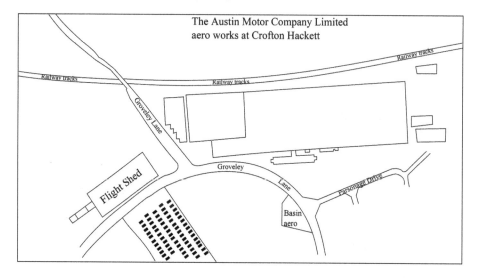

Figure 10.3 The Austin Motor Company Limited Aero Works at Crofton Hackett.[5] (Author's diagram)

Prior to writing this book, I had not considered what happened to the aircraft thought surplus to requirements by the RAF. Once decisions were made, there needed to be a process of dismantling the aircraft, which must have happened in many places. The following is an example where 270 Stirling aircraft were dismantled, ironically using shadow factory workers, some of which may have been involved in their construction in the first place!

12th November 1945

Breakdown of 270 Stirling aircraft. Austin Shadow Factory, Longbridge

On the occasion of a recent visit to Woburn Abbey, Beds, where this work is proceeding, I elicited that the average number of man hours taken was 800 per aircraft in good weather, and up to 1,000 in bad weather. The work is being undertaken in the open by a working party from Austin Shadow and I believe the order number is Con/Aircraft/5208/C.37b.

The representative of DG/SB's organisation who was present informed me that their estimate of the hours required for this work, was well under 400, and I promised to see what action could be taken to set matters right.

The work has no doubt been proceeding for some time and is expected to finish in some five months, and as we are being pressed to give up the requisitioned land on which the aircraft are parked, it is evident that there are difficulties in the way in doing anything drastic; nevertheless, I shall be obliged if you will consider the matter and take any action that appears to you likely to be fruitful.

C48[6]

Although some of the shadow factories were closed just before the end of the war, Figure 10.4 details the shadow factories still in operation almost a full year after VE Day!

Contractor	Factory	Approximate Number of Employees
Airspeed Ltd	Christchurch	393
Austin Motor Co	Crofton Hackett	407
Bristol Aeroplane Co	Weston-super-Mare	2,155
A.C. Cossor Ltd	Chadderton	917
De Havilland	Leavesden	965
Gramophone Co	Treorchy	250
Handley Page Ltd	York	570
International Alloys	Cardiff	130
ICI	Bowhouse	50
ICI (Castner Kellner)	Runcorn	12
ICI (Trimpell) Ltd	Heysham	2,100
MPRD No 1	Cowley	1,626
MPRD No 2	Eaglescliffe	3,095
Rolls-Royce	Hillington	8,000
S Smith and Son (England) Ltd	Avon House, Warwick	90
Thermal Syndicate	Workington	150

Figure 10.4 Shadow factories in operation on 1 April 1946.[7]

Of course, the whole infrastructure needed dismantling including resolving any insurance contracts.

18th July 1946

To: Mr Boddis
Ministry of Supply

Dear Mr Boddis,
Will you kindly refer to your letter of the 28th December 1945 about the various insurance matters connected with aircraft contracts. I must apologise for the long delay in letting you have this further letter dealing with flight test risks as promised in my partial reply of 28th February.

From the point of view of the insurance market, the Board of Trade do not wish to press for the continued insurance of these risks. We are, therefore, free to consider future arrangements on merits and the Treasury can certainly welcome the termination of the wartime blanket agreement with the insurance companies. As I understand the position, once a government aircraft under construction or repair at a contractor's works is cleared for flight there are the following risks during the tests:

1.   Damage to the aircraft itself.
2.   Injury to the contractor's employees.
3.   Injury to government employees.
4.   Damage to property or injury to persons other than (2) and (3) above.

And it is proposed that the contractor should be given indemnity in respect of the risks at (1), (3) and (4) (which can be clearly defined and separated from similar risks in respect of any private work which he may be carrying out) but that he should carry the risks at (2) himself. We agree with these proposals.

I understand that the Air Ministry will handle any claims in respect of (4) on behalf of the Ministry of Supply and I take it that they will consult the Treasury in advance of settlement on large or difficult claims arising out of RAF aircraft incidents. I am copying this letter to Mr Peterken at the Board of Trade, and to Mr Hawkins at the Air Ministry.

Yours sincerely,
N E Rees[8]

There was even an example of an overpayment which only came to light in 1947!

10th February 1947

Gentlemen,
The accounts of the British Thomson Houston (BTH) shadow factory at Melton Road, Leicester, are now being closed, and the payments in respect of the

structural steelwork placed with Messrs Dorman Long & Co Ltd have been under review. In this connection sums to a total of £35,825.18s.1d have been paid to your company.

It is regretted that owing to a mis-reading of the audit report the above figure represents an overpayment. The correct figure, in accordance with the agreement reached between the Government Purchasing Department and the British Structural Steelworkers Association and based on costs as revealed by the investigation is as follows (Figure 10.5):

Fabrication and erection costs	£13,111.10.8	
Profit at 7½%	£983.7.3	
		£14,094.17.11
Bought out items	£3,051.16.8	
Profit at 3¾%	£114.8.11	
		£3,166.5.7
Subcontractors		£14,679.0.3
Variations		£1,774.14.0
Association Fees		232.19.9
Dorman Long total		£33,947.17.6
Building contractors discount based on £33,947.17.6 less variations etc. £2,007.13.9	£31,940.3.9	
1/39th of £31,940.3.9		£818.19.6
		£34,766.17.0

Figure 10.5 Accounts for the British Thomson Houston (BTH) shadow factory.

Accordingly, I am to request you to forward to the Department your cheque for £1059.1s.1d, this being the difference between £35,825.1s.1d already paid, and £34,766.17s.0d revealed as due by the costing investigation. This sum of £1059.1s.1d is made up of £1026.15s.0d to be recovered from Messrs Dorman Long, and £32.6s.1d representing your Company's discount. The final figures have already been agreed between Mr Moles, the London Manager of Messrs Dorman Long & Co., and the Department's accountants.

Your cheque should be made payable to the Accounting Officer, Ministry of Supply and addressed to Branch PA9, 108-122, Westbourne Terrace, W2.

I am gentlemen,
Your obedient servant
O E N Logan[9]

Management Fees and Bonuses

We complete this account of shadow factories where the story began, that of costs and bonuses. In some cases, the bonuses related to activities in 1945, and it is therefore understandable that payments should run into 1946 for these factories.

10th August 1945

Dear Mr Neden,

Bristol Accrington Engine Shadow Factory

1. Subsequent to your loose minute to DEP dated 23rd May you stated that the management fee payable to the Bristol Aeroplane Company in respect to the Accrington Engine Shadow Factory for the first half of 1945 had been determined; the following comments are offered preparatory to consideration later in the year of the fee appropriate to the second half of 1945.
2. New Hercules engine, power plant and spares production virtually ceased at Accrington at the end of June 1945. The intention to produce Centaurus engines there has been abandoned and all dispersal units are being closed down, also 50% (i.e. 2 of the 4 main buildings) of the main engine factory. Engine and power plant repair is to be concentrated in the remaining 50%, while the exhaust ring factory carries on (without its dispersal unit) with a reduced program.
3. As only 52 new Hercules engines (and no power plants) remained due for delivery after the 30th June 1945, figures of earlier production rates are possibly not very helpful; however, that data in 6-monthly periods is as follows (Figure 10.6):

Period	Hercules Engines		Hercules Power Plants	
	Programmed	**Delivered**	**Programmed**	**Delivered**
1st half 1944	2380	2400	835	869
2nd half 1944	2300	2300	1055	1055
1st half 1945	1645	1600	486	500

Figure 10.6 Hercules engine programme.

4. Apart from the (reduced) output of the exhaust ring factory a few jobs of a sundry nature, which should be classified as new production as distinct from repair, are under way at Accrington during the second half of 1945, these comprising in the main:

    a.   Strip, rebuild and final test of a relatively small batch of Centaurus engines to that extent uncompleted at Hawthorn.

    b.   Conversion of Centaurus engines to Mark XI at a programmed rate approximating to 600 per month, although this figure has so far not been approached; 176 similar conversions were completed in the first half of 1945.

    c.   Rectification of approximately 300 Hercules 100 engines, involving mainly the embodiment of an entry casing modification – this job is so far progressing very slowly indeed.

    d.   Fireproofing, by embodiment of modifications, of 600 Hercules power plants, this job is just commencing.

5.   While these items may at first sight appear to be considerable, it is improbable that the total man hours involved during the 6 months will amount to the equivalent of 100 Hercules engines.

6.   The concentrated repair program at Accrington was, I understand, to be 400 Hercules engines per month, of which 140 were to be in power plant form. It now seems probable, however, that this program will be very considerably curtailed. You will, however, wish to consult DD/RME on this aspect.

7.   The provision of servicing squads for the northern part of the country and Ireland and their supervision remains, I believe, an Accrington charge.

8.   The no mean task of taking stock and disposing of redundant assets throughout the Accrington group of factories, and rearrangement of repair facilities, with the attendant accounting work, will occupy the whole of this half year, although at the D/POAE meeting held on 17th May (attended by Mr F Burke, PS14(d)) it was agreed that the physical work involved would be completed by 31st October 1945.

9.   The best overall computation of the changed Accrington program may perhaps be obtained from consideration of the labour force reduction; the ultimate strength is estimated to be 25% of that engaged before program reductions were initiated last winter. The floor space reduction is of the same order.

10.   To conclude, there is now some doubt as to whether there will remain sufficient work to warrant the continued operation of Accrington after the end of 1945. Certainly there is nothing envisaged beyond that date under the broadest new production classification, and the final decision as to continuance into next year will depend, as far as can be seen at present, entirely on the repair program.

DDEP1[10]

This position changed the following month.

21st September 1945

Dear Mr Neden,

I minuted you on the 10th August, quoting data as to the Bristol Accrington engine shadow factory program for the second half of 1945. Developments since that date have changed the picture extensively; the position now is that Accrington's work is being taken over by the parent factory as rapidly as possible in order that the Accrington premises may be released to Courtaulds. Of the jobs mentioned in paragraph 4 in my earlier minute:

1. The exhaust ring factory is expected to have ceased production and be cleared by the end of this month.
2. The Hawthorn Centaurus engines rebuild and final test has been completed.
3. The Centaurus conversion contract is being cancelled and Bristol parent will carry on instead.
4. The rectification of Hercules 100 engine has been stopped and the contract is being cancelled.
5. The fireproofing of Hercules Power plants is being taken over by Bristol parent at an early date.

I propose to advise you later the dates of conclusion at Accrington of work of jobs 3 and 5.

The engine and power plant repair work which had hitherto been planned for Accrington is also being taken over by Bristol, but you will wish to consult DDRM(E) on this.

It is the intention to clear the whole of the MAP work out of Accrington by the end of the year, and I understand that DDRM(E) has already intimated that he can fall in with this proposal; clearance of machine tools and plant will probably be the greatest difficulty.

DDEP1[11]

The Austin Motor Company Limited, Longbridge Works, Birmingham had many assets still needing disposal as late as 1946, Figures 10.7 and 10.8.

Fixed Capital	Airframes	Aero Engines	Total	Housing
Buildings				
Tunnel workshop		103,437	103,437	
Test house		40,000	40,000	
Flight shed	95,184		95,184	
Cofton main works	725,055	155,635	880,690	293,563
Elmdon works	471,777		471,777	
Plant and machinery	597,999	364,957	962,956	34,000
Electrical plant	21,134	11,376	32,510	
Office machinery	26,604	3,074	29,678	4,000
Furniture, fixtures etc.	131,073	35,085	156,158	6,000
Vehicles	42,476	3,215	45,691	21,000
Capital at dispersals	130,859	70,402	201,261	
Preliminary expenses	49,010	1,054	50,064	
Air raid precautions	7,224		7,224	
Factory defence	638		638	
Reparation of war damage	310		310	
Total of fixed capital	2,299,343	778,235	3,077,578	358,563

Figure 10.7 Statement of capital employed for March quarter 1946 – aero works.

16th July 1946

To A Winkles Esq
The Austin Motor Co Ltd Longbridge

Dear Mr Winkles,

Management Fees – Aircraft factory (frames)

With reference to your letter of 12th July last, I have looked up our file and find that the question of the management fees payable to your company in respect of the four years ended 31st July 1944, was one which was discussed at a meeting between Mr Payton and Sir Archibald Forbes on 25th May 1944.

Sir Archibald Forbes made an offer of £30,000 for the first year and £40,000 for each of the three subsequent years, making a total of £150,000. The extra sum of £5,000 was not actually allocated to any particular year, but the note of the meeting suggests that there was some particular discussion on the question of the fees for the first year, i.e. the year ended 31st July 1941, and I think the additional sum of £5,000 can reasonably be regarded as having been offered in respect of that particular year, although it might also be argued that the additional sum of £5,000 could be allocated proportionately to each of the four years referred to.

I think, however, that the total fee of £155,000 can reasonably be regarded as being made up as follows (Figure 10.8):

Management Fee for the Year Ended	
31st July 1941	£35,000
31st July 1942	£40,000
31st July 1943	£40,000
31st July 1944	£40,000
	£155,000

Figure 10.8 Outstanding management fees for the Austin airframe factory.

If I can be of further assistance to you in this matter no doubt you will let me know. Yours sincerely,

F W Neden[12]

The follow-up letter was just two days later.

18th July 1946

To: F W Neden Ministry of Supply

Dear Mr Neden,
I thank you for your letter of the 11th instant on the subject of Aero Factory Management Fees. Broadly speaking, we consider your proposals to be fair and reasonable and in accordance with the value of the capital employed, but there are several minor points which require attention.

As regards the Aero Factory, you suggested in your letter of the 4th October 1945, that a fee would be payable in respect of the service of care and maintenance after the main agreement was finally terminated.

There are still considerable assets in the engine factory, and as we do not know when the position will be finally cleared, we suggest that the position should be kept open and that this would be met by a fee, of say £100 for the current year and at that rate per annum until the position is clarified. The disposal of assets is being carried out by employees under our control and the out of pocket expenses are covered by the combined imprest account for the whole factory.

a. We agree to your proposal of a payment of £6,125 to cover the period from 1st January 1946 to 30th July 1946, for the clearing up of airframe production, but as the circumstances are similar to that of engines we suggest that this cannot be considered as final, and that a fee at the rate of £100 per annum from 1st July 1946 would be sufficient to keep this matter open until the position is clarified.

b. We agree to the proposal that the fee for housing work for the year ending 31st December 1946 shall be £6,500.

c. As to the care and maintenance work of the portion of the factory at present occupied by the Admiralty, we think this would be covered by a token fee of £100 per annum from 30th June 1946.

Yours sincerely,
Secretary[13]

The Vickers-Armstrongs Ltd shadow factories were terminated from 1945 with the last, the Spitfire factory at Castle Bromwich, not closing until 1947.

13th November 1947

Termination of shadow factory management agreements –
Blackpool, Chester, Castle Bromwich and South Marston Factories

As you are aware notice of termination of the shadow factory management agreements in respect of the above-named factories was given to the management company, Vickers-Armstrongs Ltd as follows (Figure 10.9):

FF No.	Factory	MOS Letter Dated	Termination as at
263	Blackpool	7th November 1945	31st October 1945
259	Chester	17th November 1945	30th November 1945
260	South Marston	28th May 1946	5th April 1946
290	Castle Bromwich	16th January 1947	31st March 1947

Figure 10.9 Termination letters for Vickers-Armstrongs shadow factories.

The management company were not happy about the retention in force of certain clauses in the agreements (e.g. re the Ministry's right to free use of patents etc., obligations of the company in regard to care and maintenance and so on after termination of the agreements) under the provisions of clause 37 in those agreements and there was at one time under consideration the question of endorsement of the agreements to meet the wishes of the managing company.

Full consideration was given to the matter by this Branch over a long period in consultation with the Treasury Solicitor but ultimately I *bearded the lion in his den* by visiting Vickers House and discussing the matter with representatives of the Contracts and Secretariat Branches of Vickers-Armstrongs Ltd. At this discussion, which was held on 16th September 1947, it was found that if only by the passing of time there was nothing of substance between the two parties (and in fact there never had been).

The Contracts Manager suggested that my formal reply to the Company's letters on the subject of termination should suggest that the terms on which the management agreements were made should be complied with and that in consequence notice of termination of the agreements should be accepted by the company without qualification, i.e. in regard to the continuance clause.

I duly wrote formally to the Company on 17th September 1947, setting out the Ministry's views in regard to the individual clauses and winding-up on the lines suggested by the Contracts Manager. In a formal letter which arrived yesterday in reply to my letter of 17th September the Company have, in effect, fully accepted without qualification the notices of termination given to them long ago.

A W Morant[14]

As the accountants worked through the seemingly endless paperwork, there were still accounts being dealt with in 1948 and 1949. Incidentally, the Tube Alloys project was the atomic bomb research undertaken by the British scientists.

30th August 1948

To: L Patrick
Imperial Chemicals Industries Ltd

Dear Mr Patrick,

Tube Alloys Agreement 294/2/7901 Overhead Charges and Profit

With reference to Mr Lyons' letter of 10th February 1948, and to the meeting held on 15th July last, the following overhead and profit arrangements are acceptable for the year 1948 commencing 1st January 1948.

Overheads

1. In respect of production work carried out at ICI works in the General Chemicals Division under the Tube Alloys Agreement, the overhead rates are those calculated by the Division as applicable to the particular factory in which production is carried out and are as follows:

a. For Works General Charges and Local Administration Expenses; the appropriate percentage to be those calculated by ICI for production work under their normal costing method, and applied to process and repair wages.

b. For Central Services; a percentage on the combined Works General Charges and Local Administration Expenses charged in the costs at an appropriate rate for the Division concerned, as calculated by ICI and agreed by Ministry of Supply accountants (AAG3).

2. In respect of research work, overheads will be calculated on the global rates agreed in my letter of 28th August 1948.

Profit or Management Fee

3. On production work under the Tube Alloy Agreement, the profit shall be £600 per month which equals £7,200 for the year (this profit is in lieu of 10% on cost). If the average capital employed on the work during the year is greater or less than £360,000, then the amount of profit shall be adjusted accordingly but no adjustment will be made if the variation is less than 5% either way.

4. On research revenue and expenditure under the Tube Alloy Agreement, the profit allowed is 10% on costs. No profit is payable on capital expenditure.

Overheads for agency plants located within divisional factories

5. The provisions of 1(a) and 1(b) above will apply to the following agency factories:
    i. Ethylene chloride – Runcorn and Burn Hall.
    ii. Sulphuric acid – Camelon and Wigg West.
    iii. Potassium carbonate – Winnington.[15]

A copy of the memorandum of agreement between the Ministry of Supply, the Ministry of Aircraft Production and Imperial Chemical Industries Limited can be found in National Archives folio AVIA 15/3753. The final trench of ICI shadow factory paperwork was some of the last to be resolved.

23rd March 1949

To: A Lyons
Imperial Chemical Industries Ltd
Nobel House

Dear Mr Lyons,

Overhead Charges on Agency Factories

In reply to your letter of the 4th January 1949 concerning the amount to be charged for the year 1948 in respect of the cost to ICI of administrative and central services rendered to Agency factories, I have consulted our accountants and I accept your proposal to settle the charge for that year at £30,000.

This amount is chargeable to the Agency Factories as follows (Figure 10.10):

ICI Division	Agency Factory	Amount (£)
General Chemicals	Randle	840
	Valley	1746
Billingham	Mossend	4966
	Dowlais	5059
	Prudhoe	7884
	Middleton	3172
Nobel	Bowhouse	1863
	Dumfries	1490
	Powfoot	1490
	Girvan	1490
		30,000

Figure 10.10 Closure of ICI shadow factories.

I am sending a copy of this letter to Mr Patrick for his information.

Yours sincerely,
H S Humphreys.[16]

It might be the case that the accountants thought that the above ICI closures were the last financial matters to needing resolution. However, there was one more matter to resolve. Some of the machine tools used by the shadow factories were bought in America (through the lend–lease arrangement with the US, Chapter 2). This paperwork was still active up until 1949, Figure 10.11!

4th November 1949

Bristol Aeroplane Company Accrington Shadow Factory

Machine tools purchased in the USA to 1941, through the British Purchasing Commission.

Vouchers on the following files:

Sect. claims 14	Claim for customs and excise duty
Sect. claims 110	Vouchers September 1940
Sect. claims 309	Vouchers April 1941
Sect. claims 363	Vouchers May 1941
Sect. claims 403	Vouchers June 1941
Sect. claims 427	Vouchers July 1941
Sect. claims 430	Vouchers August 1941
Sect. claims 495	Vouchers September 1941
Sect. claims 519	Vouchers October 1941
Sect. claims 535	Vouchers November 1941
Sect. claims 566	Vouchers December 1941
Sect. claims 586	Vouchers January 1942
Sect. claims 575	MOS claim re BAC contract with Norris and Ingram

Figure 10.11 Vouchers in respect of lend–lease arrangements.

The above files sent to Registry marked PA (Routine) 4th November 1949.[17]

Appendix I[1]

Shadow Factories: The Rationale and Early History

Reasons for Employing Firms to Manage Shadow Factories Erected and Equipped with Government Capital

The problem in connection with the employment of firms to manage factories first arose at the Air Ministry early in 1936 in connection with the so-called 'shadow factories' for the manufacture of airframes and aero-engines. These factories were projected primarily as War Potential, and they were not originally intended for extensive and continuous manufacturing use in peace time. But it was necessary to provide for their operation, as and when need arose, and for reasons into which it is not now necessary to enter it was decided to invite motor car manufacturing firms to accept the task; the agreements with the collaborating firms included terms of remuneration for the production of specified numbers of airframes and aero-engines. The progress of events resulted in twelve shadow factories being actually in production in September 1939, when war broke out, including, in addition to the airframe and aero-engine factories, one for the manufacture of airscrews and two for carburettors and one for bombs.

At a later stage, and particularly since the outbreak of war, cases arose (and are continuing to arise) when new factories required for immediate production have been provided by the Air Ministry on account of the inability of firms themselves to undertake the capital commitments involved. While, therefore, the employment of firms to manage engines and other aeronautical material first arose in connection with War Potential, it has since developed over a substantial portion of the aeronautical field.

In a strict sense, the word 'shadow' (with its connotation of War Potential) ceases to be apposite once a factory takes its full place in the country's manufacturing line, but it is a convenient term of distinction to continue to apply to that portion of productive capacity available to the Air Ministry (now or in the future) entirely financed from public funds, and the term is used in this memorandum in that sense.

Where any part of the capital is provided by the manufacturer, if only the working capital, contracts have continued to be placed on a commercial basis, due allowances being made in prices for such capital assistance as is provided by the Air Ministry.

Completeness of the Obligations Undertaken by the Government for Provision of Buildings, Plant and Working Capital for Shadow Factories

The Air Ministry pays the cost of:

i.   Acquiring the land.
ii.   The building and all building services.
iii. All plant and equipment.
iv.   All material required for manufacture.
v.   All labour and other employees including the factory management staff at the factory for administration and production.
vi.   All other costs incidental to the running of the factory.

Thus, the whole cost of the shadow factory is borne by the Air Ministry, no capital whatsoever, fixed or working, being provided by the managing company. It follows, therefore, that in managing the shadow factory, the managing firm is free of the following expenses and risks, attendant upon a commercial venture, needing to be provided for in profits:

i.   The cost of acquiring the capital.
ii.   Normal trace risks resulting in the loss of assets.
iii. Normal risks of trading losses.
iv.   Bad debts.
v.   Disappearance of goodwill from various causes.
vi.   Fall in value of patents through improvements in competitive designs and processes.
vii. Misjudgement of markets.
viii. Provision for continuity of business generally.

Hence the problem of remuneration to the managing firm is not analogous to that of estimating the profit which it would be fair to allow in a commercial venture of corresponding magnitude: it is the problem of assessing a fair return for such services as are rendered, although it is not suggested that such an assessment can fairly be arrived at without regard to a number of factors.

The nature of the services rendered by the firms is:

a.   Supervision of erection and equipment of the factory.
b.   Production.

In each case the firm selected to manage a factory in production has co-operated, as agent of the Air Ministry, in arranging for and supervising the building, equipment and laying out of the factory, a fee being negotiated for the firm's services in these matters.

So far as production is concerned, the managing firms, operating through the factory staff, are responsible, at the Ministry's expense, for the engagement of labour and the purchase of material, for the keeping of proper records and accounts, and for exercising as agents of the Air Ministry all the functions that would need to be exercised if the factory belonged to themselves and was engaged upon the same task of manufacture.

Principles Hitherto Adopted in Fixing the Remuneration of Managing Firms

The twelve shadow factories now in production were all constructed and in operation before the outbreak of war, and the terms of the agreements for what were somewhat novel enterprises were therefore negotiated under peace conditions. In short the principles followed were:

a.   A fixed fee in respect of the erection and equipping of the factory.
b.   A fixed fee for management during production, supplemented by
c.   A bonus designed to ensure and reward economical production in accordance with the degree of economy obtained.

These terms are shown in some detail below. On one case (Standard carburettors) no agreement has yet been signed and the terms are still under discussion.

Managing Firm	Shadow Factory	Remuneration
Austin Motor Company	Airframes 863 Battles and spares	a. Erection and equipment of factory: a fee of £50,000 spread over first year. b. Production fee: £200 per aeroplane (during the second year monthly advances totalling £50,000 to be made, and set off against production fee). c. Bonus: a percentage of the difference between ascertained manufacturing costs and a basic price (assessed from the first batches of 25 aeroplanes up to the fifth batch), to be debited or credited to the firm. The percentage to be 12.5% of the margin up to £300 and 17.5% above that amount. No debit to be made to the firm prior to the first credit, and in the unlikely event of the account showing a final debit this is not to be refunded to the firm.
Rootes Securities Ltd	Airframes 600 Blenheims and spares	As for the Austin factory above, except that the production fee per aeroplane was fixed at £225

Managing Firm	Shadow Factory	Remuneration
No. 1 Engine group comprising Austin Motor Co., Daimler Motor Co., Rootes Securities, Rover Motor Co., Standard Motor Co., Bristol Aeroplane Co.	Aero-engines 4,000 Bristol Mercury engines	a. Erection and equipment of factories (first year): 5 car firms – £24,000 each Bristol Co. – £20,000 b. Production (second and third years[1]): 5 car firms – £24,000 each a year Bristol Co. – £20,000 Balance on completion – £20,000 total of deliveries. c. Bonus: 20% of the saving in the ascertained cost below a basic price assessed in the light of the cost of the airscrews delivered up to 31st January 1938. If the ascertained net cost in any three monthly period is less than the basic price, then the basic price is reduced by one half of the difference and the resulting figure becomes the basic price for the following period and so on.
HM Hobson (aircraft and motor) Components Ltd	Hobson type carburettor. Original order was for 2554 carburettors.	a. Renovation etc. of factory: £5,150. b. Production fee: a fee of £7 per carburettor was agreed for the first order, with provision for the sum to be reviewed for further orders. For subsequent quantities £3.10s, £3.5s and £3 per carburettor have been agreed. c. Bonus: similar to the De Havilland Airscrew Factory except as regards the period for the assessment of the first basic price.
Machine Products Ltd	Bombs 350,000 40 lb 700,000 20 lb	a. Erection and equipment of factory: £10,000. b. Production fee: 9.5d each for first 50,000 40 lb type. 8.5d each for remaining 300,000 40 lb type. 6.5d each for first 100,000 20 lb type. 5.5d each for remaining 600,000 20 lb type. c. Bonus: 20% of savings below basic prices for each type assessed in the light of the cost of the first 50,000 40 lb bombs and first 100,000 20 lb bombs, or later batches if necessary.
Standard	Carburettors Original order 3177	a. Erection and equipment of factory: £10,000. b. Production fee: £5 per carburettor subject to limit of £10,000, after which reduced fee is to be agreed. c. Bonus: 20% of savings below basic price assessed from early batches. Note: the firm has since requested that the bonus arrangements be cancelled and the fee per carburettor increased to £7.10.0d.

Note:
1 The fee in respect of the second and third years was payable by a sum of £75 per engine (totalling £300,000 if the 4,000 engines were delivered) but in the event of failure to complete all except the final £20,000 was payable.

With the foregoing particulars in mind, it will help in an appreciation of the problem if the history of the foregoing shadow factory schemes is briefly reviewed. At their inception in the early spring of 1936, the main difficulty lay in the inducement to be offered to certain motor car manufacturers to divert a portion of their energies to the building up of a substantial airframe and aero-engine production capacity and War Potential. These firms had been allocated to the Air Ministry for use in time of war, but the new proposition went further than mere arrangements for turning over peace time production to war production in the car works. Although the position in regard to the availability of competent managing staff and skilled labour was not critical at that time, it was recognised that considerable demands would be made on the firms not only in respect of their directing personnel, but in respect also of their department heads and supervisors and some of their skilled workmen. The Air Ministry had to overcome the natural reluctance of the firms to make too great a sacrifice of their share-holders' interests, particularly when other motor car manufacturers were outside the scheme and might be expected to secure some commercial advantage by reason of undivided attention to their normal peace time business. It is not surprising, therefore, that the negotiations leading up to the inauguration of the first schemes were protracted, and that the financial terms offered reflected concessions which had to be made to secure the wholehearted co-operation of the several companies in the work. The first schemes were those for the manufacture of Fairey Battles by Austin Motor Co. in a new factory adjoining the firm's works at Birmingham, the manufacture of Bristol Blenheims at Speke, Liverpool, by Rootes Securities Ltd and the group scheme for the manufacture of Bristol engines by five motor car firms and the Bristol Aeroplane Co. at new factories adjacent to their own works. The inclusion in the latter scheme of the Bristol Aeroplane Co. was a last minute arrangement to fill the gap created by the defection of the Morris organisation.

The particular history of the aero-engine shadow scheme is a good illustration of the problem of remuneration, as it has developed in the course of the negotiations in the past year in connection with the several extensions of that scheme.

In the original scheme, it was agreed that the group should be paid £140,000 per annum for each of the three years over which the erection of the factories and the production of 4,000 engines was expected to extend. The fee for the first year was conveniently regarded as being in respect of planning, erecting and equipping the several factories. The fees in respect of each of the second and third years were regarded as advance payments of production fees based on a sum of £75 per engine. The Department was, however, obliged to concede that the advances were irrecoverable in the unlikely event of failure to produce satisfactory engines. It will be noticed that this left only a balance of £20,000 in respect of the 4,000 engines over and above the minimum advances for the second and third years.

In addition, provision was made for a bonus incentive on savings on production costs whereby the group were to receive 12.5% of the first £50 of saving and 17.5% of any further savings below an agreed basic price. This bonus incentive to cheapen production was a cardinal point of the Treasury approval of the schemes, but the firms were naturally very uncertain about their prospects of earning any appreciable sums, particularly as the Department insisted that 'debits' accruing through the costs of batches over-running the target should be off-set against any bonuses earned on earlier batches. The firms were also anxious to prevent the Department waiting until cheap production had been attained before agreeing a basic price, and were unwilling to sign an agreement which left the Department free to postpone a decision over an unspecified number of batches. It was finally agreed at a meeting with the Secretary of State that if an agreement on target costs had not been reached by the fourth batch of 100 engines, then the actual cost of that fourth batch should automatically become the agreed basic price for bonus purposes.

At the time of the agreement, it was judged that the fixed fee for remuneration would approximate to 4% of the estimated production costs at the shadow factories, any earnings in excess of this rate being dependent upon the operation of the bonus scheme. It has to be borne in mind that at that date a profit rate of 10% was being allowed in Air Ministry technical estimates of costs of production by professional firms. It was also hoped that with the special arrangements which were being made for the training of shadow factory labour during the period when the factories were in course of erection and equipment a reasonably full production stage would be attained by the fourth batch, so that the actual production costs of that batch would, in fact, approximate to the price which the two parties should be able to agree upon as a reasonable target. The Department would not in any case have objected to the prospect of high bonus earnings, provided that they were accompanied by a really substantial lowering of production costs of Bristol engines.

Accounting difficulties, more particularly a breakdown in the Austin Co.'s shadow accounting arrangements, prevented any ascertainment of actual production costs when revised proposals for remuneration, due to a series of extensions of the engine shadow schemes, were under consideration from the summer of 1938 onwards. Negotiations were therefore conducted largely in ignorance of possible bonus earnings and became more difficult with increasing attention which was being paid to armament profits and the desirability of relating shadow factory remuneration of outside firms not only to such profits, but also to the fees which professional firms were to receive in respect of shadow factories which they were commencing to manage for themselves.

A year or so ago, work to the extent of some five million pounds at the engine shadow factories in question could be foreseen for the year 1939/40 and some six million pounds for the year 1940/41. The original agreement nominally ended in July 1939. There seemed, therefore, no objection to continuing a fee of £140,000 per year, this fee representing a return of between 2% and 3% of production costs. It had been agreed that the old bonus scheme was an unsatisfactory one to work and while the companies were in favour of abolishing it altogether the Department was insistent on the retention of it or some alternative incentive to economy in production. Although precise figures of costs were not available, it had become fairly evident that the bonus earnings under the old bonus agreement would be considerable. They are now estimated at £200,000. There earnings would be partly due to the effect of straight run production, partly also to increased production and double-shift working, not foreseen in the original program, and imposed later by emergency requirements.

It was natural, therefore, that the motor car firms should wish to conserve this somewhat fortuitous large bonus earning and to base their proposals for a fixed bonus on the scale of this out-turn. It was, however, the Department's view, that whatever the justification on grounds of reduced costs for the high bonus earnings under the first agreement any further bonus earnings of fee in lieu of bonus earnings should be related to further economies in production costs. The prolonged negotiations with the motor car firms were due to this fundamental conflict of views. The Air Ministry before the outbreak of war, offered for a period of one year from the expiration of the first agreement of 30th June 1939, a fee of £150,000 and a basic bonus of £40 for each engine produced, the bonus to be variable under a formula designed to provide incentives both to rapid production and economy. The firms were unwilling to proceed on this basis and asked for a fixed fee of £150,000 and a fixed bonus of £80 for each engine produced. Since the outbreak of war there have been further negotiations culminating in an offer by the Department of £150,000 fixed fee plus a fixed bonus of £40 per engine, for the period from 1st July 1939 to 30th June 1940. This offer which amounts in all closely to 5% on estimated costs of production, was justified in that it covered a period of peace production and was the minimum to which the Ministry was virtually committed by its earlier offer. The fixed bonus was regarded as unobjectionable in view of the possibility of uncontrollable variations in cost which might arise under war conditions and also, by providing an incentive to rapid production, tending to reduce production costs. The matter has been further discussed with the firms' representatives since the offer was made and is still open. The present position is that the firms have been told that failing acceptance the offer will be withdrawn and the question referred to arbitration.

Although the history of the shadow schemes centres largely on that of the engine shadow group, the two airframe schemes merely keeping in step and awaiting a solution of the engine negotiations, there were other early schemes which require to be mentioned. One of these was the shadow factory for the manufacture of bombs by a process entirely new in this country, managed by The Plessey Co., and the other was the shadow factory for airscrews managed by de Havillands. The latter was the first instance of employment of a professional aircraft firm to manage a shadow factory for the manufacture of the firms' own product. The basis for remuneration in this case comprised a fixed fee per airscrew produced and a novel bonus on savings scheme which the department considered very favourable. This required agreement on a target price and payment of 20% of any savings on that price, and the periodic fixing of new target prices for succeeding batches mid-way between the previous target price and the ascertained cost on which the bonus had been paid. It probably required a professional firm confident in its own ability to maintain a steadily reducing cost of production to find such a scheme financially attractive. Conceivably at that time the company were prepared to make an offer attractive to the department in order to retain control and manufacture of its own product; but however that may be, there has been no attempt since to depart from the scheme or to suggest a more static bonus. Reasonable bonus payments have in fact been regularly earned.

Three other shadow schemes which followed somewhat later also deserve special mention. One was the management by Hobsons of a shadow factory at Oldham for their own design of carburettor, and in respect of which the department was able to induce the firm to accept remuneration proposals on the same basis as that of the de Havilland airscrew scheme. In this case, however, largely due to manufacturing and management difficulties, the bonus earnings so far have been negligible. The second scheme was the Nuffield scheme for airframe manufacture at Castle Bromwich. In this case management services were given free and there was a consequential absence of any associated remuneration in the form of a bonus for savings on cost of production. The other scheme was the management by Standard Motor Co. of a second shadow factory manufacturing Hobson carburettors. For the first time two rival shadow factories were to manufacture a similar product but under different arrangements for remuneration. The Standard Co. position remains unsettled pending conclusion of the revised engine negotiations.

Appendix II[1]

The Introduction to the Report Written by H. McMillan to the Chairman of the Production Council

1. The Industrial Capacity Committee was formed under my chairmanship by a decision of the Production Council on 26th June 1940. I feel that the time has come when I ought to make a full report on what we have been able to achieve during the 10 weeks of the Committee's existence and to outline the course of action which now seems to me to be necessary if further and more substantial results are to be obtained. It will be recalled that no specific terms of reference were given to me. General approval was given to the proposals contained in Papers PX (40)20 and PX (40)21 (subject to the reservations made by the Minister of Supply in the course of discussion) and to PX (40)26. In view of the larger question of policy which I shall raise later in this report it will be useful to summarise these proposals as they seem to emerge after making allowance for the modifications suggested in the discussion.

2. The Industrial Capacity Committee was charged with the duties:

    a. Of strengthening the Area Boards; of ensuring that, through the Departmental Area Officers, they were kept fully and properly informed of production needs, in order that they might make every endeavour to provide for the absorption in the war effort, whether by main or sub-contract, of firms then engaged in work of a non-essential character.

        (the Minister of Supply pointed out with prophetic wisdom, which has been confirmed by our subsequent experience, that *as regards the suggestion that the proposed local organisation should first produce a balanced plant and then arrange for it to be given work to do, this was putting the cart before the horse. The production of munitions was now so highly specialised that anything in the way of general utility was not wanted. Plant could only be organised when it was clear what work it was required to do*).

    b. Of considering the general questions relating to the utilisation of industries, as a whole, in consultation with representatives of such industries, and of co-ordinating and supervising the work of the Area Boards in this matter.

3. It was agreed that the Committee would occupy a position similar to that of the Production Council's own Committees in that it would exercise executive authority subject to appeal to the Production Council, and that in view of the importance of securing the fullest possible industrial capacity, a Minister, rather than an official, should be Chairman of the Committee.

4. These terms of reference are not free from ambiguity. It has sometimes appeared that they were being interpreted to mean that the Industrial Capacity Committee should confine itself to the task of tempting production departments with alluring offers of capacity from those branches of industry engaged in production which is non-essential in war time. I have never been able to regard this as a very intelligent interpretation of the intention of the Production Council, for there has never been any shortage of offers. On the contrary, every firm that sees its peace time market disappearing is desperately anxious to obtain war work. Indeed their solicitations have been so numerous that a large staff of civil servants has been constantly employed in the task of, for the most part, *turning them down*. The error arises from the assumption that all suitable capacity is now being fully employed on essential work, and that, therefore, the Industrial Capacity Committee should be concerned with the adaptation and recruitment of capacity which has previously been considered unsuitable and, for war purposes, useless. This is a false and impossible distinction. The extent to which adapted capacity can be used depends upon the planned use of suitable capacity. High precision plant and labour should be reserved for high precision work. The less exacting tasks should be deliberately unloaded to those sections of industry which can be adapted to perform them.

5. I have, therefore, interpreted the term of reference as being free from this false limitation. It was the intention of the Production Council, as I believe, that we should seek to bring into war production the maximum capacity which now exists, or can be created, in each Area, and to organise the use of that capacity in such a way as to obtain the highest possible output. This conclusion is logically implicit in the terms of reference. It enables us to take a more comprehensive view of the problem and to see the relation of each aspect of it to the others. Having discovered the nature of the capacity that is available, or can be made available, the question is how can it be organised and used to give us the highest output of the things we require.

6. If that is the correct approach then it is at once apparent that we cannot be content merely to seek out the ready-made, and suitably equipped, industrial concerns and give them contracts. That is the method of conducting war on a peace-time economic basis. What we are now faced with is the urgent need to organise and plan production so as to find a use for every unit of capacity. There is no difficulty in finding out what capacity is available; the difficulty lies in organising its use. It is, therefore, not a capacity problem but a production problem, and because it is a production problem it can be solved only as a result of action by the Production Departments of the Supply Ministries themselves. I shall show later in this report what the Industrial Capacity Committee is doing, and proposes to do, to facilitate a solution. But it is the Production Departments alone, with their detailed knowledge of their own needs

and day to day difficulties, with the technical and production engineering staffs at their disposal, who can solve the problem by the methods of production engineering on a group or collectivist basis.

7.   The action which has already been taken by the Industrial Capacity Committee, and the further developments that will be proposed, must, therefore, be clearly understood as auxiliary services that have been, and could be, rendered to the Production Departments to whom they report, must accept full responsibility. The Industrial Capacity Committee has not been asked, and does not wish, to create an elaborate duplicate organisation [of] the work of the Production Departments were created to do. It seeks to elaborate a plan and to create a machinery through which the work of the Production Departments could be eased and facilitated. If the responsible Ministers approve the plan and the machinery, it is for them to see that all the branches of their Ministries operate it with vigour and efficiency. The undefined *executive authority* of the Industrial Capacity Committee is certainly not great enough to enable it to relieve either Ministers or Director-Generals of Production of their responsibility.

Appendix III[1]

UK Note on the Principles Applying to Reciprocal Aid in the Prosecution of the War Against Aggression

---

3rd September 1942

Viscount Halifax to Mr Cordell Hull

British Embassy
Washington

In the United Nations Declaration of the 1st January 1942, the contracting governments pledged themselves to employ their full resources, military or economic, against those nations with which they are at war, and in the agreement of the 23rd February 1942, each contracting government undertook to provide the other with such articles, services, facilities or information, useful in the prosecution of their common war undertaking, as each may be in a position to supply. It is further the understanding of the Government of the United Kingdom of Great Britain and Northern Ireland that the general principle to be followed in providing mutual aid is set forth in the said agreement of 23rd February 1942, is that the war production and the war resources of both the Nations should be used by the armed forces of each, and of the other United Nations, in ways which most effectively utilise the available materials, manpower, production facilities and shipping space.

With a view, therefore, to supplementing Article 2 and Article 6 of the Agreement of the 23rd February 1942, between our two governments for the provision of reciprocal aid, I have the honour to set forth below the understanding of the government of the United Kingdom of Great Britain and Northern Ireland of the principles and procedures applicable to the provision of aid by the Government of the United Kingdom and Northern Ireland to the armed forces of the United States and the manner in which such aid will be correlated with the maintenance of those forces by the United States Government.

1. While each Government retains the right of final decision, in the light of its own potentialities and responsibilities, decisions as to the most effective use of resources shall so far as possible, be made in common, pursuant to common plans for winning the war.

2. As to financing the provision of such aid, within the fields mentioned below, it is the understanding of the Government of the United Kingdom of Great Britain and Northern Ireland that the general principle to be applied, to the point at which the common war effort is most effective, is that as large a portion as possible of the articles and services which each Government may authorise to be provided to the other shall be in the form of reciprocal aid so that the need of each Government for the currency of the other may be reduced to a minimum.

    It is accordingly the understanding of the Government of the United Kingdom and Northern Ireland that the United States Government will provide, in accordance with the provisions of, and to the extent authorised under, the Act of the 11th March, 1941, the share of its war production made available to the United Kingdom. The Government of the United Kingdom will provide, on the same terms and as reciprocal aid so much of its war production made available to the United States as it authorises in accordance with the Agreement of the 23rd February 1942.

3. The Government of the United Kingdom will provide the United States or its armed forces with the following types of assistance, as such reciprocal aid, when it is found that they can most effectively be procured in the United Kingdom or in the British Colonial Empire:

    a. Military equipment, munitions and military and naval stores.
    b. Other supplies, materials, facilities and services for the United States forces, except for the pay and allowances of such forces, administrative expenses, and such local purchases as its official establishments may make other than through the official establishments of the Government of the United Kingdom as specified in paragraph 4.
    c. Supplies, materials and services needed in the construction of military projects, tasks and similar capital works required for the common war effort in the United Kingdom or in the British Colonial Empire, except for the wages and salaries of United States citizens.
    d. Supplies, materials and services needed in the construction of such military projects, tasks and capital works in territory other than the United Kingdom or the British Colonial Empire or territory of the United States to the extent that the United Kingdom or the British Colonial Empire is a more practicable source of supply than the United States or another of the United Nations.

4. The practical application of the principles formulated in this note, including the procedure by which requests for aid by either Government are made and acted upon, shall be worked out as occasion may require by agreement between the two Governments, acting when possible through their appropriate military or civilian administrative authorities. Requests by the United States Government for such aid will be presented by duly authorised authorities of the United States to official agencies of the United

Kingdom which will be designated or established in London and in the areas where the United States forces are located for the purposes of facilitating the provision of reciprocal aid.

5.   It is the understanding of the Government of the United Kingdom of Great Britain and Northern Ireland that all such aid, as well as other aid, including information, received under Article 6 of the Agreement of the 23rd February 1942, accepted by the President of the United States or his authorised representatives from the Government of the United Kingdom will be received as a benefit to the United States under the Act of the 11th March 1941. In so far as circumstances will permit, appropriate record of aid received under this arrangement, except for miscellaneous facilities and services, will be kept by each Government.

If the Government of the United States concurs in the foregoing, I would suggest that the present note and your reply to that effect be regarded as placing on record the understanding of our two Governments in this matter.

I have etc.

Halifax

The reply confirmed the arrangement.

Mr Cordell Hull to Viscount Halifax

Washington
3rd September 1942

I have the honour to acknowledge receipt of your Excellency's note of today's date concerning the principles and procedures applicable to the provision of aid by the Government of the United Kingdom of Great Britain and Northern Ireland to the armed forces of the United States of America.

In reply I wish to inform you that the Government of the United States agrees with the understanding of the Government of the United Kingdom of Great Britain and Northern Ireland as expressed in that note. In accordance with the suggestion contained therein, your note and this reply will be regarded as placing on record the understanding between our two Governments in the matter.

This further integration and strengthening of our common war effort gives me great satisfaction.

Accept and etc.

Cordell Hull

Appendix IV[1]

Remuneration on Extension of the Agreement with Aero-engine Committee No 1

1. The agreement made in 1936 relates to the erection of factories and the manufacture of 4,000 Mercury engines by June 1939. It is now proposed to manufacture additional Mercury engines and also Pegasus engines, and at the same time prepare for the manufacture of Hercules engines which, however, will not come into production until about August or September 1940. It is proposed that the new agreement shall cover a period up to about July of next year.

2. The terms finally agreed with the shadow engine firms (Austin, Bristol, Daimler, Rootes, Rovers and Standard) for building and equipping the factories and producing 4,000 engines were:

	Erection of Factories (1st year)	Production (2nd and 3rd years)	Balance on completion
5 firms	£24,000 each	£24,000 each	–
Bristol	£20,000	£20,000 per year	–
Balance on completion	–	–	£20,000
Total for group	£140,000	£280,000	£20,000

3. The fee in respect of the second and third years was to be payable by a sum of £75 per engine (totalling £300,000 if 4,000 engines were delivered) but in the event of failure to deliver, all except the final £20,000 was payable.

   In addition a bonus will be paid on engines Nos 401 onwards if the cost of production of these engines is less than the average cost of the 4th 100 engines. The bonus is calculated at 12.5% on the first £50 of savings and 17.5% savings over £50.

4. Although the exact cost of the 4th 100 engines has not yet been finally ascertained, as also is the position in regard to the costs of the later engines, such information as is available shows that the amount of the bonus will be about £350,000 to £400.000.

This large sum is due to the costs of production have fallen more steeply than was anticipated after the 4th 100 had been completed – or to put it another way, the 4th 100 were not produced so economically as had been expected.

5.   Although it is stated in the Committee's letter of the 12th July 1939, that actuated by a patriotic spirit they agreed to a rate of remuneration which, in their opinion, was inadequate, it is thought that the bonus earnings, of the trend of which they are now aware, will considerably exceed their expectations. It is considered that they are out of scale with the profits made by the aircraft industry over the same period, when it is remembered that the firms have nothing at stake at all in the way of capital and the remuneration is merely in respect of management functions, with all risk eliminated.

Negotiations for extension of the agreement

6.   Negotiations were commenced by a letter of the 26th July 1938, from the Aero Engine Committee intimating their willingness to proceed with the production of the engines additional to those covered by the agreement. These negotiations have been protracted and rendered difficult firstly by the uncertainty as to the production program required from this shadow group, and secondly by the unwillingness of the Committee to recognise the reasonableness of the Department's standpoint that remuneration in the case of the shadow factories must bear some relation to the profits allowed in the aircraft industry and to the scale of the effort involved, and at the same time must take account of the fact that the whole of the capital employed in the shadow industry is provided by the Government. There have been various proposals and counter proposals leading to the following terms being provisionally agreed at a meeting on the 29th March 1939:

   i.   The present total annual payment by way of management fee of £140,000 to be continued, but not based heretofore on a fee per engine produced. The fee to cover the manufacture of any additional Mercury engines and all Pegasus and Hercules engines.

   ii.   Bonus arrangements to continue except that the Committee's share of savings would be 20% of savings up to £50 and 30% on savings beyond £50.

   iii.   Basic prices to be fixed as in the existing agreement except that in lieu of batches of 100, the Air Ministry accepted the Committee's proposal for batches of 25 in the case of Pegasus engines and batches of 50 in the case of Hercules engines.

   iv.   Owing to a variation in the arrangements for the shadow manufacture of Hercules engines, these terms were not confirmed.

7.   Modified proposals to meet the new production arrangements were sent to the Committee under cover of a letter of the 20th June 1939, in the shape of draft heads of a proposed agreement, the principal points being as follows:

   a.   The new agreement to cover all Mercury and Pegasus engines to be made by the factories.

   b.   An annual payment of £140,000 to be made as from the 1st July 1939.

    c.   A target cost to be agreed as early as practicable and subject to review at the end of the production of each 500 engines.

    d.   Bonus to be paid on savings as in the first agreement, i.e. 12.5% of savings up to £50 and 17.5% of savings beyond £50.

8.   The Committee considered these terms and proposed on the 28th June 1939, that the fee should be £150,000 for the year and that bonus on earnings should be replaced by a fee per engine which should be subject to variation according as the deliverables and cost of engines differed from standards laid down every three months. The effect of these proposals would be to give a sum per engine delivered, and since the estimates of output of cost are to be taken at short intervals there would be little room for variation. The proposals of the Committee are thus in effect a management fee (which is a commuted fee per engine) and a fee per engine delivered.

9.   The proposals at (7) and (8) represent the stage in the negotiations which had been reached when the letter of 12th July 1939 was written requesting that the net amount to be received after assessment of Armaments Profits Duty shall be the same as the Committee had provisionally agreed to accept.

10. The uncertainty as to the production requirements of the shadow engine group which, unavoidably, has been one of the principle stumbling blocks in the way of the negotiations is not in the process of being cleared up. Following discussion with AMDP and 1st DUS on 22nd July it now appears that the group may be required to manufacture about 5,000 Mercury and Pegasus engines before they will be in a position to commence production of the Hercules. On this number, if a bonus of £40 per engine is accepted in addition to a lump sum of £150,000, the revenue of the Committee would be approximately £350,000 for the year. This sum is considerably in excess of the average which is estimated will be earned in the preceding three years, namely £270,000 per annum. It represents on the estimated cost of 5,000 engines remuneration of almost exactly 5%, and compares with an estimated rate of rather more than 10% in respect of the last two years working.

11. The object of the Committee's letter and presumably of Lord Austin's meeting is to demand that payments shall be adjusted so that the net amount remaining after payment of APD shall be the same as the Committee had provisionally agreed to accept. It is not thought that this relates only to the fee of £150,000 which, in fact, is all that the Committee have so far shown a willingness to accept specifically, but relates also to bonus payments amounting in total to a figure approximating to the average anticipated receipts of the Committee under this head for each of the past two years work. It is impracticable at this stage to access the effect of APD on the earnings of the various companies, and in any case it is certain that all the firms represented by the Committee will not be affected to the same extent. Furthermore, it is presumably out of the question to accept the demand that the remuneration shall be exempt from APD or to adjust the remuneration so as to provide for the incidence of APD.

12. It may be argued by the Committee that APD will act unfairly as between the firms in that although each is allotted its proper share of the remuneration the amount

liable for duty may vary with each firm because the amount of other armament work carried out. This is a phenomenon, however, which applied throughout the armament industry, and it may be retorted that if the Committee considers the incidence of APD inequitable in relation to shadow factory remuneration, they have the remedy in their own hands, because the revenue is paid to the Committee, who may distribute it between the various firms at their discretion.

13. It is thought that remuneration in excess of 5% on the cost of production is clearly unjustified in the case of the shadow factories. Perhaps, however, it will be unnecessary in the discussion with Lord Austin to mention any particular percentage figure, and to deal generally with the question of remuneration in relation to profits in the professional industry, pointing out at the same time that the industry have accepted a substantial reduction in profit rates under the McLintock Agreement, and in addition will be subject to APD.

14. Pending a decision as to the production program it does not seem possible to say more to Lord Austin than that we are now hopeful that it will be practicable to give the shadow factories sufficient work to justify acceptance of the Committee's offer to continue at an annual fee of £150,000, with a bonus arrangement which should result in the total revenue of the Committee being substantially in excess of the average revenue of the last three years.

15. Lord Austin will probably make play with the long delay which has taken place in negotiating new terms, and will emphasise the generosity of the Committee in expressing their willingness to carry on at the same annual fee as before. The delay is very regrettable but in the circumstances it has been quite unavoidable. As regards the generosity of the offer made by the Committee in March this, of course, cannot be considered without reference to the additional remuneration which can be earned by a bonus scheme. In the circumstances in which the offer was made, however, it was undoubtedly a fair one, and deserves an expression of appreciation.

16. To recapitulate:
    a. Shadow firms in common with all other firms engaged in the armament manufacture cannot be permitted to contract out of APD.
    b. Remuneration must be related to scale of effort and must also bear comparison with profits in the professional aircraft industry, having in view shadow firms absence of risk, absence of capital commitments and absence of responsibility for design.
    c. It is now hoped (but at present a definitive guarantee to this effect cannot be given) that the number of Mercury and Pegasus engines to be manufactured at the shadow firms will be sufficient to justify a total remuneration (i.e. annual fee plus bonus earnings) appreciably in excess of the average annual revenues of the Committee over the past three years, which should ease the position in regard to the incidence of APD.
    d. Pending a definite production program it is desirable that any statements made to Lord Austin should be in general terms, mention of specific sums or profit rates being avoided.

Appendix V[1]

Agreement between the Secretary of State for Air and the Right Honourable William Richard Viscount Nuffield of Nuffield

An Agreement made the sixteenth day of September one thousand nine hundred and thirty eight between the Secretary of State for Air (hereinafter referred to as the Secretary of State) acting by Sir Donald Banks, Permanent Under-Secretary of State for Air of the one part and the Right Honourable William Richard Viscount Nuffield of Nuffield in the County of Oxford (hereinafter referred to as The Controller) of the other part.

Whereby it is agreed as follows:

1. The Controller shall on behalf of and upon terms approved by the Secretary of State contract to purchase from the Corporation of Birmingham with the concurrence of the Dunlop Rubber Company Limited in whose favour certain restrictive covenants exits certain land and premises at Tyburn Birmingham for the purpose of the erection upon such land of a factory for the manufacture of complete air frames for aeroplanes and spare parts therefor in accordance with this contract.
2. The Controller shall after completion of the contract of purchase as mentioned in clause 1 hereof procure that the said land and premises shall with his concurrence be conveyed to the Secretary of State.
3. Forthwith upon obtaining possession of the said land and premises The Controller shall on behalf of the Secretary of State and in accordance with plans and specifications to be approved by him erect thereon and equip with the necessary plant machinery and services a factory having a production capacity of three thousand air frames of the Spitfire type a year or an equivalent capacity of other types of air frames and in all other respects suitable for the manufacture of complete air frames for aeroplanes and spare parts therefor in accordance with this agreement.
4. The Controller shall also equip the factory with all jigs, gauges and other tools necessary for the manufacture of air frames and spare parts therefor required by the Secretary of State under clause 10 hereof.

5. The Controller shall obtain competitive tenders for the levelling and laying out of the site and for the erection and equipment of the factory wherever practicable save where the Secretary of State agrees that such a course is not consistent with the requirements of efficiency and urgency. The estimated cost of levelling and laying out of the site and of the erection and equipment of the factory shall be subject to the approval of the Secretary of State and the Controller shall not without the consent of the Secretary of State incur any costs in excess of the estimated cost so approved. All work shall be carried out and purchases made as economically as is consistent with efficiency and the urgency of the work and to the reasonable satisfaction of the Secretary of State.

6. All notices required to be given to local authorities or to any authorised undertakers and all licences and consents relating to the building of the factory shall be given or obtained by the Controller.

7. All plant machinery and equipment installed or provided at any time in the factory shall be of the best quality obtainable and where practicable of United Kingdom manufacture and (except as to jigs gauges and other tools) of a nature or type approved by the Secretary of State. The factory and all plant machinery and equipment shall be maintained by the Controller in good running order and condition. The Secretary of State shall have the right at all reasonable times to inspect the same and to call upon the Controller to repair the factory and any plant machinery and equipment therein if in his opinion it is not in good order and condition or to remove and if necessary replace any plant machinery or equipment which in his opinion is unsuitable or unserviceable or has become obsolete.

8. All plant machinery and equipment ordered for the purposes of this agreement shall become the property of the Secretary of State as soon as it is severally made by him for the erection of the factory or for the supply of plant and machinery and equipment *insert provisions to give effect to this clause.*

9. The factory shall be managed by the Controller on behalf of the Secretary of State with Oliver Boden or another officer appointed by the Controller with the approval of the Secretary of State as the Deputy Controller thereof and shall be used exclusively for the purposes of this agreement.

10. The Controller shall diligently and skilfully and with the utmost expedition manufacture at the factory one thousand airframes of the Spitfire type and such spare parts therefor as the Secretary of State may require. Thereafter the Controller shall as and when required by the Secretary of State manufacture to the order of the Secretary of State such airframes for aeroplanes and spare parts therefor of the Spitfire type or of such other type as the Secretary of State may require and the Secretary of State shall have the right from time to time to decide and to notify to the Controller the quantities of the airframes and spare parts respectively of the respective types to be manufactured and vary the type of airframes and spare parts so notified so far as relates to the balance or any part thereof of the quantity of airframes and spare parts so notified from time to time remaining to be manufactured.

11. The Controller shall manufacture and complete all airframes and spare parts therefor of any type so to be supplied by him to the Secretary of State as aforesaid strictly in

conformity with drawings specifications and schedules relating to that type to be supplied from time to time by the Secretary of State.

In order to increase the rate of manufacture of the efficiency of the airframes the said drawings specifications and schedules may be modified from time to time by the Secretary of State or by the Controller with the approval of the Secretary of State. Any modifications proposed by the Controller shall be submitted to the Secretary of State in such form and accompanied by such drawings as he may direct and all such modifications and drawings shall be available for the use of the Secretary of State or of any contractor employed by him without any payment to the Controller therefor.

12. The Controller shall test the airframes so manufactured in such manner and to such extent as the Secretary of State may require and the airframes when tested to the satisfaction of the Secretary of State shall forthwith be delivered in accordance with directions given by the Secretary of State.

13. Subject to the provisions relating to the termination of this agreement hereinafter contained the Controller shall be entitled to use the factory until the completion of his obligations as to manufacture, testing and delivery of airframes and spare parts therefor under this agreement.

14. The Secretary of State shall, so far as he lawfully can, authorise the Controller to make use and exercise all inventions which are necessary for the manufacture of the airframes and spare parts therefor in so far as they are now or may hereafter be protected by British letters patent.

15. The Controller shall in accordance with the terms of this agreement as agent and manager of the factory for the Secretary of State in the manufacture of the airframes and spare parts therefor:

    a.   Order and do his best to obtain on behalf of the Secretary of State at the most economical prices reasonably obtainable all material necessary for the manufacture of the airframes and spare parts therefor. All the materials used for the purposes of this agreement shall be of the best quality obtainable and where practicable of United Kingdom manufacture.

    b.   Be responsible for the engagement and employment of all the staff and workmen to be engaged in the factory and accordingly do his best in his own name to employ, instruct and pay such skilled competent managers, departmental heads and other staff and workmen as are required for the purposes of this agreement and make all proper provision for their engagement, discharge and proper conduct provided that the Secretary of State shall be entitled at any time to require the dismissal of any member of the staff or any workman engaged at the factory but shall indemnify the Controller against all actions claims and demands on the part of any such member or workmen by reason of such dismissal.

    c.   In his own name discharge all obligations incurred by an employer of labour by statute or otherwise.

    d.   Effect such insurances as the Secretary of State may require.

16. The Controller shall keep books containing such full and accurate costing and other accounts and records as are necessary to supply the information required by the

Secretary of State for the purposes of this agreement and shall render accounts to the Secretary of State on the first day of each calendar month in such form and certified in such manner as may be required by him of the expenditure incurred by the Controller in respect of the matters specified in clause 17 hereof and shall produce to the Secretary of State such vouchers and other documents as he may require for the purpose of verifying such accounts and records. The Secretary of State and the Controller and the Auditor-General and any officer authorised by them for the purpose shall at all times have access to such books records and documents.

17. The Secretary of State shall pay to the Controller and indemnify him against:

1. The net cost incurred by him in purchasing the land and premises acquired on behalf of the Secretary of State for the purposes of this agreement.

2. The net cost incurred by him in levelling and laying out the site for and in erecting and equipping the factory with the necessary plant and machinery for the purposes of this agreement and in providing services in accordance with the plans and specifications mentioned in clause 3 hereof and in the payment of all fees including architect's and other professional and technical fees incurred by the Controller under this agreement.

3. The net cost incurred by him in respect of electric light, power, gas, water, sewerage and drainage and other like services necessary for the purposes of this agreement.

4. The net cost incurred by him in equipping the factory with the jigs and other tools and in purchasing the material necessary for the manufacture of air frames and spare parts therefor in accordance with this agreement.

5. The net cost incurred by him in paying premiums on all insurance policies which the Secretary of State shall require the Controller to effect and licence fees for the use of patents or inventions which the Secretary of State may from time to time authorise the Controller to incur.

6. The net cost incurred by him from time to time in maintaining, repairing, rebuilding and reinstating the factory and maintaining, repairing and replacing the plant machinery and equipment thereof.

7. a. The net cost incurred by him in the payment of salaries and wages to and by way of insurance of persons employed by him under clause 15(b) of this agreement and of any of the personnel of his own organisations whose services he may utilise in the factory in pursuance of his obligations under clause 10 hereof but so that no payment for the services of the Controller and the Deputy Controller shall be chargeable to the Secretary of State.

   b. The fair and reasonable cost of employing in the factory any of his own personnel whom the Controller may think fit in the interests of economy and efficiency (but without any obligation to do so) to transfer from any of his own factories to the factory on a part time basis or for temporary or emergency work therein.

8. The net cost of delivering the air frames and spare parts therefor.

9.   All other expenses of whatever nature or kind which may be properly incurred by the Controller in carrying this agreement into effect.

18. The Secretary of State shall pay to the Controller any expenditure properly incurred by him in anticipation of this agreement coming into effect, credit being given to the Secretary of State for any sum already advanced by him to the Controller in respect of such expenditure.

19. An account shall be opened by the Secretary of State at Barclay's Bank Limited Aston, Birmingham under the title of the Air Council (Castle Bromwich Airframe Factory) Account and the Secretary of State may nominate for the purpose to operate the said account in accordance with directions to be given from time to time by him. The Controller shall be responsible to the Secretary of State for all operations on the account and shall make all payments in respect of any expenditure properly incurred by him on behalf of the Secretary of State in carrying out this agreement out of the account and not otherwise.

20. For the purpose of enabling the Controller to make such payments as aforesaid in due time the Secretary of State shall at or before the commencement of each calendar month during the currency of this agreement pay into the said account by way of imprest in respect of each such period such sum as (together with any money already standing to the credit of the account) he considers to be sufficient to meet the expenditure which the Controller will incur in carrying out his obligations under this agreement to the end of the said period.

21. For the purpose of enabling the Secretary of State to decide the amount to be paid into the said account as aforesaid the Controller shall not later than two days after the commencement of each period of one calendar month submit to him such form as he may require an estimate of his expenditure during the two ensuing calendar months.

22. If the Controller satisfies the Secretary of State at any time that the sum standing to the credit of the account is insufficient to enable the Controller to meet any capital or emergency payment incurred by him on behalf of the Secretary of State in carrying out the terms of this agreement, the Secretary of State will pay in to the account such additional sum as will enable the Controller to meet such capital or emergency expenditure as it falls due.

23. The Secretary of State may at all reasonable times inspect the factory and the plant machinery and equipment thereof and may in such manner as he thinks fit examine the progress and method of manufacture of the air frames and spare parts therefor and the Controller shall furnish to the Secretary of State such information relating to any of the matters provided for by this agreement as he may require. The Secretary of State may take such measures as he may from time to time think fit for the general oversight of the working of the factory and the Controller shall comply with such instructions in connection therewith as may for the general oversight of the working of the factory and the Controller shall comply with such instructions in connection therewith as may from time to time be given by the Secretary of State.

24. The Controller shall if the Secretary of State so requires assign to him on behalf of His Majesty any right of free user of any invention or design relating to air frames

to be manufactured hereunder (whether such invention or design is the subject of a patent or not) to which the controller is entitled discovered or produced in the course of or arising out of the manufacture of the airframes by any person employed in such manufacture whose salary or wages in respect of such employment are paid by the Secretary of State under this agreement.

25. The Controller shall not communicate or cause or permit to be communicated to any unauthorised person any particulars of or information relating to the terms of this agreement or to the manufacture of airframes and spare parts therefor and shall take all necessary steps to bring to the notice of their employees and of the staff employed for the purpose of this agreement the provisions of this clause and the application of the Official Secrets Acts in that behalf.

26. The Secretary of State shall be entitled at any time to give the Controller directions in writing as to:

   a. The further performance or the cessation of any work to be done under this agreement.

   b. The termination of contracts for the erection of the factory and the supply of plant machinery equipment and material therefor.

   c. Any other matters arising out of this agreement with regard to which the Secretary of State may think directions from him are necessary AND the Controller shall (so far as shall be reasonably possible) comply with any such directions.

27. 1. Upon the date when the Controller ceases to be entitled to use the factory for the purpose of this agreement the Controller shall at the expense of the Secretary of State

   a. If so required by notice in writing given by the Secretary of State maintain the factory together with the plant machinery and equipment therein in good running order and condition for such period as the Secretary of State may require.

   b. If not so required deliver up in good running order and condition to the Secretary of State or as he may direct the factory and the plant machinery equipment and material therein fair wear and tear and damage by fire explosion accident or tempest excepted.

   In either case:

   c. Hand over to the Secretary of State all plans of the factory and schedules of all the plant machinery equipment and material therein together with all books costing or other accounts and working plans and drawings and records made or kept for the purpose of this agreement.

   d. Assign in accordance with the directions of the Secretary of State all contracts entered into by the Controller for the purposes of this agreement in such manner that the Controller shall be completely released from and indemnified against all his obligations properly incurred thereunder.

   2. The Secretary of State or the Controller may terminate the period during which the Controller is required to maintain the factory under paragraph (a) of this clause by giving the other of them twelve calendar month' notice in writing of

his intention so to do and on the expiration of such notice the Controller shall deliver up in good running order and condition to the Secretary of State or as he may direct the factory and the plant machinery equipment and material therein fair wear and tear and damage by fire explosion accident or tempest excepted.

28. Without prejudice to any indemnity implied by law the Secretary of State shall effectually indemnify and keep indemnified the Controller and his employees and agents both before and after the termination of this agreement from and against all action proceedings claims demands costs expenses and liabilities whatsoever taken or made against or incurred by the Controller or to which the Controller may be or become liable in carrying out any of his obligations under this agreement or incidental to the proper performance of his obligations hereunder.

29. The Controller or the Deputy Controller shall not be entitled to any profit or personal remuneration whatsoever for the carrying out of this agreement.

30. Any dispute under this agreement shall be referred to the arbitration of a single arbitrator to be agreed upon between the Secretary of State and the Controller and in default of agreement to be appointed by the Lord Chief Justice of England.

31. Clauses 27 and 28 hereof shall remain in full force notwithstanding the termination of this agreement and the provisions of clause 30 shall continue for the purposes of such clauses.

32. So far as they are not inconsistent with the express terms of this agreement the Special Contract Conditions (AM Form 838) and the General Contract Conditions (AM Form 705) both of which are hereto annexed shall be incorporated in and form part of this agreement provided that the said General Contract Conditions shall not be so incorporated so far as they are inconsistent with the said Special Contract Conditions.

33. In witness whereof the parties have hereunto set their hands and seals the day and year first written.

Signed, sealed and delivered by the said Sir Donald Banks

Signed, sealed and delivered by the Right Honourable William Richard Viscount Nuffield in the presence of O Boden, Morris Motors Ltd, Cowley

Appendix VI[1]

A Compiled List of Shadow Factories

The following list of shadow factories has been compiled from several National Archives folios. The lists in the Archives are often undated, and in some cases mention the name of the company and not the product made at that factory during the war. I have chosen to include these companies for completeness, even though a search in the National Archives database did not solicit any further information. The compilation is therefore the best representation of the many shadow factories that existed. During the war, the term agency factory was often used, particularly in the Admiralty. Some of these factories have also been added, the reason being that strictly speaking the term 'Shadow Factory' was initially used to denote factories established to run alongside the existing factories producing like materials in the immediate pre-war period.

Parent Company	Shadow Factories	Product and Estimated Capacity (where Known)
No. 1 Engine Group		
Standard	Coventry	Engines Bristol (inc. spare parts) Mercury and Pegasus 10,400 per annum
Austin	Longbridge	
Rootes	Coventry	
Rover	Birmingham	
Daimler	Coventry	
Bristol	Filton	
No. 2 Engine Group		
Rover	Birmingham	Engines Bristol inc. spare parts Hercules 4,400 per annum
Standard	Coventry	
Daimler	Coventry	
Rootes	Coventry	
No. 3 Shadow		

Parent Company	Shadow Factories	Product and Estimated Capacity (where Known)
Bristol	Accrington	Engines Hercules Engine exhaust rings Capacity 400 per month
AC Cossor Ltd, London N5	Oldham and High Wycombe	RDF equipment
Aeronautical & Panel Plywood Co	Lydney	Plywood 10 million Sq. ft. per annum Veneers 30 million Sq. ft. per annum
Airspeed (1934) Ltd, Portsmouth	Christchurch	Oxfords
Alvis Ltd, Coventry	Mountsorrel	Armaments
Amalgamated Banket Areas Ltd	Ejuanema, Gold Coast	Metals
Armstrong Whitworth	Coventry	Lancasters
Austin	Longbridge	Airframes Battle inc. spares Hurricanes 25 Stirlings per month
Automotive Products Co Ltd	Leicester	Airframes
AV Roe Ltd	Stoke	Airframes
AV Roe Ltd	Yeadon	Ansons, Lancaster bombers
Birmetals Ltd, Birmingham	Stourbridge	Metals
Briggs Motor Bodies Ltd	Stoke	Parts for Spitfires
Bristol Aeroplane Co Ltd	Accrington	Engines
Bristol Aeroplane Co Ltd	Weston, Hawthorne and No. 1 Engine Group	Beaufighters, engines
British Aluminium Co.	Sefwi Bakwai, Gold Coast	Bauxite 50,000 per annum
British Aluminium Co Ltd, Shrewsbury	Swansea, Northern Ireland and Scheme 8, Warrington	Metals
British Insulated Cables Ltd, High Wycombe	High Wycombe	Unknown product
British Manufacturing and Research Co. (MARC)	Grantham	Cannon Guns 600 per month
British Piston Ring Co Ltd, Coventry	Edinburgh	Engine components
BSA Guns Ltd	Newcastle-under-Lyne	Hispana-Suiza guns 750 per month
BTH Ltd, Rugby	Leicester	Magnetos

Parent Company	Shadow Factories	Product and Estimated Capacity (where Known)
Burtonwood Repair Depot, Hayes	Warrington	Repair and recovery depot
C Napier and Sons Ltd Acton	Liverpool	Engines for the navy and some trucks
Castner-Kellner Alkalai Co Ltd	Runcorn	Chemicals
Castle Bromwich Aeroplane Factory	Castle Bromwich	Lancasters
Daimler Co Ltd, Coventry	No. 1 and 2 Engine Groups	Engines
De Havilland	Lostock	Airscrews 10–12,000 per annum
De Havilland Aircraft Co Ltd, Hatfield	Factory No. 2 Leavesden Aerodrome, Leavesden, Herts	Airframes
Dowty Equipment Ltd	Cheltenham, Tewkesbury	Undercarriages
English Electric Co Ltd	Preston	Hampden and Halifax aircraft
Expanded Rubber Co Ltd, Croydon	Dundee	Unknown product
Factories Direction Ltd, London	Lydney	Unknown product
Fairey	Burtonwood	Repairs and assembly
	Stockport	Airframes Beaufighters 60 per month Halifax also
Fairey Aviation Ltd, Hayes	Errwood Park	Beaufighters
Ford Motor Co Ltd	Trafford Park	Engines Merlins 400 per month
Gramophone Co Ltd	Treorchy, Glamorgan	Unknown product
General Electric Co Ltd, London WC2	Shaw (Oldham)	Wireless valves
Hadfields Ltd	Swinton	Bombs 1,000 500 lb bombs per week
Handley Page Ltd, Cricklewood	York Aircraft Depot	Halifax
	Duple Bodies & Motors Ltd Chrysler Motors Ltd Express Motors Park Royal Coach Works LPTB 1 other	Halifax components

Parent Company	Shadow Factories	Product and Estimated Capacity (where Known)
HM Hobson (Aircraft and Motor), Coventry	Oldham	Carburettors and spares Types AVT 85MB AIT 122MB
ICI (Explosives) Ltd, Mill Hill	Hawick, Kilmarnock and Springfields (Nr Preston)	Aviation fuel, light alloys, incendiary bombs, ethyl chloride, monomer and Perspex
ICI (General Chemicals), Liverpool	Widness	
ICI (Metals), Birmingham	Gowerton	
ICI (Plastics) Ltd, Welwyn	Rawtenstall	
ICI Ltd, London SW1		
Integral Auxiliary Equipment	Witney	Pumps 1,000 per month
International Alloys Ltd, Slough	Aylesbury and Cardiff	Metals
J Stone and Co Ltd, Deptford	Bardsley	Unknown product
Joseph Lucas Ltd, Willesden Junction	High Wycombe, Cwmbran and Warwick	Unknown product
KLG Sparking Plugs Ltd, London SW15	Treforest, nr Pontypridd, Glam	Engine components
Leyland Motors, Leyland	Leeds	Carburettor castings
Lockheed Hydraulic Brake Co.	Leicester	Undercarriages
Joseph Lucas	Cwmbran	Cannon turrets BP type
Machine Products Ltd	Cardiff	Bombs
Magnesium Elektron Ltd	Burnley	Unknown product
Metal Box Co Ltd	Apperley Bridge, nr Bradford	Hand grenades
Metropolitan Vickers	Manchester	Lancasters
Morris Motors	Cowley and Eaglescliffe (nr Stockton-on-Tees)	Metals Salvage (including melting) 50-70 tons per week
Murex Ltd, Essex	Mossend	Thorium powder
Napier	West Derby	Engines Sabre 2,000 per annum
Northern Aluminium Co Ltd	Adderbury	Metal 15,000 tons scrap and virgin aluminium melting per annum
Phillips and Powis	South Marston	Masters, 70 per month

Parent Company	Shadow Factories	Product and Estimated Capacity (where Known)
Plessey Co Ltd	Swindon	Complete wiring systems for all services, cartridge starters, fuel pumps, conduit systems, vacuum pumps, ignition harnesses, etc.
Rolls-Royce, Derby	Hillington, Barnoldswick and Clitheroe	Engines Merlin
Rolls-Royce from 5th January 1943	Barnoldswick and Clitheroe	Development of the jet engine
Rootes	Speke (also covers Stock-on-Trent shadow factory)	Airframes Halifax from Nov 1941 32 Halifax per month 5 Blenheim per week inc. spares
Rover Co Ltd	No. 1 and 2 Engine Groups	Engines
Rover Co Ltd until 5th January 1943	Barnoldswick and Clitheroe	Development of the jet engine
Rubery Owen Messier	Darlington and Warrington	Undercarriages
Shell Refineries Ltd	Stanlow (Cheshire) and Ardrossan (Scotland)	Petrol and oil containers
Standard Carburettors	Coventry	Carburettors 22/2/40–8/3/41 4959 carburettors 2624 boost and mixture controls 500 (spares equivalent to)
Standard Motor Co Ltd, Coventry	No. 1 and 2 Engine Groups and Nottingham Carburettor	Engines
Stirling Metals Ltd, Coventry	Burton Latimer, Kettering	Metals
SU Carburettors Ltd, Ilkley	Addingham, Yorks	Carburettors
Trimpell Ltd	Heysham (nr Morecambe)	Aviation fuel
United Africa Co Ltd	Dunkwa, Gold Coast	Metal ore
Vickers Armstrongs Ltd, Bath	South Marston	Airframes
Vickers-Armstrongs	Chester	Wellingtons 80 per month
Vickers-Armstrongs	Blackpool	Wellingtons 80 per month Warwicks 40 per month
Vickers-Armstrongs	Castle Bromwich	Spitfires 180 per month
Vickers-Armstrongs	Weybridge	Wellingtons

Appendix VII[1]

Lancaster and York Production and Development

Visit to Avros, Manchester on 19th–21st July 1943

During my visit to Avros the following company representatives were consulted:

Mr RH Dobson	Managing Director
Mr E Fielding	General Manager
Mr R Chadwick	Chief Designer
Mr SD Davies	Experimental Engineer
Mr Wm Meacock	Assistant Experimental Engineer

Avro manufacturing facilities consist of 9 large factories in and around Manchester, varying from new plant such as the Chadderton works to converted cotton mills like the Laurel works and Ashton works. They are producing about 120 Lancasters monthly now and expect eventually to reach a peak production of about 150 monthly. In addition to the large Lancaster manufacturing program they are also building a few York transports, about 130 Anson twin engined trainers monthly, bomber turrets, and bomb carriers and bomb slips. Final assembly of the Lancaster is being done at Yeadon and Woodford and parts sub-assemblies are being manufactured there as well as at other Avro factories.

Avros have produced approximately 1,300 Lancasters to date and a study of their present production factors indicate that they are now producing Lancasters at approximately 2.34 man hours per lb. This was calculated from the following figures furnished by Mr Fielding.

Airframe weight	20,800lbs
Percentage sub-contracting (approx.)	15%
Percent spares (approx.)	15%
Working hours per man per month (approx.)	200
Total employees on Lancaster production in April 1943	26,200
June production of Lancasters	105

Using the above figures it appears that the present production rate is 83.5 lbs per employee per month. Incidentally, Mr Dobson advised that they are now building the airplane in a total of 27,000 man hours and expect to get this down to about 24,700 hours by the end of 1943.

The production records as of July 15th 1943 show the following figures on total labour strength and total area.

Section	Labour Strength	Area	Square feet per labour unit
Production area	28,692	2,633,000	92
Stores area	2,656	667,000	251
Office area	4,534	322,000	71
Total	35,882	3,622,000	103

The above production area includes tool room, experimental section and flight hangers, and the stores includes dispersal stores. The labour strength shown for the production area is more than direct labour as it includes inspection, maintenance, production planning etc., in fact all except office and stores personnel. Of the total production labour strength about 1000 are unskilled part-time workers, mostly women, each of whom works only 5 hours daily. The plants are now working two 10 hour shifts daily, approximately 5½days per week.

It is interesting to note that in March 1943 the hires totalled 1,185 and the quits totalled 695, of whom 400 were women and 295 were men. Since Avros has a total employment of about 35,000 at that time, the quit rate was only about 2% monthly. This was typical of the first 4 months of 1943.

The tempo of work at Avros seemed very good and the percentage of unskilled and female labour very high. This percentage was 72% at the Ashton works and 75% at Wythenshawe. In the Ashton plant all machine tools are run by unskilled or semi-skilled operators and they have only a very few skilled workers for machine tool set up.

Conveyor belts are used to good advantage, particularly in the manufacture and assembly of bomb slips and bomb carriers. Their equipment for working drawn sections and extrusions is not so elaborate as that in some American factories, for instance North American, but the final results are good. Two years ago, when it appeared that an extrusion shortage was imminent, Avros succeeded in changing 66% of their Lancaster extrusions by length to tolled and drawn sections. The only members kept as extrusions were wing beam spar caps, main fuselage longerons, and a few heavy cross members and transport joints.

Automatic riveting is not widely used and the few Erco riveting machines in use at Avros have had the hole punching apparatus and automatic rivet feeds removed. Consideration is being given to increasing the use of such equipment particularly on the large flat skin panels of the York. The quality of hand riveting is generally not up to the American standards.

Their material position is good and in general there are very few shortages. It is estimated that they are running on a 9½week cycle from raw material to finished airplane, plus about one month's supply of material in stores, making a total of about 3 to 3½ months flow time on the average.

The machine tools and fixtures position is good as is also their labour position. In this connection dispersal has not proven so great a problem to Avros as they have taken over numerous old cotton mills and their labour was drawn from former cotton mill employees living in the vicinity of each mill. Plant housekeeping seemed quite good at Newton Heath and Wythenshawe but in most of the other plants it was not up to American standards.

Assembly and sub-assembly fixtures are in a constant state of change to improve the efficiency of output and also to permit adjustment of wage incentive rates when bonuses run too high. It is very difficult to establish new rates without changing the process as there is otherwise considerable resentment on the part of labour.

Certain of the assembly operations are still hindered by the brick blast walls and bomb shelters which have been built in the factories, and which have prevented the location of assembly stations and line production, as they would wish them. However, this is not a serious factor.

For female unskilled labour, the weekly salary based on a 47 hour week is 22 shillings plus the wage incentive bonus based on this salary and a 16 shilling weekly cost of living bonus. Overtime of 33⅓ paid after 5 pm, 50% on Saturdays and 100% on Sundays. Wage incentive bonus is running as high as 100% in several shops but it should be noted that this brings the unskilled female weekly wage to only 58 s or $22.60, not including overtime payment.

The comparative rates for unskilled male labour are 34 shillings weekly basic rate, to which wage incentive bonus is added, and 22 shillings weekly cost of living bonus – with the same percentage overtime payments.

The first 20 York transports are being built in the experimental shop at Chadderton. The prototype and the No 1 production airplane (VIP) are now in flying condition at Ringway and the No 2 production airplane is expected out of Chadderton within the next 2 or 3 weeks.

The York has a square cross section fuselage with a built in wing centre section of somewhat greater span than the Lancaster. The outer wings are regular Lancaster wings and the gross weight and performance is practically identical to the standard Lancaster as the drag of the larger York fuselage just about equals that of the bomber with turrets. The construction is very simple and the flat side and top fuselage skin panels are made up in large sections of about 30 × 7 ft and the stringers of these panels are then bolted to the fuselage bulk heads.

Among the interesting Lancaster developments are the mail planes for trans-Atlantic and possibly trans-Canada operations, and the new long span Lancaster bomber.

The mail planes are cleaned up bombers with no turrets and a small quantity is being built with the following specifications:

Gross weight	63,000 lbs
Range	4,300 miles
Cruising speed (at 2100 rpm)	230 mph
Fuel	2,900 Imperial Gallons
Crew	4
Mail load	7,000 lbs
Take-off run (over 50 ft obstacle)	1,200 yards

The new long span Lancaster bomber will not be in production until 1944 and will have extended outer wings to make the span 102 ft. Other changes include a strengthened centre section and a modified fuselage mid-section to accommodate an improved upper turret with increased armament. This will be located somewhat forward of the present turret position.

Avros are also working on the design of a large civil air transport but this has only reached the weight estimate and lay-out drawing stage to date.

The attached (to original copy only) Avro brochures show the breakdown of Lancaster production factors by component and the complete basis production data which is furnished by Avros to new firms being brought into the Lancaster production program.

Edwin C Walton

Appendix VIII[1]

Responsibilities of the Ministry of Home Security and the Air Ministry at Aerodromes Used Jointly by the RAF and Contractors

Notes of a meeting at the Air Ministry on 5th February 1941 Present: Chairman: L G S Reynolds

Air Ministry: Wing Commander F Carpenter, C J Galpin, A H Matheson and J A Robertson.

MAP: R C Carline and W P Hildred.

Ministry of Home Security: W E Curtis, Captain L M Glasson, W S Imrie, P James, C S Petheram and W T Thornington.

The Chairman explained that the meeting was being held to clear up the position as it had been left after three meetings held in October and December 1940, viz. on the 3rd October, 31st October and 9th December. After the December meeting a list of aerodromes had been produced, divided into:

1. Class I – where the Royal Air Force had the predominating interest.
2. Class 2A – where there was no Air Ministry present or prospective interest.
    Class 2B – where the Air Ministry had an interest in the landing ground and certain buildings.

The result of these meetings as seen by the Air Minister had been reported to him after an Inter-Departmental conference with Sir Alan Barlow on the 14th Report from the Select Committee on National Expenditure, and he had written to Mr Petheram on the 14th January. He suggested that the conference should now examine do novo the division of responsibility as suggested in his letter to Mr Petheram and then consider the list of aerodromes.

He must, however, warn the Minister of Home Security that on the previous day he had heard that there was a very large requirement for additional aerodromes for the RAF and it seemed very unlikely that this could be satisfied with new sites; it might, therefore, prove that the list of aerodromes at 2A would have to be very much cut down.

The meeting adopted this procedure and the following conclusions were agreed to after discussion.

1 Definitions

1.   Class 1 – where the Air Ministry has a predominating interest.

In such cases:
   i.   The Air Ministry will prepare the design of the whole scheme including landing ground and buildings.
   ii.   The Air Ministry will execute camouflage to RAF buildings.
   iii. The Air Ministry will execute camouflage to the landing ground.
   iv. The Ministry of Home Security will arrange for execution of camouflage of civil buildings in accordance with the Air Ministry scheme.

2.   Class 2 – where the Ministry of Home Security has the predominating interest.
   (These are cases where the aerodrome is primarily a civil aerodrome constructed either for the purposes of civil aviation or for a factory working for the MAP).
   This class is divided into two sub-classes, where the following also details the division of responsibilities between the two Ministries:
   a.   Class 2A – where the Air Ministry has not declared any present or prospective interest in the aerodrome.
      i.   The Ministry of Home Security will be responsible for the design, execution and maintenance of the complete scheme.
      ii.   The Ministry of Home Security can use three-dimensional camouflage devices, provided that these are removed within 24 hours without detriment to the serviceability of the aerodrome.should the aerodrome be required for RAF purposes.
      iii. The Ministry of Home Security will consult the Superintending Engineer of the appropriate works area as to the effect on the serviceability of the aerodrome of the proposed camouflage scheme and of its removal under (ii) above.
      iv. It is understood that removal of three-dimensional camouflage devices will be the responsibility of the Air Ministry, as the Ministry of Home Security cannot arrange for this.

Note: The Ministry of Home Security explained that they were very anxious to try three-dimensional camouflage on an aerodrome, but had not hitherto been able to do so. The Air Ministry explained that, while it might be possible to have part of the aerodrome camouflaged in this way if it was only being used by expert testing and ferry pilots, it would not be practicable to have three-dimensional camouflage at aerodromes being used for instructional purposes or probably for operational purposes where pilots have to make night landings.

b.   Class 2B – where regular use of the aerodrome by the RAF is contemplated.
    i.   The Ministry of Home Security will design the whole scheme for the landing ground and all the buildings.
    ii.   Three dimensional camouflage devices will not be used.
    iii. The Ministry of Home Security will consult the appropriate Superintending Engineer who must be satisfied that the proposed scheme will not affect the serviceability of the aerodrome for RAF purposes or conflict with Service requirements. The Superintending Engineer will normally act in consultation with the Commanding Officer.
    iv.   The Air Ministry will execute at their own expense the camouflage scheme on the landing ground and RAF buildings: the Ministry of Home Security will arrange for the execution of the scheme on other buildings.
    v.   The Air Ministry will maintain the camouflage scheme on the aerodrome and will give the highest priority to the maintenance of camouflage schemes on Class B aerodromes.
    vi.   The Ministry of Home Security will have the right to see how camouflage is maintained, and if not satisfied with its condition will communicate in the first instance with the appropriate Superintending Engineer. If such representations fail to secure the necessary improvement, the Ministry of Home Security will communicate with W. War B. semi-officially.
    vii. Claims for compensation from aerodromes or factory owners in respect of camouflage already executed etc. should be sent direct to the Air Ministry (Under Secretary of State for Air, Department F5). The Air Ministry will then consult the Ministry of Home Security (Department L3) as necessary.

2 List of Aerodromes

a.   Class 1. It was pointed out by the Air Ministry that Hucknall should be included in this list. The Ministry of Home Security said that Rolls-Royce had a factory there; but Operational Intelligence said that this was a very minor affair, occupying one or two hangers, whereas Hucknall was a large RAF station.

b.   Class 2A.
    i.   It was agreed that Operational Intelligence and W.War.B. would go through this list and revise it in light of developments since the meeting of the 9th December 1940.

ii.   The Ministry of Home Security raised the question of the inclusion of Yeovil, Yeovilton and Eastleigh in the list. They said that the Admiralty were definitely interested in Yeovilton and Eastleigh but that the position of Yeovil was uncertain. It was agreed that Operational Intelligence should clear up the position of these aerodromes, and that for the sake of completeness they might then put a note at the bottom of the agreed list.

c.   Class 2B. At some of these aerodromes there were factories of major importance, while at others there was little of great importance from the MAP point of view. It was agreed that the MAP (Mr Carline) should send Mr Robertson a list of the aerodromes at which there were factories of importance from the MAP point of view, with the name of the firm in each case.

Notes

Introduction

1 The National Archives (TNA) AIR 19/10. This document can also be found in AIR 19/9.
2 *Spitfires to Jaguars at Castle Bromwich*. A booklet published by Jaguar Heritage.
3 Crosby, Frances, *The World Encyclopedia of Bombers* (London: Annes Publishing Limited, 2007).
4 Oliver, David, *Fighter Command 1939–45* (St Helens: The Book People Limited, 2000).
5 Jackson, Robert, *The Encyclopedia of Military Aircraft* (Bath: Parragon Books, 2002).
6 RAF Museum Hendon information board.
7 RAF Museum Hendon information board.
8 *Encyclopaedia Britannica Ultimate Reference Suite* (Chicago: Encyclopaedia Britannica, 2011).
9 *Biographical Memoirs of Fellows of the Royal Society*, vol. 12, 1966, pp. 394–95.
10 *Who was Who 1961–1970* (London: A. & C. Black Limited, 1967), pp. 975–76.

Chapter 1 Key Ministries in the National War Cabinet

1. The National Archives (TNA) CAB 21/1108.
2. The National Archives (TNA) AVIA 12/24.
3. The National Archives (TNA) AVIA 12/24.
4. The National Archives (TNA) AVIA 22/145.
5. The National Archives (TNA) T 161/1157.
6. The National Archives (TNA) SUPP 14/686.
7. The National Archives (TNA) CAB 80/25/100.
8 The National Archives (TNA) AVIA 22/1199.
9. The National Archives document lists this entry as just 'Northern'. This word is also used in several other tables in the same reference.
10. The National Archives (TNA) AVIA 22/1270.
11. Joseph Rogers and David Rogers (ed.), *Civilians in Silsden* (London: Danercon Ltd 2009).
12. The National Archives (TNA) AVIA 22/1265.
13. The National Archives (TNA) SUPP 14/656.
14. The National Archives (TNA) AVIA 15/564.
15. The National Archives (TNA) AVIA 15/564.
16. *Encyclopaedia Britannica*, 2011.
17. The National Archives (TNA) AVIA 33/1.
18. *Who was Who 1951–1960* (London: A. & C. Black Limited, 1967), pp. 1090–91.
19. The National Archives (TNA) BT 168/127.
20. National Archives AVIA 15/3802.

21. The National Archives (TNA) AVIA 15/1929.
22. The National Archives (TNA) AVIA 15/1929.
23. The National Archives (TNA) T 273/119.
24. The National Archives (TNA) T 273/119.
25. The National Archives (TNA) BT 87/68.
26. The National Archives (TNA) BT 87/68.

Chapter 2   Overseas Capacity and Infrastructure

1. The National Archives (TNA) CAB 21/1531.
2. The National Archives (TNA) CAB 21/1531.
3. The National Archives (TNA) BT 96/191.
4. The National Archives (TNA) BT 96/191 and HLG 7/185.
5. The National Archives (TNA) ADM 1/10313.
6. The National Archives (TNA) ADM 1/10313.
7. The National Archives (TNA) ADM 116/4897.
8. The National Archives (TNA) BT 96/190.
9. The National Archives (TNA) BT 96/199.
10. The National Archives (TNA) BT 168/135.
11. The National Archives (TNA) BT 168/135.
12. *Biographical Memoirs of Fellows of the Royal Society* vol 18 (1972), p. 543.
13. Rogers, D.N., *Men Amidst the Madness: British Technology Development in World War II* (Solihull: Helion & Company, 2014).
14. National Archives BT 96/191.
15. The National Archives (TNA) BT 96/191.
16. The National Archives (TNA) AVIA 38/1032.
17. The National Archives (TNA) BT 11/1979.
18. The National Archives (TNA) AVIA 15/3639.
19. The National Archives (TNA) AVIA 15/3639.
20. The National Archives (TNA) MH 79/541.
21. The National Archives (TNA) ADM 1/12110.
22. The National Archives (TNA) CAB 115/540.
23. *Encyclopaedia Britannica Ultimate Reference Edition* (2011 DVD version).
24. The National Archives (TNA) SUPP 14/658.
25. The National Archives (TNA) WORK 6/401/3.
26. The National Archives (TNA) WORK 6/401/3.
27. The National Archives (TNA) ADM 1/14895.
28. The National Archives (TNA) WORK 6/401/3.
29. The National Archives (TNA) SUPP 14/671.
30. The National Archives (TNA) WO 32/10567.
31. The National Archives (TNA) AVIA 38/592.
32. The National Archives (TNA) SUPP 14/670.
33. The National Archives (TNA) AVIA 38/14.
34. The National Archives (TNA) AVIA 38/14.
35. The National Archives (TNA) AVIA 38/14.
36. The National Archives (TNA) AVIA 38/725.
37. The National Archives (TNA) AVIA 38/725.
38. RAF Museum Hendon information board.
39. RAF Museum Hendon information board.
40. RAF Museum Hendon information board.

Chapter 3 Set-up and Contracts

1. The National Archives (TNA) AIR 19/3.
2. The National Archives (TNA) AIR 19/9.
3. The National Archives (TNA) AIR 19/3.
4. The National Archives (TNA) AIR 19/5.
5. The National Archives (TNA) AIR 19/5.
6. The National Archives (TNA) AIR 19/9.
7. The National Archives (TNA) AIR 19/5.
8. The National Archives (TNA) AIR 19/5.
9. The National Archives (TNA) T 161/1070.
10. The National Archives (TNA) AVIA 15/3724.
11. The National Archives (TNA) T 161/1070.
12. The National Archives (TNA) AIR 2/2174.
13. The National Archives (TNA) AIR 2/2174.
14. The National Archives (TNA) AIR 2/2174.
15. The National Archives (TNA) AVIA 15/853.
16. The National Archives (TNA) AVIA 22/2912.
17. The National Archives (TNA) AIR 19/5.
18. RAF Museum Hendon information board.
19. The National Archives (TNA) AIR 19/9.
20. The National Archives (TNA) AIR 15/3766.
21. The National Archives (TNA) AVIA 15/19.
22. The National Archives (TNA) AVIA 15/354.
23. The National Archives (TNA) AVIA 15/354.
24. The National Archives (TNA) AVIA 15/3775.
25. The National Archives (TNA) AVIA 15/3775.
26. The National Archives (TNA) AVIA 15/3775.
27. The National Archives (TNA) AVIA 15/3874.
28. The National Archives (TNA) AVIA 15/3733.
29. The National Archives (TNA) AVIA 15/3733.
30. Jackson, Robert, *The Encyclopedia of Military Aircraft* (Bath: Parragon Books, 2002).
31. The National Archives (TNA) 15/320.
32. The National Archives (TNA) AVIA 15/3802.
33. The National Archives (TNA) AIR 15/320.
34. The National Archives (TNA) AVIA 15/414.
35. The National Archives (TNA) AVIA 15/3825.

Chapter 4 Finance and Administration

1. The National Archives (TNA) AIR 19/3.
2. The National Archives (TNA) AIR 19/3.
3. The National Archives (TNA) AIR 19/3.
4. The National Archives (TNA) AIR 19/9.
5. The National Archives (TNA) AVIA 15/3765.
6. The National Archives (TNA) AIR 19/9.
7. The National Archives (TNA) AIR 20/2395.
8. The National Archives (TNA) AVIA 15/320.
9. The National Archives (TNA) AIR 19/9.
10. The National Archives (TNA) AVIA 15/2401.

11. The National Archives (TNA) AIR 2/2873.
12. The National Archives (TNA) AIR 2/3683.
13. The National Archives (TNA) AIR 2/2873.
14. The National Archives (TNA) AVIA 15/3719.
15. The National Archives (TNA) AVIA 15/3719.
16. The National Archives (TNA) AVIA 15/3719.
17. The National Archives (TNA) AVIA 15/3719.
18. The National Archives (TNA) AVIA 15/3719.
19. The National Archives (TNA) AVIA 15/2313.
20. The National Archives (TNA) AVIA 15/2313.
21. The National Archives (TNA) AVIA 15/2313.
22. The National Archives (TNA) AVIA 15/724.
23. The National Archives (TNA) AVIA 15/724.
24. RAF Museum Hendon information board.
25. The National Archives (TNA) AVIA 15/2288.
26. The National Archives (TNA) AIR 2/1738.
27. The National Archives (TNA) AIR 2/1738.
28. The National Archives (TNA) AVIA 15/414.
29. The National Archives (TNA)AVIA 15/3723.

Chapter 5 Building Work

1. The National Archives (TNA) AIR 2/2424.
2. The National Archives (TNA) AVIA 15/3768.
3. The National Archives (TNA) AIR 3309.
4. The National Archives (TNA) AVIA 15/2.
5. The National Archives (TNA) AVIA 15/3765.
6. The National Archives (TNA) AVIA 15/2302.
7. The National Archives (TNA) AVIA 9/7.
8. The National Archives (TNA) AVIA 15/1657.
9. The National Archives (TNA) AVIA 15/320.
10. The National Archives (TNA) AVIA 15/320.
11. RAF Museum Hendon information board.
12. The National Archives (TNA) AVIA 15/2306.
13. The National Archives (TNA) AVIA 15/3765.
14. The National Archives (TNA) AIR 19/2.
15. The National Archives (TNA) AIR 19/2.

Chapter 6 Research and Development

1. *Encyclopaedia Britannica Ultimate Reference Edition*(2001, DVD version).
2. RAF Museum Hendon information board.
3. The National Archives (TNA) AIR 20/4617.
4. RAF Museum Hendon information board.
5. RAF Museum Hendon information board.
6. The National Archives (TNA) AVIA 10/108.
7. *Encyclopaedia Britannica Ultimate Reference Edition* (2011 DVD version).
8. The National Archives (TNA) AVIA 15/1397.
9. The National Archives (TNA) AVIA 15/1397.
10. The National Archives (TNA) AVIA 15/1397.

11. The National Archives (TNA) AVIA 15/1397.
12. The National Archives (TNA) AVIA 15/1120.
13. The National Archives (TNA) AVIA 15/1120.
14. The National Archives (TNA) AVIA 15/1120.
15. The National Archives (TNA) AVIA 15/1120.
16. The National Archives (TNA) AVIA 15/1120.
17. RAF Museum Hendon information board.
18. The National Archives (TNA) AVIA 9/5.
19. The National Archives (TNA) AVIA 9/5.

Chapter 7 Forecasts and Planning

1. The National Archives (TNA) AIR 19/4.
2. The National Archives (TNA) AVIA 9/5.
3. The National Archives (TNA) AIR 19/3.
4. The National Archives (TNA) AIR 2/1842.
5. The National Archives (TNA) AIR 19/8.
6. The National Archives (TNA) AIR 19/9.
7. The National Archives (TNA) AVIA 10/108.
8. The National Archives (TNA) AVIA 9/26.
9. RAF Museum at Hendon information board.
10. RAF Museum Hendon information board.
11. The National Archives (TNA) AVIA 9/5.
12. The National Archives (TNA) AVIA 9/26.
13. The National Archives (TNA) AVIA 9/5.

Chapter 8 Parts Manufacture and Aircraft Assembly

1. The National Archives (TNA) AIR 19/3, also in The National Archives (TNA) 19/9.
2. The National Archives (TNA) AIR 19/9.
3. The National Archives (TNA) AIR 19/9.
4. The National Archives (TNA) AIR 19/8.
5. The National Archives (TNA) AVIA 9/5.
6. The National Archives (TNA) AVIA 9/25.
7. The National Archives (TNA) AVIA 9/39.
8. The National Archives (TNA) AVIA 9/39.
9. The National Archives (TNA) AVIA 9/39.
10. The National Archives (TNA) AVIA 9/39.
11. The National Archives (TNA) AVIA 9/5.
12. The National Archives (TNA) AIR 19/1.
13. The National Archives (TNA) AIR 19/1.
14. Alex Henshaw, *Spitfires to Jaguars*, an in-house publication by Jaguar Cars
15. The National Archives (TNA) AIR 10/312.
16. The National Archives (TNA) AVIA 10/312.
17. The National Archives (TNA) AVIA 10/312.
18. RAF Museum Hendon information board.
19. The National Archives (TNA) AIR 20/4617.
20. The National Archives (TNA) AIR 20/4617.
21. The National Archives (TNA) AIR 20/4617.
22. The National Archives (TNA) AIR 19/1.

23. The National Archives (TNA) AVIA 15/414.
24. The National Archives (TNA) AVIA 9/5.
25. The National Archives (TNA) AVIA 9/5.
26. The National Archives (TNA) AIR 2/2873.

Chapter 9 Visitors: Unwanted and Wanted

1. The National Archives (TNA) AVIA 15/706.
2. The National Archives (TNA) AVIA 15/706.
3. The National Archives (TNA) AVIA 15/320.
4. The National Archives (TNA) AVIA 15/1584.
5. The National Archives (TNA) AVIA 15/1584.
6. The National Archives (TNA) AVIA 15/1584.
7. The National Archives (TNA) WO 199/2532.
8. The National Archives (TNA) WO 199/2532.
9. The National Archives (TNA) WO 199/2532.
10. *Telegraph and Argus*, Saturday June 20, 2012 p. 23.
11. The National Archives (TNA) AIR 19/2.
12. RAF Museum Hendon information board.
13. The National Archives (TNA) AIR 19/2.
14. The National Archives (TNA) AIR 19/2.
15. RAF Museum at Hendon, information board.

Chapter 10 Post-war Costs/Sales of Factories

1. The National Archives (TNA) AVIA 15/3825.
2. The National Archives (TNA) AVIA 15/2288.
3. The National Archives (TNA) AIR 2/2326.
4. The National Archives (TNA) AVIA 15/3765.
5. The National Archives (TNA) AVIA 15/3765.
6. The National Archives (TNA) AIR 15/320.
7. The National Archives (TNA) AVIA 15/3825.
8. The National Archives (TNA) AVIA 15/2313.
9. The National Archives (TNA) AVIA 15/20.
10. The National Archives (TNA) AVIA 15/414.
11. The National Archives (TNA) AVIA 15/414.
12. The National Archives (TNA) AVIA 13/320.
13. The National Archives (TNA) AVIA 15/320.
14. The National Archives (TNA) AIR 2/1738.
15. The National Archives (TNA) AVIA 15/3753.
16. The National Archives (TNA) AVIA 15/3753.
17. The National Archives (TNA) AIR 2/3683.

Appendix I Shadow Factories: The Rationale and Early History

1. The National Archives TNA) AIR 19/9.

Appendix II The Introduction to the Report Written by H. McMillan to the Chairman of the Production Council

1. The National Archives (TNA) ADM 116/4897.

Appendix III UK Note on the Principles Applying to Reciprocal Aid in the Prosecution of the War Against Aggression

1. The National Archives (TNA) AVIA 38/592.

Appendix IV Remuneration on Extension of the Agreement with Aero-engine Committee No 1

1. The National Archives (TNA) AIR 19/9.

Appendix V Agreement between the Secretary of State for Air and the Right Honourable William Richard Viscount Nuffield of Nuffield

1. The National Archives (TNA) AIR 19/1.

Appendix VI A Compiled List of Shadow Factories

1. The National Archives (TNA) AVIA 15/3874, AVIA 15/483, AVIA 15/3772, AVIA 15/19, AVIA 15/2346, AVIA 15/2313, AVIA 15/1852 and AVIA 15/1120.

Appendix VII Lancaster and York Production and Development

1. The National Archives (TNA) AVIA 10/108.

Appendix VIII Responsibilities of the Ministry of Home Security and the Air Ministry at Aerodromes Used Jointly by the RAF and Contractors

1. The National Archives (TNA) AVIA 15/1584.

Bibliography

Archive Documents

The National Archives (TNA): ADM 1/10313, ADM 1/12110, ADM 1/14895, ADM 116/4897, AIR 10/312, AIR 15/320, AIR 15/3766, AIR 19/1, AIR 19/10, AIR 19/2, AIR 19/3, AIR 19/4, AIR 19/5, AIR 19/8, AIR 19/9, AIR 2/1738, AIR 2/1842, AIR 2/2174, AIR 2/2326, AIR 2/2424, AIR 2/2873, AIR 2/3683, AIR 20/2395, AIR 20/4617, AIR 3309, AVIA 10/108, AVIA 10/312, AVIA 12/24, AVIA 13/320, AVIA 15/1120, AVIA 15/1120, AVIA 15/1397, AVIA 15/1584, AVIA 15/1657, AVIA 15/1852, AVIA 15/19, AVIA 15/19, AVIA 15/1929, AVIA 15/2, AVIA 15/20, AVIA 15/2288, AVIA 15/2302, AVIA 15/2306, AVIA 15/2313, AVIA 15/2313, AVIA 15/2346, AVIA 15/2401, AVIA 15/320, AVIA 15/354, AVIA 15/3639, AVIA 15/3719, AVIA 15/3723, AVIA 15/3724, AVIA 15/3733, AVIA 15/3753, AVIA 15/3765, AVIA 15/3768, AVIA 15/3772, AVIA 15/3775, AVIA 15/3802, AVIA 15/3825, AVIA 15/3874, AVIA 15/414, AVIA 15/483, AVIA 15/564, AVIA 15/706, AVIA 15/724, AVIA 15/853, AVIA 22/1199, AVIA 22/1265, AVIA 22/1270, AVIA 22/145, AVIA 22/2912, AVIA 33/1, AVIA 38/1032, AVIA 38/14, AVIA 38/592, AVIA 38/725, AVIA 9/25, AVIA 9/26, AVIA 9/39, AVIA 9/39, AVIA 9/5, AVIA 9/7, BT 11/1979, BT 168/127, BT 168/135, BT 87/68, BT 96/190, BT 96/191, BT 96/199, CAB 115/540, CAB 21/1108, CAB 21/1531, CAB 80/25/100, HLG 7/185, MH 79/541, SUPP 14/656, SUPP 14/658, SUPP 14/67, SUPP 14/671, SUPP 14/686, T 161/1070, T 161/1157, T 273/119, T 273/119, WO 199/2532, WO 32/10567, WORK 6/401/3

Newspapers

Telegraph and Argus, Saturday, 20 June 2012, p. 23.

Printed Books

Crosby, Frances, *The World Encyclopedia of Bombers* (London: Annes Publishing Limited, 2007).

Encyclopædia Britannica Ultimate Reference Suite (Chicago: Encyclopædia Britannica, 2011).

Henshaw, Alex, *Spitfires to Jaguars*, an undated in-house publication by Jaguar Cars.

Jackson, Robert, *The Encyclopedia of Military Aircraft* (Bath: Parragon Books, 2002).

Oliver, David, *Fighter Command 1939-45* (St Helens: The Book People Limited, 2000).

Rogers, David, *Men Amidst the Madness British Technology Development in World War II* (Solihull: Helion & Company, 2014).

Rogers, Joseph and Rogers, David (ed.), *Civilians in Silsden* (London: Danercon Ltd 2009).

Who was Who 1951-1960 (London: A. & C. Black Limited, 1967).

Who was Who 1961-1970 (London: A. & C. Black Limited, 1967).

Royal Society Publications

Biographical Memoirs of Fellows of the Royal Society vol 18 (1972).

Biographical Memoirs of Fellows of the Royal Society vol 12 (1966).

Index

Lightning Source UK Ltd.
Milton Keynes UK
UKHW051016200220
358983UK00010B/114